The Science of Getting Rich,
Living Well
And Being Great
By
Wallace D. Wattles
Originally published in 1910

3 Classics in One Convenient Volume
Compiled and Edited
By
Richard B. Lanoue

The Science of Living the Life You've Always Wanted

© 2007 Richard B. Lanoue
ISBN: 978-0-6151-6914-9

All rights reserved. No part of this book, including interior design, cover design, and icons, may be reproduced or transmitted in any form, by any means (Electronic, photocopying, recording, or otherwise) without prior written permission of the publisher.

The advice and strategies contained herein may not be suitable for your situation. You should consult with a professional where appropriate. Neither the publisher nor the author shall be liable for any loss of profit or any commercial damages, including but not limited to incidental, consequential, or other damages.

Printed in the United States of America by Lulu.com

Dedication

This book is dedicated to my best friend and supporter, my wife of 20 years, Stephanie Lanoue who always supports me in any of my endeavors and to the memory of my greatest mentors Earl Nightingale and Dottie Walters.

Table of Contents

Dedication	iii
Introduction	1
The Science of Getting Rich	4
The Right to Be Rich	5
There Is a Science of Getting Rich	7
Is Opportunity Monopolized?	10
The First Principle in the Science of Getting Rich	12
Increasing Life	16
How Riches Come To You	20
Gratitude	24
Thinking in the Certain Way	27
How to Use the Will	30
Further Use of the Will	34
Acting in the Certain Way	37
Efficient Action	41
Getting Into the Right Business	44
The Impression of Increase	47
The Advancing Personality	50
Some Cautions and Concluding Observations	53
A Summary of the Science of Getting Rich	56
Author's Preface to the Science of Living Well	59
The Principle of Health	61
The Foundations of Faith	65
Life and Its Organisms	69
What to Think	73
Faith	78
Use of the Will	83
Health from God	87
Summary of the Mental Actions	91
When to Eat	94
What to Eat	98
How to Eat	105

The Science of Living the Life You've Always Wanted by Richard Lanoue

Hunger and Appetites	109
In a Nutshell	113
Breathing	117
Sleep	121
Supplementary Instructions	124
A Summary of the Science of Living Well	129
The Science of Being Great	131
Any Person May Become Great	132
Heredity and Opportunity	135
The Source of Power	138
The Mind of God	141
Preparation	144
The Social Point of View	146
The Individual Point of View	150
Consecration	152
Identification	155
Idealization	157
Realization	159
Hurry and Habit	162
Thought	165
Action at Home	168
Action Abroad	171
Some Further Explanations	174
More About Thought	176
Jesus' Idea of Greatness	179
A View of Evolution	182
Serving God	184
A Mental Exercise	187
A Summary of The Science of Being Great	190
About Wallace D. Wattles	195
Supplemental Material by Prentice Mulford	197
The God in You	198
Positive and Negative Thought	209
Some Practical Mental Recipes	218
Self Teaching; or, the Art of Learning How To Learn	227

Love Thyself	237
The Art of Forgetting	246
The Law of Change	254
Being Born Again	263
About Prentice Mulford	272
About the Compiler and Editor	274

Introduction

Wallace Delois Wattles wrote a number of books. The most famous being *The Science of Getting Rich*. He followed this with two more books, The Science of Being Great, and The Science of Being Well, as well as, many others. The books are meant to be read in order so this compilation has kept them in the preferred order. The reader is encouraged to read from front to back.

The *Science of Getting Rich* was written in 1910. It is more than any self help book has ever been, linking God, Einstein, spiritual and universal laws in a manual that was shunned by the church at the time, and is still relevant today.

These works are still read by intelligent people today because his books have been rediscovered in the public domain and republished for the general public.

Little is known about his life except that he was born in the United States after the Civil War. He experienced poverty and failure in his earlier years.

Later he studied the various religions and philosophies.

Through his study, he discovered the truth of the Law of Attraction principles and put them into practice in his own life. We are only now rediscovering these ancient teachings that originated from the ancient Upanishads (Hindu). Now that Quantum Physics has explained how the observer influences the experiences through the particle/wave experiments, we are finally coming to realize what most of the ancient religions discussed in their more esoteric books.

Wallace wrote books outlining these principles and practiced the technique of creative visualization.

His ideas were controversial in his day. He was even fired from a high position in the Methodist Church because he spoke about how the power of our destiny is within us.

His teachings were considered heresy because he outlined how to use the law of attraction to live a happy, prosperous, and fulfilled life. The Law of Attraction is a law of nature. It is impersonal. It does not break up the world into good things or bad things. It receives your thoughts and reflects back to you those thoughts as your life experience. The law of attraction simply gives you what you think about.

Wallace Wattles taught how to think "in a certain way" to attract wealth, health, love, and success.

His daughter Florence relates, "He wrote almost constantly. It was then that he formed his mental picture. He saw himself as a successful writer, a personality of power, an advancing man, and he began to work toward the realization of this vision. He lived every page ... His life was truly the powerful life."

Wattles' best known book, The Science of Getting Rich is a mental and spiritual approach on how to become rich.

Wattles said his book was "Intended for the men and women whose most pressing need is for money; who wish to get rich first, and philosophize afterward. It is pragmatic, not philosophical; a practical manual, not a lot of theory. It is for those who have, so far, found neither the time, the means, nor the opportunity, to go deeply into the study of metaphysics, but who want prosperous results and who are willing to take the conclusions of science as a basis for action.

Wattles died not long after the 1910 publication of The Science of Getting Rich, but his books, like those of Orison Swett Marden, another famous prosperity teacher, was the stimulus behind much of the self-development literature of the past 100 years.

His ideas have influenced many contemporary people, transforming their lives entirely.

Fundamentally, except for the Bible, this is the only book you need to achieve, Wealth, Health and Well Being in your life.

One remarkable example of his influence is how it transformed the life of Rhonda Byrne.

Rhonda Byrne, an Australian woman, was at the end of her rope. Her father had died suddenly. Her relationships were in turmoil. And she had worn herself into exhaustion by her work. After reading *The Science of Getting Rich*, a book given to her by her daughter to lift her spirits, she created the sensationally popular movie, **The Secret.** By applying the principles in The Science of Getting Rich,

Rhonda Byrne created a mental image of what she wanted to accomplish and the rest, can we say, is history.

Earl Nightingale, the original spoken word recording great, summed it up in his work titled, "The Strangest Secret", by reducing everything to 6 words. "We become what we think about". How profound!

The many copycats who have reworked Wallace Wattles' tome have jumped on Rhonda Byrne's Law of Attraction bandwagon and blazed their own trail; but the original, I feel, is still the best because you can arrive at your own conclusions without the filter of someone else's interpretation.

I have attempted to preserve the original language, however dated, correcting only the archaic spelling of common words like favour to favor, endeavour to endeavor, etc. and changing a few words, which mean the same but make for easier understanding of the text.

The reader is cautioned to consider the contents of these books with an open mind as a closed mind will only read the words and refuse to believe anything he reads. I urge the reader to read slowly and absorb the material; seek to understand so as to successfully implement the principles outlined herein.

Words like God and Spirit may be confused with religious zealousness but, I assure you, there is a God and Wallace Wattles believed this. His chapter on evolution makes sense but he attributes our lives as an extension of God.

In this age of political correctness, I have to mention that words like man and men refer to both genders. It is prudent to remember that when this book was written, women hadn't even gotten the right to vote and the way she dressed was a matter of public scrutiny and judgment (by men). There were no female politicians or corporate leaders. Times have changed but the book remains a favorite to men and women alike.

These books should be required reading in every high school in America with colleges around the world implementing courses in the science of living.

At the end of the 3 books by Wallace Wattles, there is a bonus lesson by Prentice Mulford who wrote during the same approximate timeframe of Wallace Wattles and is worth studying to clarify the thought process.

The Science of Getting Rich

By

Wallace D. Wattles

CHAPTER 1

The Right to Be Rich

Whatever may be said in praise of poverty, the fact remains that it is not possible to live a really complete or successful life unless one is rich. No one can rise to his greatest possible height in talent or soul development unless he has plenty of money, for to unfold the soul and to develop talent he must have many things to use, and he cannot have these things unless he has money to buy them with. A person develops in mind, soul, and body by making use of things, and society is so organized that man must have money in order to become the possessor of things.

Therefore, the basis of all advancement must be the science of getting rich. The object of all life is development, and everything that lives have an inalienable right to all the development it is capable of attaining. A person's right to life means his right to have the free and unrestricted use of all the things which may be necessary to his fullest mental, spiritual, and physical unfolding; or, in other words, his right to be rich. In this book, I shall not speak of riches in a figurative way. To be really rich does not mean to be satisfied or contented with a little. No one ought to be satisfied with a little if he is capable of using and enjoying more. The purpose of nature is the advancement and unfolding of life and everyone should have all that can contribute to the power, elegance, beauty, and richness of life. To be content with less is sinful. The person who owns all he wants for the living of all the life he is capable of living is rich, and no person who has not plenty of money can have all he wants. Life has advanced so far and become so complex that even the most ordinary man or woman requires a great amount of wealth in order to live in a manner that even approaches completeness.

Every person naturally wants to become all that they are capable of becoming. This desire to realize innate possibilities is inherent in human nature; we cannot help wanting to be all that we can be. Success in life is becoming what you want to be. You can become what you want to be only by making use of things, and you can have the free use of things only as you become rich enough to buy them. To understand the science of getting rich is therefore the most essential of all knowledge. There is nothing wrong in wanting to get rich. The desire for riches is really the desire for a richer, fuller, and more abundant life — and that desire is praiseworthy. The person who does not desire to live more abundantly is abnormal, and so the person who does not desire to have money enough to buy all he wants is abnormal. There are three motives for which we live: We live for the body, we live for the mind, and we live for the soul. No one of these is better or holier than the other; all are alike desirable, and no one of the three — body, mind, or soul — can live fully if either of the others is cut short of full life and expression. It is not right or noble to live only for the soul and deny mind or body, and it is wrong to live for the intellect and deny body or soul. We are all acquainted with the loathsome consequences of living for the body and denying both mind and soul, and we see that real life means the complete expression of all that a person can give forth through body, mind, and soul. Whatever he can say, no one can be really happy or satisfied, that unless his body is living fully in its every function, and unless the same is true of his mind and his soul. Wherever there is unexpressed possibility or function not performed, there is unsatisfied desire. Desire is possibility seeking expression or function seeking performance.

A person cannot live fully in body without good food, comfortable clothing, and warm shelter, and without freedom from excessive toil. Rest and recreation are also necessary to his physical life. One cannot live fully in mind without books and time to study them, without opportunity for travel and observation, or without intellectual companionship. To live fully in mind a person must have intellectual recreations, and must surround himself with all the objects of art and beauty he is capable of using and appreciating. To live fully in soul, a person must have love, and love is denied fullest expression by poverty. A person's highest happiness is found in the bestowal of benefits on those he loves; love finds its most natural and spontaneous expression in giving. The individual who has nothing to give cannot fill his place as a spouse or parent, as a citizen, or as a human being. It is in the use of material things that a person finds full life for his body, develops his mind, and unfolds his soul. It is therefore of supreme importance to each individual to be rich. It is perfectly right that you should desire to be rich. If you are a normal man or woman you cannot help doing so. It is perfectly right that you should give your best attention to the science of getting rich, for it is the noblest and most necessary of all studies. If you neglect this study, you are derelict in your duty to yourself, to God and humanity, for you can render to God and humanity no greater service than to make the most of yourself.

CHAPTER 2

There Is a Science of Getting Rich

There is a science of getting rich and it is an exact science, like algebra or arithmetic. There are certain laws that govern the process of acquiring riches, and once these laws are learned and obeyed by anyone, that person will get rich with mathematical certainty. The ownership of money and property comes as a result of doing things in a certain way, and those who do things in this certain way — whether on purpose or accidentally — get rich, while those who do not do things in this certain way — no matter how hard they work or how able they are — remain poor. It is natural laws that like causes always produce like effects, and, therefore, any man or women who learns to do things in this certain way will infallibly get rich. That the above statement is true is shown by the following facts: Getting rich is not a matter of environment, for if it were, all the people in certain neighborhoods would become wealthy. The people of one city would all be rich, while those of other towns would all be poor, or all the inhabitants of one state would roll in wealth, while those of an adjoining state would be in poverty. But everywhere we see rich and poor living side-by-side, in the same environment, and often engaged in the same vocations. When two people are in the same locality and in the same business, and one gets rich while the other remains poor, it shows that getting rich is not primarily a matter of environment. Some environments may be more favorable than others, but when two people in the same business are in the same neighborhood and one gets rich while the other fails, it indicates that getting rich is the result of doing things in a certain way. And further, the ability to do things in this certain way is not due solely to the possession of talent, for many people who have great talent remain poor, while others who have very little talent get rich.

Studying the people who have gotten rich, we find that they are an average lot in all respects, having no greater talents and abilities than other people have. It is evident that they do not get rich because they possess talents and abilities that others do not have, but because they happen to do things in a certain way. Getting rich is not the result of saving, or thrift. Many very impecunious people are poor, while free spenders often get rich. Nor is getting rich due to doing things which others fail to do, for two people in the same business often do almost exactly the same things, and one gets rich while the other remains poor or becomes bankrupt. From all these things, we must come to the conclusion that getting rich is the result of doing things in a certain way. If getting rich is the result of doing things in a certain way, and if like causes always produce like effects, then any man or woman who can do things in that way can become rich, and the whole matter is brought within the domain of exact science. The question arises here as to whether this certain way may not be so difficult that only a few may follow it. As we have seen, this cannot be true (as far as natural ability is concerned). Talented people get rich, and blockheads get rich, intellectually brilliant people get rich, and very stupid people get rich; physically strong people get rich, and weak and sickly people get rich. Some degree of ability to think and understand is, of course, essential, but insofar as natural ability is concerned, any man or woman who has sense enough to read and understand these words can certainly get rich. Also, we have seen that it is not a matter of environment. Yes, location counts for something. One would not go to the heart of the Sahara and expect to do successful business.

Getting rich involves the necessity of dealing with people and of being where there are people to deal with, and if these people are inclined to deal in the way you want to deal, so much the better. But that is about as far as environment goes. If anybody else in your town can get rich, so can you, and if anybody else in your state can get rich, so can you. Again, it is not a matter of choosing some particular business or profession. People get rich in every business and in every profession, while their next-door neighbors in the very same vocation remain in poverty.

It is true that you will do best in a business you like and which is congenial to you. And if you have certain talents that are well developed, you will do best in a business that calls for the exercise of those talents. Also, you will do best in a business which is suited to your locality: An ice cream parlor would do better in a warm climate than in Greenland, and a salmon fishery will succeed better in the northwest than in Florida, where there are no salmon. But, aside from these general limitations, getting rich is not dependent upon your engaging in some particular business, but upon your learning to do things in a certain way. If you are now in business and anybody else in your locality is getting rich in the same business, while you are not getting rich, it is simply because you are not doing things in the same way that the other person is doing them.

No one is prevented you from getting rich by lack of capital. True, as you get capital the increase becomes easier and rapid, but one who has capital is already rich and does not need to consider how to become so. No matter how poor you may be, if you begin to do things in the certain way you will begin to get rich and you will begin to have capital. The getting of capital is a part of the process of getting rich and it is a part of the result that invariably follows the doing of things in the certain way. You may be the poorest person on the continent and be deeply in debt. You may not have friends, influences, or resources, but if you begin to do things in this way, you must infallibly begin to get rich, for like causes must produce like effects. If you have no capital, you can get capital. If you are in the wrong business, you can get into the right business. If you are in the wrong location, you can go to the right location. And you can do so by beginning in your present business and in your present location to do things in the certain way that always causes success. You must begin to live in harmony with the laws governing the universe.

CHAPTER 3

Is Opportunity Monopolized?

No one is kept poor because other people have monopolized the wealth and have put a fence around it. You may be shut off from engaging in business in certain lines, but there are other channels open to you. At different periods the tide of opportunity sets in different directions, according to the needs of the whole and the particular stage of social evolution, which has been reached. There is abundance of opportunity for the person who will go with the tide, instead of trying to swim against it. So workers, either as individuals or as a class, are not deprived of opportunity. The workers are not being "kept down" by their masters; they are not being "ground" by the trusts and big business. As a class, they are where they are because they do not do things in a certain way. The working class may become the master class whenever they will begin to do things in a certain way. The law of wealth is the same for them as it is for all others. This they must learn, and they will remain where they are as long as they continue to do as they do.

The individual worker, however, is not held down by an entire class's ignorance of these laws; he can follow the tide of opportunity to riches, and this book will tell him how. No one is kept in poverty by shortness in the supply of riches; there is more than enough for all. A palace as large as the capitol at Washington might be built for every family on earth from the building material in the United States alone, and under intensive cultivation this country would produce wool, cotton, linen, and silk enough to clothe each person in the world finer than Solomon was arrayed in all his glory, together with food enough to feed them all luxuriously. The visible supply is practically inexhaustible, and the invisible supply really is inexhaustible. Everything you see on earth is made from one original substance, out of which all things proceed. New forms are constantly being made, and older ones are dissolving, but all are shapes assumed by one thing. There is no limit to the supply of formless stuff, or original substance. The universe is made out of it, but it was not all used in making the universe. The spaces in, through, and between the forms of the visible universe are permeated and filled with the original substance, with the formless stuff — with the raw material of all things.

Ten thousand times as much as has been made might still be made, and even then we should not have exhausted the supply of universal raw material. No one, therefore, is poor because nature is poor or because there is not enough to go around.

Nature is an inexhaustible storehouse of riches; the supply will never run short. Original substance is alive with creative energy, and is constantly producing more forms. When the supply of building material is exhausted, more will be produced. When the soil is exhausted so that foodstuffs and materials for clothing will no longer grow upon it, it will be renewed or more soil will be made. When all the gold and silver has been dug from the earth, if humanity is still in such a stage of social development that it needs gold and silver, more will produced from the formless. The formless stuff responds to the needs of mankind; it will not let the world be without any good thing. This is true of man collectively. The race as a whole is always abundantly rich, and if individuals are poor it is because they do not follow the certain way of doing things that makes the individual rich. The formless stuff is intelligent; it is stuff which thinks. It is alive and is always impelled toward more life. It is the natural and inherent impulse of life to seek to live more; it is the nature of intelligence to enlarge itself, and of consciousness to seek to extend its boundaries and find fuller expression. The universe of forms has been made by formless living substance throwing itself into form in order to express itself more fully. The universe is a great living presence, always moving inherently toward more life and fuller functioning.

Nature is formed for the advancement of life, and its impelling motive is the increase of life. Because of this, everything, which can possibly minister to life, is bountifully provided. There can be no lack unless God is to contradict himself and nullify his own works. You are not kept poor by lack in the supply of riches. It is a fact that I shall demonstrate a little farther on that even the resources of the formless supply are at the command of the man or woman who will act and think in a certain way.

CHAPTER 4

The First Principle in the Science of Getting Rich

Thought is the only tangible power that produces riches from the formless substance. The stuff from which all things are made is a substance that thinks, and a thought of form in this substance produces the form. Original substance moves according to its thoughts; every form and process you see in nature is the visible expression of a thought in original substance. As the formless stuff thinks of a form, it takes that form; as it thinks of a motion, it makes that motion. That is the way all things were created. We live in a thought world, which is part of a thought universe. The thought of a moving universe extended throughout formless substance, and the thinking stuff — moving according to that thought — took the form of systems of planets, and maintains that form. Thinking substance takes the form of its thought, and moves according to the thought. Holding the idea of a circling system of suns and worlds, it takes the form of these bodies, and moves them as it thinks.

Thinking the form of a slow-growing oak tree, it moves accordingly, and produces the tree, though centuries may be required to do the work. In creating, the formless seems to move according to the lines of motion it has established. In other words, the thought of an oak tree does not cause the instant formation of a full-grown tree, but it does start in motion the forces, which will produce the tree, along established lines of growth. Every thought of form, held in thinking substance, causes the creation of the form, but always, or at least generally, along lines of growth and action already established. The thought of a house of a certain construction, if it were impressed upon formless substance, might not cause the instant formation of the house, but it would cause the turning of creative energies already working in trade and commerce into such channels as to result in the speedy building of the house. And if there were no existing channels through which the creative energy could work, then the house would be formed directly from primal substance, without waiting for the slow processes of the organic and inorganic world. No thought of form can be impressed upon original substance without causing the creation of the form. A person is a thinking center and can originate thought.

All the forms that a person fashions with his hands must first exist in his thought. He cannot shape a thing until he has thought that thing. So far, humankind has confined its efforts wholly to the work of its hands, applying manual labor to the world of forms and seeking to change or modify those already existing. Humankind has never thought of trying to cause the creation of new forms by impressing thought upon formless substance. When a person has a thought-form, he takes material from the forms of nature and makes an image of the form which is in his mind. People have, so far, made little or no effort to cooperate with formless intelligence — to work "with the Father." The individual has not dreamed that he can "do what he sees the Father doing." An individual reshapes and modifies existing forms by manual labor and has given no attention to the question of whether he may produce things from formless substance by communicating his thoughts to it. We propose to prove that he may do so — to prove that any man or woman may do so — and to show how. As our first step, we must lay down three fundamental propositions.

First, we assert that there is one original formless stuff or substance from which all things are made. All the seemingly many elements are but different presentations of one element. All the many forms found in organic and inorganic nature are but different shapes, made from the same stuff. And this stuff is thinking stuff — a thought held in it produces the form of the thought. Thought, in thinking substance, produces shapes. A human being is a thinking center, capable of original thought. If a person can communicate his thought to original thinking substance, he can cause the creation, or formation, of the thing he thinks about.

To summarize this: There is a thinking stuff from which all things are made, and which, in its original state, permeates, penetrates, and fills the interspaces of the universe. A thought in this substance produces the thing that is imaged by the thought. A person can form things in his thought, and, by impressing his thought upon formless substance, can cause the thing he thinks about to be created. It may be asked if I can prove these statements, and without going into details I answer that I can do so, both by logic and experience.

Reasoning back from the phenomena of form and thought, I come to one original thinking substance, and reasoning forward from this thinking substance, I come to a person's power to cause the formation of the thing he thinks about. And by experiment, I find the reasoning true. This is my strongest proof. If one person who reads this book gets rich by doing what it tells him to do, that is evidence in support of my claim, but if every person who does what it tells him to do gets rich, that is positive proof until someone goes through the process and fails.

The theory is true until the process fails, and this process will not fail, for everyone who does exactly what this book tells him to do will get rich. I have said that people get rich by doing things in a certain way, and in order to do so, people must become able to think in a certain way. A person's way of doing things is the direct result of the way he thinks about things. To do things in the way you want to do them, you will have to acquire the ability to think the way you want to think. This is the first step toward getting rich. And to think what you want to think is to think **TRUTH**, regardless of appearances. Every individual has the natural and inherent power to think what he wants to think, but it requires far more effort to do so than it does to think the thoughts, which are suggested by appearances. To think according to appearances is easy; to think truth regardless of appearances is laborious and requires the expenditure of more power than any other work we are called upon to perform.

There is no labor from which most people shrink as they do from that of sustained and consecutive thought. It is the hardest work in the world. This is especially true when truth is contrary to appearances. Every appearance in the visible world tends to produce a corresponding form in the mind that observes it, and this can only be prevented by holding to the thoughts of **TRUTH**. To look upon the appearances of poverty will produce corresponding forms in your own mind, unless you hold to the truth that there is no poverty; there is only abundance. To think health when surrounded by the appearances of disease or to think riches when in the midst of the appearances of poverty requires power, but whoever acquires this power becomes a mastermind. That person can conquer fate and can have what he wants. This power can only be acquired by getting hold of the basic fact which is behind all appearances, and that fact is that there is one thinking substance from which and by which all things are made. Then we must grasp the truth that every thought held in this substance becomes a form, and that man can so impress his thoughts upon it as to cause them to take form and become visible things. When we realize this we lose all doubt and fear, for we know that we can create what we want to create, we can get what we want to have, and can become what we want to be.

As a first step toward getting rich, you must believe the three fundamental statements given previously in this chapter, and in order to emphasize them, I repeat them here: There is a thinking stuff from which all things are made, and which, in its original state, permeates, penetrates, and fills the interspaces of the universe. A thought in this substance produces the thing that is imaged by the thought. A person can form things in his thought, and, by impressing his thought upon formless substance, can cause the thing he thinks about to be created. You must lay aside all other concepts of the universe, and you must dwell upon this until it is fixed in your mind and has become your habitual thought. Read these statements over and over again. Fix every word upon your memory and meditate upon them until you firmly believe what they say. If a doubt comes to you, cast it aside. Do not listen to arguments against this idea. Do not go to churches or lectures where a contrary concept of things is taught or preached. Do not read magazines or books that teach a different idea. If you get mixed up in your understanding, belief, and faith, all your efforts will be in vain. Do not ask why these things are true nor speculate as to how they can be true. Simply take them on trust. The science of getting rich begins with the absolute acceptance of this.

CHAPTER 5

Increasing Life

You must get rid of the last vestige of the old idea that there is a Deity whose will it is that you should be poor or whose purposes may be served by keeping you in poverty. The intelligent substance, which is all, and in all, and which lives in all and lives in you, is a consciously living substance. Being a consciously living substance, it must have the nature and inherent desire of every living intelligence for increase of life.

Every living thing must continually seek for the enlargement of its life, because life, in the mere act of living, must increase itself. A seed, dropped into the ground, springs into activity, and in the act of living produces a hundred more seeds; life, by living, multiplies itself. It is forever becoming more. It must do so, if it continues to be at all. Intelligence is under this same necessity for continuous increase. Every thought we think makes it necessary for us to think another thought; consciousness is continually expanding. Every fact we learn leads us to the learning of another fact; knowledge is continually increasing. Every talent we cultivate brings to the mind the desire to cultivate another talent; we are subject to the urge of life, seeking expression, which ever drives us on to know more, to do more, and to be more. In order to know more, do more, and be more we must have more. We must have things to use, for we learn, and do, and become only by using things. We must get rich so that we can live more. The desire for riches is simply the capacity for larger life seeking fulfillment. Every desire is the effort of an unexpressed possibility to come into action. It is power seeking to manifest, which causes desire. That which makes you want more money is the same as that which makes the plant grow; it is life seeking fuller expression. The one living substance must be subject to this inherent law of all life. It is permeated with the desire to live more, and that is why it is under the necessity of creating things.

The one substance desires to live more in and through you. Therefore it wants you to have all the things you can use. It is the desire of God that you should get rich. He wants you to get rich because he can express himself better through you if you have plenty of things to use in giving him expression. He can live more in you if you have unlimited command of the means of life. The universe desires you to have everything you want to have. Nature is friendly to your plans. Everything is naturally for you. Make up your mind that this is true. It is essential, however, that your purpose should harmonize with the purpose that is in all. You must want real life, not mere pleasure or sensual gratification. Life is the performance of function, and the individual really lives only when he performs every function — physical, mental, and spiritual — of which he is capable, without excess in any. You do not want to get rich in order to live swinishly, for the gratification of animal desires. That is not life. But the performance of every physical function is a part of life, and no one lives completely who denies the impulses of the body a normal and healthful expression. You do not want to get rich solely to enjoy mental pleasures, to get knowledge, to gratify ambition, to outshine others, to be famous.

All these are a legitimate part of life, but the person who lives for the pleasures of the intellect alone will only have a partial life, and he will never be satisfied with his lot. You do not want to get rich solely for the good of others, to lose yourself for the salvation of mankind, to experience the joys of philanthropy and sacrifice. The joys of the soul are only a part of life, and they are no better or nobler than any other part. You want to get rich in order that you may eat, drink, and be merry when it is time to do these things; in order that you may surround yourself with beautiful things, see distant lands, feed your mind, and develop your intellect; in order that you may love others and do kind things, and be able to play a good part in helping the world to find truth. But remember that extreme altruism is no better and no nobler than extreme selfishness; both are mistakes.

Get rid of the idea that God wants you to sacrifice yourself for others and that you can secure his favor by doing so. God requires nothing of the kind. What God wants is that you should make the most of yourself, for yourself, and for others. And you can help others more by making the most of yourself than in any other way. You can make the most of yourself only by getting rich, so it is right and praiseworthy that you should give your first and best thought to the work of acquiring wealth. Remember, however, that the desire of substance is for all, and its movements must be for more life to all. It cannot be made to work for less life to any, because it is equally in all, seeking riches and life. Intelligent substance will make things for you, but it will not take things away from someone else and give them to you. You must get rid of the thought of competition. You are to create, not to compete for what is already created.

You do not have to take anything away from anyone. You do not have to drive sharp bargains. You do not have to cheat or to take advantage. You do not need to let anyone work for you for less than he earns. You do not have to covet the property of others or to look at it with wishful eyes. No one has anything of which you cannot have the like and that without taking what he has away from him. You are to become a creator, not a competitor. You are going to get what you want, but in such a way that when you get it every other person whom you affect will have more than he has now. I am aware that there are those who get a vast amount of money by proceeding in direct opposition to the statements in the paragraph above, and may add a word of explanation here. Individuals of that type who become very rich do so sometimes purely by their extraordinary ability on the plane of competition, and sometimes they unconsciously relate themselves to substance in its great purposes and movements for the general up building through industrial evolution. Rockefeller, Carnegie, Morgan, et al., have been the unconscious agents of the supreme in the necessary work of systematizing and organizing productive industry, and in the end their work will contribute immensely toward increased life for all. But their day is nearly over. They have organized production and will soon be succeeded by the agents of the multitude, who will organize the machinery of distribution. They are like the monster reptiles of the prehistoric eras. They play a necessary part in the evolutionary process, but the same power, which produced them, will dispose of them. And it is well to bear in mind that they have never been really rich; a record of the private lives of most of this class will show that they have really been most abject and wretched. Riches secured on the competitive plane are never satisfactory and permanent. They are yours today and another's tomorrow. Remember, if you are to become rich in a scientific and certain way, you must rise entirely out of competitive thought. You must never think for a moment that the supply is limited. Just as soon as you begin to think that all the money is being "cornered" and controlled by others, and that you must exert yourself to get laws passed to stop this process, and so on — in that moment you drop into the competitive mind and your power to cause creation is gone for the time being. And what is worse, you will probably arrest the creative movements you have already begun. **KNOW** that there are countless millions of dollars' worth of gold in the mountains of the earth, not yet brought to light. And know that if there were not, more would be created from thinking substance to supply your needs. **KNOW** that the money you need will come, even if it is necessary for a thousand men to be led to the discovery of new gold mines tomorrow. Never look at the visible supply. Look always at the limitless riches in formless substance, and **KNOW** that they are coming to you as fast as you can receive and use them. Nobody, by cornering the visible supply, can prevent you from getting what is yours. So never allow yourself to think for an instant that all the best building spots will be taken before you get ready to build your house, unless you hurry. Never worry about the trusts and combines, and get anxious for fear they will soon come to own the whole earth. Never get afraid that you will lose what you want because some other person "beats you to it." That cannot possibly happen. You are not seeking anything that is possessed by anybody else; you are causing what you want to be created from formless substance, and the supply is without limits. Stick to the formulated statement: There is a thinking stuff from which all things are made, and which, in its original state, permeates, penetrates, and fills the interspaces of the universe. A thought, in this substance produces the thing that is imaged by the thought. A person can form things in his thought, and, by impressing his thought upon formless substance, can cause the thing he thinks about to be created.

CHAPTER 6

How Riches Come To You

When I say that you do not have to drive sharp bargains, I do not mean that you do not have to drive any bargains at all or that you are above the necessity for having any dealings with your fellow men. I mean that you will not need to deal with them unfairly. You do not have to get something for nothing, but can give to every person more than you take from him. You cannot give everyone more in cash market value than you take from him, but you can give him more in use value than the cash value of the thing you take from him. The paper, ink, and other material in this book may not be worth the money you pay for it, but if the ideas suggested by it bring you thousands of dollars, those who sold it to you have not wronged you. They have given you a great use value for a small cash value.

Let us suppose that I own a picture by one of the great artists, which, in a developed society, is worth thousands of dollars. I take it to Baffin Bay and by "salesmanship" induce a native dweller to give a bundle of furs worth $500 for it. I have really wronged him, for he has no use for the picture. It has no use value to him; it will not add to his life. But suppose I give him a gun worth $50 for his furs. Then he has made a good bargain. He has use for the gun. It will get him many more furs and much food; it will add to his life in every way. It will make him rich. When you rise from the competitive to the creative plane, you can scan your business transactions very strictly, and if you are selling any person anything which does not add more to his life than the thing he give you in exchange, you can afford to stop it. You do not have to beat anybody in business.

And if you are in a business, which does beat people, get out of it at once. Give everyone more in use value than you take from him in cash value. Then you are adding to the life of the world by every business transaction. If you have people working for you, you must take from them more in cash value than you pay them in wages, but you can so organize your business that it will be filled with the principle of advancement, and so that each employee who wishes to do so may advance a little every day. You can make your business do for your employees what this book is doing for you. You can so conduct your business that it will be a sort of ladder by which every employee who will take the trouble may climb to riches himself. And given the opportunity, if he will not do so, it is not your fault.

And finally, just because you are to cause the creation of your riches from formless substance which permeates all your environment, it does not follow that they are to take shape from the atmosphere and come into being before your eyes. If you want a sewing machine, for instance, I do not mean to tell you that you are to impress the thought of a sewing machine on thinking substance until the machine is formed without hands, in the room where you sit or elsewhere. But if you want a sewing machine, hold the mental image of it with the most positive certainty that it is being made or is on its way to you. After once forming the thought, have the most absolute and unquestioning faith that the sewing machine is coming. Never think of it or speak of it in any other way than as being sure to arrive. Claim it as already yours. It will be brought to you by the power of the supreme intelligence, acting upon the minds of men. If you live in Maine, it may be that a person will be brought from Texas or Japan to engage in some transaction that will result in your getting what you want. If so, the whole matter will be as much to that person's advantage as it is to yours.

Do not forget for a moment that the thinking substance is through all, in all, communicating with all, and can influence all. The desire of thinking substance for fuller life and better living has caused the creation of all the sewing machines already made, and it can cause the creation of millions more — and will, whenever people set it in motion by desire and faith and by acting in a certain way. You can certainly have a sewing machine in your house, and it is just as certain that you can have any other thing or things which you want and which you will use for the advancement of your own life and the lives of others. You need not hesitate about asking largely. "It is your Father's pleasure to give you the kingdom," said Jesus. Original substance wants to live all that is possible in you, and wants you to have all that you can use and will use for the living of the most abundant life. If you fix upon your consciousness the fact that your desire for the possession of riches is one with the desire of the supreme power for more complete expression, your faith becomes invincible. Once I saw a little boy sitting at a piano, vainly trying to bring harmony out of the keys. I saw that he was grieved and provoked by his inability to play real music. I asked him the cause of his vexation, and he answered, "I can feel the music in me, but I can't make my hands go right." The music in him was the URGE of original substance, containing all the possibilities of all life. All that there is of music was seeking expression through the child. God, the one substance, is trying to live and do and enjoy things through humanity. He is saying "I want hands to build wonderful structures, to play divine harmonies, to paint glorious pictures. I want feet to run my errands, eyes to see my beauties, tongues to tell mighty truths and to sing marvelous songs," and so on. All that there is of possibility is seeking expression through people. God wants those who can play music to have pianos and every other instrument and to have the means to cultivate their talents to the fullest extent. He wants those who can appreciate beauty to be able to surround themselves with beautiful things. He wants those who can discern truth to have every opportunity to travel and observe. He wants those who can appreciate dress to be beautifully clothed, and those who can appreciate good food to be luxuriously fed. He wants all these things because it is himself that enjoys and appreciates them; they are his creation. It is God who wants to play, and sing, and enjoy beauty, and proclaim truth, and wear fine clothes, and eat good foods. "It is God that worketh in you to will and to do," said the apostle Paul. The desire you feel for riches is the infinite, seeking to express himself in you as he sought to find expression in the little boy at the piano. So you need not hesitate to ask largely. Your part is to focus on and express that desire to God.

This is a difficult point with most people. They retain something of the old idea that poverty and self-sacrifice are pleasing to God. They look upon poverty as a part of the plan, a necessity of nature. They have the idea that God has finished his work, and made all that he can make, and that the majority of people must stay poor because there is not enough to go around. They hold to so much of this erroneous thought that they feel ashamed to ask for wealth. They try not to want more than a very modest competence, just enough to make them fairly comfortable. I recall now the case of one student who was told that he must get in mind a clear picture of the things he desired, so that the creative thought of them might be impressed on formless substance. He was a very poor man, living in a rented house and having only what he earned from day today, and he could not grasp the fact that all wealth was his. So, after thinking the matter over, he decided that he might reasonably ask for a new rug for the floor of his best room and a coal stove to heat the house during the cold weather. Following the instructions given in this book, he obtained these things in a few months. And then it dawned upon him that he had not asked enough. He went through the house in which he lived, and planned all the improvements he would like to make in it. He mentally added a bay window here and a room there, until it was complete in his mind as his ideal home, and then he planned its furnishings. Holding the whole picture in his mind, he began living in the certain way and moving toward what he wanted — and he owns the house now and is rebuilding it after the form of his mental image. And now, with still larger faith, he is going on to get greater things. It has been unto him according to his faith, and so it is with you — and with all of us.

CHAPTER 7

Gratitude

The illustrations given in the last chapter will have conveyed to the reader the fact that the first step toward getting rich is to convey the idea of your wants to the formless substance. This is true, and you will see that in order to do so it becomes necessary to relate yourself to the formless intelligence in a harmonious way. To secure this harmonious relation is a matter of such primary and vital importance that I shall give some space to its discussion here and give you instructions, which, if you will follow them, will be certain to bring you into perfect unity of mind with the supreme power, or God. The whole process of mental adjustment can be summed up in one word: Gratitude. First, you believe that there is one intelligent substance, from which all things proceed. Second, you believe that this substance gives you everything you desire. And third, you relate yourself to it by a feeling of deep and profound gratitude. Many people who order their lives rightly in all other ways are kept in poverty by their lack of gratitude. Having received one gift from God, they cut the wires, which connect them with him by failing to make acknowledgment.

It is easy to understand that the nearer we live to the source of wealth, the more wealth we shall receive, and it is easy also to understand that the soul that is always grateful lives in closer touch with God than the one, which never looks to him in thankful acknowledgment. The more gratefully we fix our minds on the supreme when good things come to us, the more good things we will receive, and the more rapidly they will come. And the reason simply is that the mental attitude of gratitude draws the mind into closer touch with the source from which the blessings come.

If it is a new thought to you that gratitude brings your whole mind into closer harmony with the creative energies of the universe, consider it well, and you will see that it is true. The good things you have already have come to you along the line of obedience to certain laws. Gratitude will lead your mind out along the ways by which things come, and it will keep you in close harmony with creative thought and prevent you from falling into competitive thought. Gratitude alone can keep you looking toward the all, and prevent you from falling into the error of thinking of the supply as limited — and to do that would be fatal to your hopes. There is a law of gratitude, and it is absolutely necessary that you should observe the law if you are to get the results you seek. The law of gratitude is the natural principle that action and reaction are always equal and in opposite directions. The grateful outreaching of your mind in thankful praise to the supreme intelligence is a liberation or expenditure of force. It cannot fail to reach that to which it addressed, and the reaction is an instantaneous movement toward you. "Draw nigh unto God, and he will draw nigh unto you." That is a statement of psychological truth. And if your gratitude is strong and constant, the reaction in formless substance will be strong and continuous; the movement of the things you want will be always toward you. Notice the grateful attitude that Jesus took, how he always seems to be saying, "I thank thee, Father, that thou hearest me."

You cannot exercise much power without gratitude, for it is gratitude that keeps you connected with power. But the value of gratitude does not consist solely in getting you more blessings in the future. Without gratitude you cannot long keep from dissatisfied thought regarding things as they are. The moment you permit your mind to dwell with dissatisfaction upon things as they are, you begin to lose ground. You fix attention upon the common, the ordinary, the poor, the squalid, and the mean — and your mind takes the form of these things. Then you will transmit these forms or mental images to the formless. And the common, the poor, the squalid, and the mean will come to you. To permit your mind to dwell upon the inferior is to become inferior and to surround yourself with inferior things. On the other hand, to fix your attention on the best is to surround yourself with the best, and to become the best. The creative power within us makes us into the image of that to which we give our attention. We are of thinking substance, too, and thinking substance always takes the form of that which it thinks about. The grateful mind is constantly fixed upon the best.

Therefore it tends to become the best. It takes the form or character of the best, and will receive the best. Also, faith is born of gratitude. The grateful mind continually expects good things, and expectation becomes faith. The reaction of gratitude upon one's own mind produces faith, and every outgoing wave of grateful thanksgiving increases faith. The person who has no feeling of gratitude cannot long retain a living faith, and without a living faith you cannot get rich by the creative method, as we shall see in the following chapters. It is necessary, then, to cultivate the habit of being grateful for every good thing that comes to you and to give thanks continuously. And because all things have contributed to your advancement, you should include all things in your gratitude. Do not waste a lot of time thinking or talking about the shortcomings or wrong actions of those in power. Their organization of the world has created your opportunity; all you get really comes to you because of them. Do not rage against corrupt politicians. If it were not for politicians we should fall into anarchy and your opportunity would be greatly lessened. God has worked a long time and very patiently to bring us up to where we are in industry and government, and he is going right on with his work. There is not the least doubt that he will do away with plutocrats, trust magnates, captains of industry, and politicians as soon as they can be spared, but in the meantime, they are all very necessary. Remember that they are all helping to arrange the lines of transmission along which your riches will come to you, and be grateful. This will bring you into harmonious relations with the good in everything, and the good in everything will move toward you.

CHAPTER 8

Thinking in the Certain Way

Turn back to Chapter 6 and read again the story of the man who formed a mental image of his house and you will get a fair idea of the initial step toward getting rich. You must form a clear and definite mental picture of what you want. You cannot transmit an idea unless you have it yourself. You must have it before you can give it, and many people fail to impress thinking substance because they have themselves only a vague and misty concept of the things they want to do, to have, or to become. It is not enough that you should have a general desire for wealth "to do good with."

Everybody has that desire. It is not enough that you should have a wish to travel, see things, live more, etc. Everybody has those desires also. If you were going to send a wireless message to a friend, you would not send the letters of the alphabet in their order and let him construct the message for himself, nor would you take words at random from the dictionary. You would send a coherent sentence, one, which meant something. When you try to impress your wants upon the thinking substance, remember that it must be done with a coherent statement. You must know what you want and be specific and definite. You can never get rich or start the creative power into action by sending out unformed longings and vague desires. Go over your desires just as the man I have described went over his house. See just what you want and get a clear mental picture of it as you wish it to look when you get it. That clear mental picture you must have continually in mind. As the sailor has in mind the port toward which he is sailing the ship, you must keep your face toward it all the time. You must no more lose sight of it than the helmsman loses sight of the compass. It is not necessary to take exercises in concentration, nor to set apart special times for prayer and affirmation, nor to "go into the silence," nor to do occult stunts of any kind. Some of these things are well enough, but all you need is to know what you want and to want it badly enough so that it will stay in your thoughts. Spend as much of your leisure time as you can in contemplating your picture. But no one needs to take exercises to concentrate his mind on a thing, which he really wants. It is the things you do not really care about which require effort to fix your attention upon them. And unless you really want to get rich, so that the desire is strong enough to hold your thoughts directed to the purpose as the magnetic pole holds the needle of the compass, it will hardly be worthwhile for you to try to carry out the instructions given in this book.

The methods set forth here are for people whose desire for riches is strong enough to overcome mental laziness and the love of ease, and to make them work. The more clear and definite you make your picture then, and the more you dwell upon it, bringing out all its delightful details, the stronger your desire will be. And the stronger your desire, the easier it will be to hold your mind fixed upon the picture of what you want. Something more is necessary, however, than merely to see the picture clearly. If that is all you do, you are only a dreamer, and will have little or no power for accomplishment. Behind your clear vision must be the purpose to realize it, to bring it out in tangible expression. And behind this purpose must be an invincible and unwavering **FAITH** that the thing is already yours that it is "at hand" and you have only to take possession of it. Live in the new house, mentally, until it takes form around you physically. In the mental realm, enter at once into full enjoyment of the things you want. "Whatsoever things ye ask for when ye pray, believe that ye receive them, and ye shall have them," said Jesus.

See the things you want as if they were actually around you all the time. See yourself as owning and using them. Make use of them in imagination just as you will use them when they are your tangible possessions. Dwell upon your mental picture until it is clear and distinct, and then take the mental attitude of ownership toward everything in that picture. Take possession of it, in mind, in the full faith that it is actually yours. Hold to this mental ownership. Do not waiver for an instant in the faith that it is real. And remember what was said in a proceeding chapter about gratitude: Be as thankful for it all the time as you expect to be when it has taken form. The person who can sincerely thank God for the things that as yet he owns only in imagination has real faith. He will get rich. He will cause the creation of whatever he wants. You do not need to pray repeatedly for things you want. It is not necessary to tell God about it every day. Your part is to intelligently formulate your desire for the things which make for a larger life and to get these desire arranged into a coherent whole, and then to impress this whole desire upon the formless substance, which has the power and the will to bring you what you want.

You do not make this impression by repeating strings of words; you make it by holding the vision with unshakable **PURPOSE** to attain it and with steadfast **FAITH** that you do attain it. The answer to prayer is not according to your faith while you are talking, but according to your faith while you are working. Keep yourself focused and thinking in the certain way with of words; you make it by holding the vision with unshakable **PURPOSE** to attain it and with steadfast **FAITH** that you do attain it. The answer to prayer is not according to your faith while you are talking, but according to your faith while you are working. You cannot impress the mind of God by having a special Sabbath day set apart to tell him what you want, and then forgetting him during the rest of the week. You cannot impress him by having special hours to go into your closet and pray, if you then dismiss the matter from your mind until the hour of prayer comes again. Oral prayer is well enough, and has its effect, especially upon yourself, in clarifying your vision and strengthening your faith, but it is not your oral petitions that get you what you want. In order to get rich you do not need a "sweet hour of prayer;" you need to "pray without ceasing." And by prayer I mean holding steadily to your vision, with the purpose to cause its creation into solid form, and the faith that you are doing so. "Believe that ye receive them."

Once you have clearly formed your vision, the whole matter turns on receiving. When you have formed it, it is well to make an oral statement, addressing the supreme in gratitude. Then, from that moment on you must, in mind, receive what you ask for. Live in the new house, wear the fine clothes, ride in the automobile, go on the journey, and confidently plan for greater journeys.

Think and speak of all the things you have asked for in terms of actual present ownership. Imagine an environment and a financial condition exactly as you want them, and live all the time in that mental environment and financial condition until they take physical shape. Mind, however, that you do not do this as a mere dreamer and castle builder. Hold to the **FAITH** that the imaginary is being realized and to your **PURPOSE** to realize it. Remember that it is faith and purpose in the use of the imagination that make the difference between the scientist and the dreamer. And having learned this fact, it is here that you must learn the proper use of the will.

CHAPTER 9

How to Use the Will

To set about getting rich in the certain way, you do not try to apply your will power to anything outside of yourself. You have no right to do so, anyway. It is wrong to apply your will to other men and women in order to get them to do what you wish done. It is as flagrantly wrong to coerce people by mental power, as it is to coerce them by physical power. If compelling people by physical force to do things for you reduces them to slavery, compelling them by mental means accomplishes exactly the same thing; the only difference is in methods. If taking things from people by physical force is robbery, them taking things by mental force is robbery also.

There is no difference in principle. You have no right to use your will power upon another person, even "for his own good," for you do not know what is for his good. The science of getting rich does not require you to apply power or force to any other person, in any way whatsoever. There is not the slightest necessity for doing so. Indeed, any attempt to use your will upon others will only tend to defeat your purpose. You do not need to apply your will to things in order to compel them to come to you. That would simply be trying to coerce God and would be foolish and useless. You do not have to try to compel God to give you good things, any more than you have to use your will power to make the sun rise. You do not have to use your will power to conquer an unfriendly Deity, or to make stubborn and rebellious forces do your bidding. Substance is friendly to you, and is more anxious to give you what you want than you are to get it.

To get rich, you need only to use your will power upon yourself. When you know what to think and do, then you must use your will to compel yourself to think and do the right things. That is the legitimate use of the will in getting what you want — to use it in holding yourself to the right course. Use your will to keep yourself thinking and acting in the certain way. Do not try to project your will, or your thoughts, or your mind out into space to "act" on things or people. Keep your mind at home. It can accomplish more there than elsewhere. Use your mind to form a mental image of what you want and to hold that vision with faith and purpose.

And use your will to keep your mind working in the right way. The more steady and continuous your faith and purpose, the more rapidly you will get rich because you will make only **POSITIVE** impressions upon substance, and you will not neutralize or offset them by negative impressions. The picture of your desires, held with faith and purpose, is taken up by the formless, and permeates it to great distances — throughout the universe, for all we know. As this impression spreads, all things are set moving toward its realization. Every living thing, every inanimate thing, and the things yet uncreated are stirred toward bringing into being that which you want.

All force begins to be exerted in that direction. All things begin to move toward you. The minds of people everywhere are influenced toward doing the things necessary to the fulfilling of your desires, and they work for you, unconsciously. But you can check all this by starting a negative impression in the formless substance. Doubt or unbelief is as certain to start a movement away from you, as faith and purpose are to start one toward you. It is by not understanding this that most people make their failure. Every hour and moment you spend in giving heed to doubts and fears, every hour you spend in worry, every hour in which your soul is possessed by unbelief, sets a current away from you in the whole domain of intelligent substance. All the promises are unto them that believe and unto them only. Since belief is all-important, it behooves you to guard your thoughts, and as your beliefs will be shaped to a very great extent by the things you observe and think about, it is important that you should carefully govern to what you give your attention. And here the will comes into use, for it is by your will that you determine upon what things your attention shall be fixed. If you want to become rich, you must not make a study of poverty. Things are not brought into being by thinking about their opposites.

Health is never to be attained by studying disease and thinking about disease; righteousness is not to be promoted by studying sin and thinking about sin; and no one ever got rich by studying poverty and thinking about poverty. Medicine as a science of disease has increased disease; religion as a science of sin has promoted sin, and economics as a study of poverty will fill the world with wretchedness and want. Do not talk about poverty, do not investigate it, or concern yourself with it. Never mind what its causes are; you have nothing to do with them. What concerns you is the cure. Do not spend your time in so-called charitable work Do some of these bold statements challenge or confuse you? Get the insights and thoughts of other like-minded people in the or charity movements; most charity only tends to perpetuate the wretchedness it aims to eradicate. I do not say that you should be hard-hearted or unkind and refuse to hear the cry of need, but you must not try to eradicate poverty in any of the conventional ways. Put poverty behind you, and put all that pertains to it behind you, and "make good." Get rich. That is the best way you can help the poor.

And you cannot hold the mental image that is to make you rich if you fill your mind with pictures of poverty and all its attendant ills. Do not read books or papers which give circumstantial accounts of the wretchedness of the tenement dwellers, of the horrors of child labor, and so on. Do not read anything that fills your mind with gloomy images of want and suffering. You cannot help the poor in the least by knowing about these things, and the widespread knowledge of them does not tend at all to do away with poverty. What tends to do away with poverty is not the getting of pictures of poverty into your mind, but getting pictures of wealth, abundance, and possibility into the minds of the poor. You are not deserting the poor in their misery when you refuse to allow your mind to be filled with pictures of that misery.

Poverty can be done away with, not by increasing the number of well-to-do people who think about poverty, but by increasing the number of poor people who purpose with faith to get rich. The poor do not need charity; they need inspiration. Charity only sends them a loaf of bread to keep them alive in their wretchedness, or gives them an entertainment to make them forget for an hour or two. But inspiration can cause them to rise out of their misery. If you want to help the poor, demonstrate to them that they can become rich. Prove it by getting rich yourself. The only way in which poverty will ever be banished from this world is by getting a large and constantly increasing number of people to practice the teachings of this book. People must be taught to become rich by creation, not by competition. Every person who becomes rich by competition knocks down the ladder by which he rises, and keeps others down, but every person who gets rich by creation opens a way for thousands to follow — and inspires them to do so. You are not showing hardness of heart or an unfeeling disposition when you refuse to pity poverty, see poverty, read about poverty, or think or talk about it, or to listen to those who do talk about it. Use your will power to keep your mind

OFF the subject of poverty and to keep it fixed with faith and purpose **ON** the vision of what you want and are creating.

CHAPTER 10

Further Use of the Will

You cannot retain a true and clear vision of wealth if you are constantly turning your attention to opposing pictures, whether they are external or imaginary. Do not tell of your past troubles of a financial nature, if you have had them. Do not think of them at all. Do not tell of the poverty of your parents or the hardships of your early life. To do any of these things is to mentally class yourself with the poor for the time being, and it will certainly check the movement of things in your direction. Put poverty and all things that pertain to poverty completely behind you. You have accepted a certain theory of the universe as being correct, and are resting all your hopes of happiness on its being correct. What can you gain by giving heed to conflicting theories? Do not read books which tell you that the world is soon coming to an end, and do not read the writing of muckrakers and pessimistic philosophers who tell you that it is going to the devil. The world is not going to the devil; it is going to God who already owns everything!. It is a wonderful becoming.

True, there may be a good many things in existing conditions that are disagreeable, but what is the use of studying them when they are certainly passing away and when the study of them only tends to slow their passing and keep them with us? Why give time and attention to things that are being removed by evolutionary growth, when you can hasten their removal only by promoting the evolutionary growth as far as your part of it goes? No matter how horrible in seeming may be the conditions in certain countries, sections, or places, you waste your time and destroy your own chances by dwelling on them. You should interest yourself in the world's becoming rich. Think of the riches the world is coming into instead of the poverty it is growing out of, and bear in mind that the only way in which you can assist the world in growing rich is by growing rich yourself through the creative method, not the competitive one. Give your attention wholly to riches. Do not focus on poverty. Whenever you think or speak of those who are poor, think and speak of them as those who are becoming rich, as those who are to be congratulated rather than pitied. Then they and others will catch the inspiration, and begin to search for the way out. Because I say that you are to give your whole time and mind and thought to riches, it does not follow that you are to be sordid or mean. To become really rich is the noblest aim you can have in life, for it includes everything else. On the competitive plane, the struggle to get rich is a Godless scramble for power over others, but when we come into the creative mind, all this is changed.

All that is possible in the way of greatness, of service and lofty endeavor, comes by way of getting rich, because all is made possible by the use of things. You can aim at nothing so great or noble, I repeat, as to become rich, and you must fix your attention upon your mental picture of wealth to the exclusion of all that may tend to dim or obscure the vision. Some people remain in poverty because they are ignorant of the fact that there is wealth for them, and these can best be taught by showing them the way to affluence in your own person and practice. Others are poor because, while they feel that there is a way out, they are too intellectually indolent to put forth the mental effort necessary to find that way and travel it. For these, the very best thing you can do is to arouse their desire by showing them the happiness that comes from being rightly rich. Others still are poor because, while they have some notion of science, they have become so swamped and lost in the maze of theories that they do not know which road to take. They try a mixture of many systems and fail in all. For these, again, the very best thing to do is to show the right way in your own person and practice. An ounce of doing things is worth a pound of theorizing. The very best thing you can do for the whole world is to make the most of yourself. You can serve God and humanity in no more effective way than by getting rich; that is, if you get rich by the creative method and not by the competitive one.

Another thing. We assert that this book gives in detail the principles of the science of getting rich, and if that is true, you do not need to read any other book upon the subject. This may sound narrow and egotistical, but consider: There is no more scientific method of computation in mathematics than by addition, subtraction, multiplication, and division; no other method is possible. There can be but one shortest distance between two points. There is only one way to think scientifically, and that is to think in the way that leads by the most direct and simple route to the goal. No one has yet formulated a briefer or less complex "system" than the one set forth here. It has been stripped of all non-essentials. When you commence on this, lay all others aside. Put them out of your mind altogether. Read this book every day. Keep it with you. Commit it to memory, and do not think about other "systems" and theories. If you do, you will begin to have doubts and to be uncertain and wavering in your thought, and then you will begin to make failures. After you have made good and become rich, you may study other systems as much as you please. And read only the most optimistic comments on the world's news — those in harmony with your picture. Also, do not dabble in theosophy, spiritualism, or kindred studies. Perhaps the dead still live and are near, but if they are, let them alone; mind your own business. Wherever the spirits of the dead may be, they have their own work to do, and we have no right to interfere with them. We cannot help them, and it is very doubtful whether they can help us, or whether we have any right to trespass upon their time if they can. Let the dead and the hereafter alone, and solve your own problem: Get rich. If you begin to mix with the occult, you will start mental crosscurrents that will surely bring your hopes to shipwreck.

Now, this and the preceding chapters have brought us to the following statement of basic facts: There is a thinking stuff from which all things are made, and which, in its original state, permeates, penetrates, and fills the interspaces of the universe. A thought in this substance produces the thing that is imaged by the thought. A person can form things in his thought, and, by impressing his thought upon formless substance, can cause the thing he thinks about to be created. In order to do this, a person must pass from the competitive to the creative mind; he must form a clear mental picture of the things he wants, and hold this picture in his thoughts with the fixed **PURPOSE** to get what he wants, and the unwavering **FAITH** that he does get what he wants, closing his mind against all that may tend to shake his purpose, dim his vision, or quench his faith. And in addition to all this, we shall now see that he must live and act in a certain way.

CHAPTER 11

Acting in the Certain Way

Thought is the creative power or the impelling force which causes the creative power to act. Thinking in a certain way will bring riches to you, but you must not rely upon thought alone, paying no attention to personal action. That is the rock upon which many otherwise scientific thinkers meet shipwreck — the failure to connect thought with personal action. We have not yet reached the stage of development, even supposing such a stage to be possible, in which a person can create directly from formless substance without nature's processes or the work of human hands. A person must not only think, but his personal action must supplement his thought. By thought you can cause the gold in the hearts of the mountains to be impelled toward you, but it will not mine itself, refine itself, coin itself into double eagles, and come rolling along the roads, seeking its way into your pocket. Under the impelling power of the supreme spirit, people's affairs will be so ordered that someone will be led to mine the gold for you.

Other people's business transactions will be so directed that the gold will be brought toward you. And you must so arrange your own business affairs that you may be able to receive it when it comes to you. Your thought makes all things, animate and inanimate, work to bring you what you want, but your personal activity must be such that you can rightly receive what you want when it reaches you. You are not to take it as charity, nor to steal it. You must give every man more in use value than he gives you in cash value. The scientific use of thought consists in forming a clear and distinct mental image of what you want, in holding fast to your purpose to get what you want, and in realizing with grateful faith that you do get what you want. Do not try to "project" your thought in any mysterious or occult way, with the idea of having it go out and do things for you. That is wasted effort and will weaken your power to think with sanity. The action of thought in getting rich is fully explained in the preceding chapters:

Your faith and purpose positively impress your vision upon formless substance, which has the same desire for more life that you have, and this vision, received from you, sets all the creative forces at work in and through their regular channels of action, but directed toward you. It is not your part to guide or supervise the creative process. All you have to do with that is to retain your vision, stick to your purpose, and maintain your faith and gratitude. But you must act in a certain way, so that you can appropriate what is yours when it comes to you and so that you can meet the things you have in your picture and put them in their proper places as they arrive. You can really see the truth of this. When things reach you, they will be in the hands of others, who will ask an equivalent for them. And you can only get what is yours by giving the other person what is rightfully his. Your pocketbook is not going to be transformed into a Fortunata's purse, which shall be always full of money without effort on your part. This is the crucial point in the science of getting rich — right here, where thought and personal action must be combined. There are very many people who, consciously or unconsciously, set the creative forces in action by the strength and persistence of their desires, but who remain poor because they do not provide for the reception of the thing they want when it comes. By thought, the thing you want is brought to you. By action, you receive it. Whatever your action is to be, it is evident that you must act **NOW**. You cannot act in the past, and it is essential to the clearness of your mental vision that you dismiss the past from your mind. You cannot act in the future, for the future is not here yet. And you cannot tell how you will want to act in any future contingency until that contingency has arrived. Because you are not in the right business or the right environment now, do not think that you must postpone action until you get into the right business or environment. And do not spend time in the present taking thought as to the best course in possible future emergencies; have faith in your ability to meet any emergency when it arrives. If you act in the present with your mind on the future, your present action will be with a divided mind, and will not be effective. Put your whole mind into present action. Do not give your creative impulse to original substance, and then sit down and wait for results. If you do, you will never get them. Act now. There is never any time but now, and there never will be any time but now. If you are ever to begin to make ready for the reception of what you want, you must begin **NOW**. And your action, whatever it is, must most likely be in your present business or employment, and must be upon the persons and things in your present environment. You cannot act where you are not, you cannot act where you have been, and you cannot act where you are going to be. You can act only where you are.

Do not bother as to whether yesterday's work was well done or ill done; do today's work well. Do not try to do tomorrow's work now; there will be plenty of time to do that when you get to it. Do not try, by occult or mystical means, to act on people or things that are out of your reach. Do not wait for a change of environment, before you act; get a change of environment by action. You can so act upon the environment in which you are now, as to cause yourself to be transferred to a better environment. Hold with faith and purpose the vision of yourself in the better environment, but act upon your present environment with all your heart, and with all your strength, and with all your mind. Do not spend any time in daydreaming or castle building; hold to the one vision of what you want, and act **NOW**. Do not cast about, seeking some new thing to do or some strange, unusual, or remarkable action to perform as a first step toward getting rich. It is probable that your actions, at least for some time to come, will be the same ones you have been performing for some time past, but you are to begin now to perform these actions in the certain way, which will surely make you rich. If you are engaged in some business, and feel that it is not the right one for you, do not wait until you get into the right business before you begin to act. Do not feel discouraged or sit down and lament because you are misplaced. No one is so misplaced that he cannot find the right place, and no one is so involved in the wrong business that he cannot get into the right business. Hold the vision of yourself in the right business, with the purpose to get into it and the faith that you will get into it and are getting into it, but **ACT** in your present business. Use your present business as the means of getting a better one, and use your present environment as the means of getting into a better one. Your vision of the right business, if held with faith and purpose, will cause the supreme power to move the right business toward you. And your action, if performed in the certain way, will cause you to move toward the business.

If you are an employee or wage earner and feel that you must change places in order to get what you want, do not "project" your thought into space and rely upon it to get you another job. It will probably fail to do so. Hold the vision of yourself in the job you want while you **ACT** with faith and purpose on the job you have, and you will certainly get the job you want. Your vision and faith will set the creative force in motion to bring it toward you, and your action will cause the forces in your own environment to move you toward the place you want. In closing this chapter, we will add another statement to our syllabus: There is a thinking stuff from which all things are made, and which, in its original state, permeates, penetrates, and fills the interspaces of the universe. A thought in this substance produces the thing that is imaged by the thought. A person can form things in his thought, and, by impressing his thought upon formless substance, can cause the thing he thinks about to be created. In order to do this, a person must pass from the competitive to the creative mind; he must form a clear mental picture of the things he wants, and hold this picture in his thoughts with the fixed **PURPOSE** to get what he wants, and the unwavering **FAITH** that he does get what he wants, closing his mind to all that may tend to shake his purpose, dim his vision, or quench his faith. So that he may receive what he wants when it comes, a person must act **NOW** upon the people and things in his present environment.

CHAPTER 12

Efficient Action

You must use your thought as directed action in previous chapters and begin to do what you can do where you are, and you must do **ALL** that you can do where you are. You can advance only by being larger than your present place, and no one is larger than his present place that leaves undone any of the work pertaining to that place. Only those who more than fill their present places advance the world. If no one quite filled his present place, you can see that there must be a going backward in everything. Those who do not quite fill their present places are dead weight upon society, government, commerce, and industry. Others must carry them along at a great expense. Only those who do not fill the places they are holding slow the progress of the world. They belong to a former age and their tendency is toward degeneration. No society could advance if everyone was smaller than his place; the law of physical and mental evolution guides social evolution.

In the animal world, evolution is caused by excess of life. When an organism has more life than can be expressed in the functions of its own plane, it develops the organs of a higher plane, and a new species is originated. There never would have been new species had there not been organisms that more than filled their places. The law is exactly the same for you: Your getting rich depends upon your applying this principle to your own affairs. Every day is either a successful day or a day of failure, and it is the successful days that get you what you want. If every day is a failure you can never get rich, while if every day is a success, you cannot fail to get rich.

If there is something that may be done today and you do not do it, you have failed insofar as that thing is concerned — and the consequences may be more disastrous than you imagine. You cannot foresee the results of even the most trivial act. You do not know the workings of all the forces that have been set moving in your behalf. Much may be depending on your doing some simple act, and it may be the very thing that is to open the door of opportunity to very great possibilities. You can never know all the combinations which supreme intelligence is making for you in the world of things and of human affairs. Your neglect or failure to do some small thing may cause a long delay in getting what you want. Do, every day **ALL** that can be done that day. There is, however, a limitation or qualification of the above that you must take into account. You are not to overwork, nor to rush blindly into your business in the effort to do the greatest possible number of things in the shortest possible time.

You are not to try to do tomorrow's work today, nor to do a week's work in a day. It is really not the number of things you do, but the **EFFICIENCY** of each separate action that counts. Every act is, in itself, either a success or a failure. Every act is, in itself, either effective and efficient or ineffective and inefficient. Every inefficient act is a failure, and if you spend your life in doing inefficient acts, your whole life will be a failure. The more things you do, the worse for you — if all your acts are inefficient ones. On the other hand, every efficient act is a success in itself, and if every act of your life is an efficient one, your whole life must be a success. The cause of failure is doing too many things in an inefficient manner and not doing enough things in an efficient manner. You will see that it is a self-evident proposition that if you do not do any inefficient acts and if you do a sufficient number of efficient acts, you will become rich. If, now, it is possible for you to make each act an efficient one, you see again that the getting of riches is reduced to an exact science, like mathematics.

The matter turns, then, on the question of whether you can make each separate act a success in itself. And this you can certainly do. You can make each act a success, because **ALL** power is working with you, and **ALL** power cannot fail. Power is at your service, and to make each act efficient you have only to put power into it. Every action is either strong or weak, and when every action is strong, you are acting in the certain way that will make you rich. Every act can be made strong and efficient by holding your vision while you are doing it and putting the whole power of your **FAITH** and **PURPOSE** into it. It is at this point that the people who separate mental power from personal action fail. They use the power of mind in one place and at one time, and they act in another way in another place and at another time. So their acts are not successful in themselves; too many of them are inefficient.

But if **ALL** power goes into every act, no matter how commonplace, every act will be a success in itself. And since it is the nature of things that every success opens the way to other successes, your progress toward what you want and the progress of what you want toward you will become increasingly rapid.

Remember that successful action is cumulative in its results. Since the desire for more life is inherent in all things, when a person begins to move toward larger life, more things attach themselves to him, and the influence of his desire is multiplied. Do, every day, all that you can do that day, and do each act in an efficient manner. In saying that you must hold your vision while you are doing each act, however trivial or commonplace, I do not mean to say that it is necessary at all times to see the vision distinctly to its smallest details. It should be the work of your leisure hours to use your imagination on the details of your vision and to contemplate them until they are firmly fixed upon memory.

If you wish speedy results, spend practically all your spare time in this practice. By continuous contemplation you will get the picture of what you want — even to the smallest details — so firmly fixed upon your mind and so completely transferred to the mind of formless substance, that in your working hours you need only to mentally refer to the picture to stimulate your faith and purpose and cause your best effort to be put forth. Contemplate your picture in your leisure hours until your consciousness is so full of it that you can grasp it instantly. You will become so enthused with its bright promises that the mere thought of it will call forth the strongest energies of your whole being. Let us again repeat our syllabus, and by slightly changing the closing statements bring it to the point we have now reached.

There is a thinking stuff from which all things are made, and which, in its original state, permeates, penetrates, and fills the interspaces of the universe. A thought in this substance produces the thing that is imaged by the thought. A person can form things in his thought, and, by impressing his thought upon formless substance, can cause the thing he thinks about to be created. In order to do this, a person must pass from the competitive to the creative mind. He must form a clear mental picture of the things he wants, and must do — with faith and purpose — all that can be done each day, doing each separate thing in an efficient manner.

CHAPTER 13

Getting Into the Right Business

Success in any particular business depends for one thing upon your possessing, in a well-developed state, the faculties required in that business. Without good musical faculty no one can succeed as a teacher of music. Without well-developed mechanical faculties no one can achieve great success in any of the mechanical trades. Without tact and the commercial faculties no one can succeed in mercantile pursuits. But to possess in a well-developed state the faculties required in your particular vocation does not insure getting rich.

There are musicians who have remarkable talent, and who yet remain poor. There are blacksmiths, carpenters, and so on who have excellent mechanical ability, but who do not get rich. And there are merchants with good faculties for dealing with people who nevertheless fail. The different faculties are tools. It is essential to have good tools, but it is also essential that the tools should be used in the right way. One man can take a sharp saw, a square, a good plane, and so on, and build a handsome article of furniture. Another man can take the same tools and set to work to duplicate the article, but his production will be a botch. He does not know how to use good tools in a successful way. The various faculties of your mind are the tools with which you must do the work that is to make you rich. So it will be easier for you to succeed if you get into a business for which you are well equipped with mental tools.

Generally speaking, you will do best in that business which will use your strongest faculties — the one for which you are naturally "best fitted." But there are limitations to this statement also. No one should regard his vocation as being irrevocably fixed by the tendencies with which he was born. You can get rich in **ANY** business, for if you have not the right talent, you can develop that talent. It merely means that you will have to make your tools as you go along, instead of confining yourself to the use of those with which you were born. It will be **EASIER** for you to succeed in a vocation for which you already have the talents in a well-developed state; but you **CAN** succeed in any vocation, for you can develop any rudimentary talent, and there is no talent of which you have not at least the rudiment. You will get rich most easily in terms of effort, if you do that for which you are best fitted, but you will get rich most satisfactorily if you do that which you **WANT** to do. Doing what you want to do is life, and there is no real satisfaction in living if we are compelled to be forever doing something which we do not like to do and can never, do what we want to do. And it is certain that you can do what you want to do. The desire to do it is proof that you have within you the power that can do it. Desire is a manifestation of power. The desire to play music is the power that can play music seeking expression and development. The desire to invent mechanical devices is the mechanical talent seeking expression and development.

Where there is no power, either developed or undeveloped, to do a thing, there is never any desire to do that thing, and where there is strong desire to do a thing, it is certain proof that the power to do it is strong and only requires to be developed and applied in the right way. All other things being equal, it is best to select the business for which you have the best developed talent, but if you have a strong desire to engage in any particular line of work, you should select that work as the ultimate end at which you aim.

You can do what you want to do, and it is your right and privilege to follow the business or avocation that will be most congenial and pleasant. You are not obliged to do what you do not like to do, and should not do it except as a means to bring you to the doing of the thing you want to do. If there are past mistakes whose consequences have placed you in an undesirable business or environment, you may be obliged for some time to do what you do not like to do, but you can make the doing of it pleasant by knowing that it is making it possible for you to come to the doing of what you want to do. If you feel that you are not in the right vocation, do not act too hastily in trying to get into another one.

The best way, generally, to change business or environment is by growth. Do not be afraid to make a sudden and radical change if the opportunity is presented and you feel after careful consideration that it is the right opportunity, but never take sudden or radical action when you are in doubt as to the wisdom of doing so. There is never any hurry on the creative plane, and there is no lack of opportunity. When you get out of the competitive mind you will understand that you never need to act hastily. No one else is going to beat you to the thing you want to do; there is enough for all. If one space is taken, another and a better one will be opened for you a little farther on; there is plenty of time. When you are in doubt, wait. Fall back on the contemplation of your vision, and increase your faith and purpose.

And by all means, in times of doubt and indecision, cultivate gratitude. A day or two spent in contemplating the vision of what you want and in earnest thanksgiving that you are getting it will bring your mind into such close relationship with the supreme that you will make no mistake when you do act. There is a mind that knows all there is to know, and you can come into close unity with this mind by faith and the purpose to advance in life, if you have deep gratitude. Mistakes come from acting hastily or from acting in fear or doubt or in forgetfulness of the right motive, which is more life to all, and less to none. As you go on in the certain way, opportunities will come to you in increasing number, and you will need to be very steady in your faith and purpose, and to keep in close touch with the supreme mind by reverent gratitude.

Do all that you can do in a perfect manner every day, but do it without haste, worry, or fear. Go as fast as you can, but never hurry. Remember that in the moment you begin to hurry you cease to be a creator and become a competitor. You drop back upon the old plane again. Whenever you find yourself hurrying, call a halt. Fix your attention on the mental image of the thing you want and begin to give thanks that you are getting it. The exercise of **GRATITUDE** will never fail to strengthen your faith and renew your purpose.

CHAPTER 14

The Impression of Increase

Whether you change your vocation or not, your actions for the present must be those pertaining to the business in which you are now engaged. You can get into the business you want by making constructive use of the business you are already established in — by doing your daily work in the certain way. And insofar as your business consists in dealing with other people, whether personally or by letter, the key thought of all your efforts must be to convey to their minds the impression of increase. Increase is what all men and all women are seeking; it is the urge of the formless intelligence within them seeking fuller expression. The desire for increase is inherent in all nature; it is the fundamental impulse of the universe.

All human activities are based on the desire for increase. People are seeking more food, more clothes, better shelter, more luxury, more beauty, more knowledge, more pleasure — increase in something, more life. Every living thing is under this necessity for continuous advancement; where increase of life ceases, dissolution and death set in at once. Man instinctively knows this, and therefore he is forever seeking more. Jesus sets this law of perpetual increase forth in the parable of the talents: Only those who gain more retain any; from him who has not shall be taken away even that which he has. The normal desire for increased wealth is not an evil or a reprehensible thing. It is simply the desire for more abundant life. It is aspiration. And because it is the deepest instinct of their natures, all men and women are attracted to those who can give them more of the means of life.

In following the certain way as described in the foregoing pages, you are getting continuous increase for yourself, and you are giving it to all with whom you deal. You are a creative centre from which increase is given off to all. Be sure of this, and convey assurance of the fact to every man, woman, and child with whom you come in contact. No matter how small the transaction, even if it be only the selling of a stick of candy to a little child, put into it the thought of increase, and make sure that the customer is impressed with the thought. Convey the impression of advancement with everything you do, so that all people shall receive the impression that you are an "advancing personality," and that you advance all who deal with you. Even to the people whom you meet in a social way — without any thought of business and to whom you do not try to sell anything — give the thought of increase. You can convey this impression by holding the unshakable faith that you, yourself, are in the way of increase and by letting this faith inspire, fill, and permeate every action.

Do everything that you do in the firm conviction that you are an advancing personality and that you are giving advancement to everybody. Feel that you are getting rich, and that in so doing you are making others rich and conferring benefits on all. Do not boast or brag of your success or talk about it unnecessarily; true faith is never boastful. Wherever you find a boastful person, you find one who is secretly doubtful and afraid. Simply feel the faith, and let it work out in every transaction. Let every act and tone and look express the quiet assurance that you are getting rich — that you are already rich. Words will not be necessary to communicate this feeling to others. They will feel the sense of increase when in your presence, and will be attracted to you again. You must so impress others that they will feel that in associating with you they will get increase for themselves. See that you give them a use value greater than the cash value you are taking from them.

Take an honest pride in doing this and let everybody know it, and you will have no lack of customers. People will go where they are given increase, and the supreme, which desires increase in all and which knows all, will move toward you men and women who have never heard of you. Your business will increase rapidly, and you will be surprised at the unexpected benefits that will come to you. You will be able from day to day to make larger combinations, secure greater advantages, and to go on into a more congenial vocation if you desire to do so. But doing thing all this, you must never lose sight of your vision of what you want or your faith and purpose to get what you want. Let me here give you another word of caution in regard to motives: Beware of the insidious temptation to seek for power over other people.

Nothing is so pleasant to the unformed or partially developed mind as the exercise of power or dominion over others. The desire to rule for selfish gratification has been the curse of the world. For countless ages kings and lords have drenched the earth with blood in their battles to extend their dominions — not to seek more life for all, but to get more power for themselves. Today, the main motive in the business and industrial world is the same: Men marshal their armies of dollars and lay waste the lives and hearts of millions in the same mad scramble for power over others. Commercial kings, like political kings, are inspired by the lust for power. Look out for the temptation to seek for authority, to become a "master," to be considered as one who is above the common herd, to impress others by lavish display, and so on. The mind that seeks for mastery over others is the competitive mind, and the competitive mind is not the creative one. In order to master your environment and your destiny, it is not at all necessary that you should rule over your fellow men, and, indeed, when you fall into the world's struggle for the high places, you begin to be conquered by fate and environment and your getting rich becomes a matter of chance and speculation. Beware of the competitive mind! No better statement of the principle of creative action can be formulated than the favorite declaration of the late "Golden Rule" Jones of Toledo: "What I want for myself, I want for everybody."

CHAPTER 15

The Advancing Personality

What I have said in the last chapter applies, as well, to the professional person and the wage-earner as to the person who is engaged in selling or any other form of business. No matter whether you are a physician, a teacher, or a clergyman, if you can give increase of life to others and make them sensible of that fact, they will be attracted to you, and you will get rich.

The physician who holds the vision of himself as a great and successful healer, and who works toward the complete realization of that vision with faith and purpose, as described in former chapters, will come into such close touch with the source of life that he will be phenomenally successful; patients will come to him in throngs. No one has a greater opportunity to carry into effect the teaching of this book than the practitioner of medicine. It does not matter to which of the various schools he may belong, for the principle of healing is common to all of them and may be reached by all alike. The "advancing man" in medicine, who holds to a clear mental image of himself as successful, and who obeys the laws of faith, purpose, and gratitude, will cure every curable case he undertakes. In the field of religion, the world cries out for the clergyman who can teach his hearers the true science of abundant life. He who masters the details of the science of getting rich, together with the allied sciences of being well, of being great, and of winning love, and who teaches these details from the pulpit, will never lack for a congregation. This is a gospel that the world needs; it will give increase of life, and people will hear it gladly and give liberal support to the person who brings it to them. What is now needed is a demonstration of the science of life from the pulpit. We want preachers who can not only tell us how, but who in their own persons will show us how. We need the preacher who will himself be rich, healthy, great, and beloved, to teach us how to attain to these things, and when he comes he will find a numerous and loyal following.

The same is true of the teacher who can inspire the children with the faith and purpose of the advancing life. He will never be "out of a job." And any teacher who has this faith and purpose can give it to his pupils. He cannot help giving it to them if it is part of his own life and practice. What is true of the teacher, preacher, and physician is true of the lawyer, dentist, real estate agent, and insurance agent — of everybody. The combined mental and personal action I have described is infallible; it cannot fail. Every man and woman, who follows these instructions steadily, perseveringly, and to the letter, will get rich. The law of the increase of life is as mathematically certain in its operation as the law of gravity. Getting rich is an exact science.

The wage earner will find this as true of his case as of any of the others mentioned. Do not feel that you have no chance to get rich because you are working where there is no visible opportunity for advancement, where wages are small and the cost of living high. Form your clear mental vision of what you want, and begin to act with faith and purpose. Do all the work you can do, every day, and do each piece of work in a perfectly successful manner. Put the power of success and the purpose to get rich into everything that you do. But do not do this merely with the idea of currying favor with your employer, in the hope that he, or those above you, will see your good work and advance you. It is not likely that they will do so.

The person who is merely a "good" worker, filling his place to the very best of his ability and satisfied with that, is valuable to his employer, and it is not to the employer's interest to promote him. He is worth more where he is. To secure advancement, something more is necessary than to be too large for your place. The person who is certain to advance is the one who is too big for his place, who has a clear concept of what he wants to be, who knows that he can become what he wants to be, and who is determined to **BE** what he wants to be. Do not try to more than fill your present place with a view to pleasing your employer. Do it with the idea of advancing yourself. Hold the faith and purpose of increase during work hours, after work hours, and before work hours. Hold it in such a way that every person who comes in contact with you, whether foreman, fellow worker, or social acquaintance, will feel the power of purpose radiating from you — so that everyone will get the sense of advancement and increase from you. People will be attracted to you, and if there is no possibility for advancement in your present job, you will very soon see an opportunity to take another job.

There is a power that never fails to present opportunity to the advancing personality who is moving in obedience to law. God cannot help helping you if you act in a certain way. He must do so in order to help himself. There is nothing in your circumstances or in the industrial situation that can keep you down. If you cannot get rich working for the steel trust, you can get rich on a ten-acre farm. And if you begin to move in the certain way, you will certainly escape from the "clutches" of the steel trust and get on to the farm or wherever else you wish to be. If a few thousands of its employees would enter upon the certain way, the steel trust would soon be in a bad plight. It would have to give its workers more opportunity or go out of business. Nobody has to work for a trust. The trusts can keep people in so called hopeless conditions only so long as there are people who are ignorant of the science of getting rich or too intellectually slothful to practice it.

Begin this way of thinking and acting, and your faith and purpose will make you quick to see any opportunity to better your condition. Such opportunities will speedily come, for the supreme power, working in all and working for you, will bring them before you. Do not wait for an opportunity to be all that you want to be. When an opportunity to be more than you are now is presented and you feel impelled toward it, take it. It will be the first step toward a greater opportunity. There is no such thing possible in this universe as a lack of opportunities for the person who is living the advancing life. It is inherent in the constitution of the cosmos that all things shall be for him and work together for his good, and he must certainly get rich if he acts and thinks in the certain way. So let wage-earning men and women study this book with great care and enter with confidence upon the course of action it prescribes. It will not fail.

CHAPTER 16

Some Cautions and Concluding Observations

Many people will scoff at the idea that there is an exact science of getting rich. Holding the impression that the supply of wealth is limited, they will insist that social and governmental institutions must be changed before even any considerable number of people can acquire a competence. But this is not true. It is true that existing governments keep the masses in poverty, but this is because the masses do not think and act in the certain way. If the masses begin to move forward as suggested in this book, neither governments nor industrial systems can check them; all systems must be modified to accommodate the forward movement. If the people have the advancing mind, have the faith that they can become rich, and move forward with the fixed purpose to become rich, nothing can possibly keep them in poverty. Individuals may enter upon the certain way at any time and under any government and make themselves rich. And when any considerable number of individuals does so under any government, they will cause the system to be so modified as to open the way for others. The more people who get rich on the competitive plane, the worse for others. The more who get rich on the creative plane, the better for others. The economic salvation of the masses can only be accomplished by getting a large number of people to practice the scientific method set down in this book and become rich. These will show others the way and inspire them with a desire for real life, with the faith that it can be attained, and with the purpose to attain it.

For the present, however, it is enough to know that neither the government under which you live nor the capitalistic or competitive system of industry can keep you from getting rich. When you enter upon the creative plane of thought you will rise above all these things and become a citizen of another kingdom. But remember that your thought must be held upon the creative plane. You are never for an instant to be betrayed into regarding the supply as limited or into acting on the moral level of competition. Whenever you do fall into old ways of thought, correct yourself instantly. For when you are in the competitive mind, you have lost the cooperation of the supreme mind. Do not spend any time in planning as to how you will meet possible emergencies in the future, except as the necessary policies may affect your actions today. You are concerned with doing today's work in a perfectly successful manner and not with emergencies that may arise tomorrow. You can attend to them as they come. Do not concern yourself with questions as to how you shall surmount obstacles that may loom upon your business horizon unless you can see plainly that your course must be altered today in order to avoid them. No matter how tremendous an obstruction may appear at a distance, you will find that if you go on in the certain way it will disappear as you approach it, or that a way over, under, through, or around it will appear. No possible combination of circumstances can defeat a man or woman who is proceeding to get rich along strictly scientific lines. No man or woman who obeys the law can fail to get rich, any more than one can multiply two by two and fail to get four. Give no anxious thought to possible disasters, obstacles, panics, or unfavorable combinations of circumstances. There is time enough to meet such things when they present themselves before you in the immediate present, and you will find that every difficulty carries with it the wherewithal for its overcoming.

Guard your speech. Never speak of yourself, your affairs, or of anything else in a discouraged or discouraging way. Never admit the possibility of failure or speak in a way that infers failure as a possibility. Never speak of the times as being hard or of business conditions as being doubtful. Times may be hard and business doubtful for those who are on the competitive plane, but they can never be so for you. You can create what you want, and you are above fear. When others are having hard times and poor business, you will find your greatest opportunities.

Train yourself to think of and to look upon the world as a something which is becoming, which is growing, and to regard seeming evil as being only that which is undeveloped. Always speak in terms of advancement. To do otherwise is to deny your faith, and to deny your faith is to lose it. Never allow yourself to feel disappointed. You may expect to have a certain thing at a certain time and not get it at that time, and this will appear to you like failure. But if you hold to your faith you will find that the failure is only apparent.

Go on in the certain way, and if you do not receive that thing, you will receive something so much better that you will see that the seeming failure was really a great success. A student of this science had set his mind on making a certain business combination that seemed to him at the time to be very desirable, and he worked for some weeks to bring it about. When the crucial time came, the thing failed in a perfectly inexplicable way. It was as if some unseen influence had been working secretly against him. But he was not disappointed. On the contrary, he thanked God that his desire had been overruled, and went steadily on with a grateful mind. In a few weeks an opportunity so much better came his way that he would not have made the first deal on any account, and he saw that a mind which knew more than he knew had prevented him from losing the greater good by entangling himself with the lesser. That is the way every seeming failure will work out for you, if you keep your faith, hold to your purpose, and have gratitude, and do, every day all that can be done that day, doing each separate act in a successful manner. When you make a failure, it is because you have not asked for enough. Keep on, and a larger thing then you were seeking will certainly come to you.

Remember this. You will not fail because you lack the necessary talent to do what you wish to do. If you go on as I have directed, you will develop all the talent that is necessary to the doing of your work. It is not within the scope of this book to deal with the science of cultivating talent, but it is as certain and simple as the process of getting rich. However, do not hesitate or waver for fear that when you come to any certain place you will fail for lack of ability. Keep right on, and when you come to that place, the ability will be furnished to you. The same source of ability that enabled the untaught Lincoln to do the greatest work in government ever accomplished by a single man is open to you. You may draw upon all the mind there is for wisdom to use in meeting the responsibilities which are laid upon you.

Go on in full faith. Study this book. Make it your constant companion until you have mastered all the ideas contained in it. While you are getting firmly established in this faith, you will do well to give up most recreations and pleasure and to stay away from places where ideas conflicting with these are advanced in lectures or sermons.

Do not read pessimistic or conflicting literature or get into arguments upon the matter. Spend most of your leisure time in contemplating your vision, in cultivating gratitude, and in reading this book. It contains all you need to know of the science of getting rich, and you will find all the essentials summed up in the following chapter.

CHAPTER 17

A Summary of the Science of Getting Rich

There is a thinking stuff from which all things are made, and which, in its original state, permeates, penetrates, and fills the interspaces of the universe. A thought in this substance produces the thing that is imaged by the thought. A person can form things in his thought, and by impressing his thought upon formless substance can cause the thing he thinks about to be created. In order to do this, a person must pass from the competitive to the creative mind. Otherwise he cannot be in harmony with formless intelligence, which is always creative and never competitive in spirit.

A person may come into full harmony with the formless substance by entertaining a lively and sincere gratitude for the blessings it bestows upon him. Gratitude unifies the mind of man with the intelligence of substance, so that man's thoughts are received by the formless. A person can remain upon the creative plane only by uniting himself with the formless intelligence through a deep and continuous feeling of gratitude. A person must form a clear and definite mental image of the things he wishes to have, to do, or to become, and he must hold this mental image in his thoughts, while being deeply grateful to the supreme that all his desires are granted to him. The person who wishes to get rich must spend his leisure hours in contemplating his vision, and in earnest thanksgiving that the reality is being given to him.

Too much stress cannot be laid on the importance of frequent contemplation of the mental image, coupled with unwavering faith and devout gratitude. This is the process by which the impression is given to the formless and the creative forces set in motion. The creative energy works through the established channels of natural growth, and of the industrial and social order. All that is included in his mental image will surely be brought to the person who follows the instructions given above, and whose faith does not waver. What he wants will come to him through the ways of established trade and commerce. In order to receive his own when it is ready to come to him, a person must be in action in a way that causes him to more than fill his present place. He must keep in mind the purpose to get rich through realization of his mental image. And he must do, every day, all which can be done that day, taking care to do each act in a successful manner. He must give to every person a use value in excess of the cash value he receives, so that each transaction makes for more life, and he must hold the advancing thought so that the impression of increase will be communicated to all with whom he comes into contact. The men and women who practice the foregoing instructions will certainly get rich, and the riches they receive will be in exact proportion to the definiteness of their vision, the fixity of their purpose, the steadiness of their faith, and the depth of their gratitude.

Please Study the Science of Getting Rich first.

The Science of Living Well

By

Wallace D. Wattles

Author's Preface to the Science of Living Well

This volume is the second of a series, the first of which is ***The Science of Getting Rich***. As that book is intended solely for those who want money, so this is for those who want health, and who want a practical guide and handbook, not a philosophical treatise.

It is an instructor in the use of the universal Principle of Life, and my effort has been to explain the way in so plain and simple a fashion that the reader, though he may have given no previous study to New Thought or metaphysics, may readily follow it to perfect health. While retaining all essentials, I have carefully eliminated all non-essentials. I have used no technical, abstruse, or difficult language, and have kept the one point in view at all times.

As its title asserts the book deals with science, not speculation. The monistic theory of the universe the theory that matter, mind, consciousness, and life are all manifestations of One Substance is now accepted by most thinkers, and if you accept this theory, you cannot deny the logical conclusions you will find here.

Best of all, the methods of thought and action prescribed have been tested by the author in his own case and in the case of hundreds of others during twelve years of practice, with continuous and unfailing success.

I can say of the Science of Being Well that it works, and that wherever its laws are complied with, it can no more fail to work than the science of geometry can fail to work. If the tissues of your body have not been so destroyed that continued life is impossible, you can get well, and if you will think and act in a Certain Way, you will get well.

Those who wish more detailed information as to the performance of the voluntary function of eating, I would recommend the writings of Horace Fletcher and of Edward Hooker Dewey. Read these, if you like, as a sort of buttress to your faith, but let me warn you against making the mistake of studying many conflicting theories, and practicing, at the same time, parts of several different systems. For if you get well, it must be by giving your **WHOLE MIND** to the right way of thinking and living.

Remember that the Science of Being Well claims to be a complete and sufficient guide in every particular. Concentrate upon the way of thinking and acting it prescribes, and follow it in every detail, and you will get well, or if you are already well, you will remain so.

Trusting that you will go on until the priceless blessing of perfect health is yours, I remain,

Truly Yours,

- Wallace D. Wattle

CHAPTER 1

The Principle of Health

In the personal application of the Science of Being Well, as in that of *The Science of Getting Rich*, certain fundamental truths must be known in the beginning, and accepted without question. Some of these truths we state here:

The perfectly natural performance of function constitutes health, and the perfectly natural performance of function results from the natural action of the Principle of Life.

1. There is a Principle of Life in the universe, and it is the One Living Substance from which all things are made. This Living Substance permeates, penetrates, and fills the interspaces of the universe. It is in and through all things, like very refined and diffusible ether. All life comes from it, its life is all the life there is.

2. A human being is a form of this Living Substance, and has within him a Principle of Health. (The word Principle is used as meaning source.) The Principle of Health in a person, when in full constructive activity, causes all the voluntary functions of his life to be perfectly performed. It is the Principle of Health in a person which really works all healing, no matter what or remedy is employed, and this Principle of Health is brought into Constructive Activity by thinking in a Certain Way.

I proceed now to prove this last statement. We all know that cures are wrought by all the different, and often opposite, methods employed in the various branches of the healing art. The allopath, who gives a strong dose of a counter-poison, cures his patient. And the homeopath, who gives a diminutive dose of the poison most similar to that of the disease, also cures it. If allopath ever cured any given disease, it is certain that homeopathy never cured that disease. And if homeopathy ever cured an ailment, allopath could not possibly cure that ailment.

The two systems are radically opposite in theory and practice, and yet both cure most diseases. And even the remedies used by physicians in any one school are not the same.

Go with a case of indigestion to half a dozen doctors, and compare their prescriptions. It is more than likely that none of the ingredients of any one of them will also be in the others. Must we not conclude that their patients are healed by a Principle of Health within themselves, and not by something in the varying remedies?

Not only this, but we find the same ailments cured by the osteopath with manipulations of the spine, by the faith healer with prayer, by the food scientist with bills of fare, by the Christian Scientist with a formulated creed statement, by the mental scientist with affirmation, and by the hygienists with differing plans of living.

What conclusion can we come to in the face of all these facts but that there is a Principle of Health which is the same in all people, and which really accomplishes all the cures; and that there is something in all the systems which, under favorable conditions, arouses the Principle of Health to action? That is, medicines, manipulations, prayers, bills of fare, affirmations, and hygienic practices cure whenever they cause the Principle of Health to become active, and fail whenever they do not cause it to become active.

Does not all this indicate that the results depend upon the way the patient thinks about the remedy, rather than upon the ingredients in the prescription?

There is an old story which furnishes so good an illustration on this point that I will give it here. It is said that in the middle ages, the bones of a saint, kept in one of the monasteries, were working miracles of healing. On certain days a great crowd of the afflicted gathered to touch the relics, and all who did so were healed.

On the eve of one of these occasions, some sacrilegious rascal gained access to the case in which the wonder-working relics were kept and stole the bones, and in the morning, with the usual crowd of sufferers waiting at the gates, the fathers found themselves shorn of the source of the miracle-working power.

They resolved to keep the matter quiet, hoping that by doing so they might find the thief and recover their treasures, and hastening to the cellar of the convent they dug up the bones of a murderer, who had been buried there many years before. These they placed in the case, intending to make some plausible excuse for the failure of the saint to perform his usual miracles on that day; and then they let in the waiting assemblage of the sick and infirm.

To the intense astonishment of those in on the secret, the bones of the malefactor proved as effective as those of the saint, and the healing went on as before. One of the fathers is said to have left a history of the occurrence, in which he confessed that, in his judgment, the healing power had been in the people themselves all the time, and never in the bones at all.

Whether the story is true or not, the conclusion applies to all the cures wrought by all the systems. The Power that Heals is in the patient himself, and whether it shall become active or not does not depend upon the physical or mental means used, but upon the way the patient thinks about these means. There is a Universal Principle of Life, as Jesus taught a great spiritual Healing Power and there is a Principle of Health in every human being which is related to this Healing Power. This is dormant or active, according to the way a person thinks. He can always quicken it into activity by thinking in a Certain Way.

Your getting well does not depend upon the adoption of some system, or the finding of some remedy; people with your identical ailments have been healed by all systems and all remedies. It does not depend upon climate; some people are well and others are sick in all climates. It does not depend upon avocation, unless in case of those who work under poisonous conditions; people are well in all trades and professions.

Your getting well depends upon your beginning to think" and act" in a Certain Way.

The way a person thinks about things is determined by what he believes about them. His thoughts are determined by his faith, and the results depend upon his making a personal application of his faith.

If a person has faith in the efficacy of a medicine, and is able to apply that faith to himself, that medicine will certainly cause him to be cured. But though his faith be great, he will not be cured unless he applies it to himself. Many sick people have faith for others but none for themselves. So, if he has faith in a system of diet, and can personally apply that faith, it will cure him. And if he has faith in prayers and affirmations and personally applies his faith, prayers and affirmations will cure him.

Faith, personally applied, cures. And no matter how great the faith or how persistent the thought, it will not cure without personal application. The Science of Being Well, then, includes the two fields of thought and action.

To be well it is not enough that a person should merely think in a Certain Way. He must apply his thought to himself, and he must express and externalize it in his outward life by acting in the same way that he thinks.

CHAPTER 2

The Foundations of Faith

Before a person can think in the Certain Way which will cause his diseases to be healed, he must believe in certain truths which are here stated:

All things are made from one Living Substance, which, in its original state, permeates, penetrates, and fills the interspaces of the universe. While all visible things are made from It, yet this Substance" in its first formless condition" is in and through all the visible forms that It has made. Its life is in All, and its intelligence is in All.

This Substance creates by thought, and its method is by taking the form of that which it thinks about. The thought of a form held by this substance causes it to assume that form; the thought of a motion causes it to institute that motion. Forms are created by this substance in moving itself into certain orientations or positions.

When original Substance wishes to create a given form, it thinks of the motions which will produce that form. When it wishes to create a world, it thinks of the motions, perhaps extending through ages, which will result in its coming into the attitude and form of the world" and these motions are made. When it wishes to create an oak tree, it thinks of the sequences of movement, perhaps extending through ages, which will result in the form of an oak tree" and these motions are made. The particular sequences of motion by which differing forms should be produced were established in the beginning; they are changeless. Certain motions instituted in the Formless Substance will forever produce certain forms.

The human body is formed from the Original Substance, and is the result of certain motions, which first existed as thoughts of Original Substance. The motions which produce, renew, and repair the body are called functions, and these functions are of two classes: voluntary and involuntary.

The involuntary functions are under the control of the Principle of Health in a person, and are performed in a perfectly healthy manner so long as a person thinks in a certain way. The voluntary functions of life are eating, drinking, breathing, and sleeping. These, entirely or in part, are under the direction of a person's conscious mind, and he can perform them in a perfectly healthy way if he will. If he does not perform them in a healthy way, he cannot long be well.

So we see that if a person thinks in a certain way, and eats, drinks, breathes and sleeps in a corresponding way, he will be well.

The involuntary functions of a person's life are under the direct control of the Principle of Health, and so long as a person thinks in a perfectly healthy way, these functions are perfectly performed, for the action of the Principle of Health is largely directed by a person's conscious thought, affecting his subconscious mind of originating thought, and as he does not know everything, he makes mistakes and thinks error. Not knowing everything, he believes things to be true which are not true. A person holds in his thought the idea of diseased and abnormal functioning and conditions, and so perverts the action of the Principle of Health, causing diseased and abnormal functioning and conditions within his own body.

In the Original Substance there are held only the thoughts of perfect motion, perfect and healthy function, and complete life. God never thinks disease or imperfection. But for countless ages people have held thoughts of disease, abnormality, old age, and death. And the perverted functioning resulting from these thoughts has become a part of the inheritance of the human race. Our ancestors have, for many generations, held imperfect ideas concerning human form and functioning, and we begin life with racial sub-conscious impressions of imperfection and disease.

This is not natural, not a part of the plan of nature.

The purpose of nature can be nothing else than the perfection of life. This we see from the very nature of life itself. It is the nature of life to continually advance toward more perfect living; advancement is the inevitable result of the very act of living. Increase is always the result of active living; whatever lives must live more and more.

The seed, lying in the granary, has life, but it is not living. Put it into the soil and it becomes active, and at once begins to gather to itself from the surrounding substance, and to build a plant form. It will so cause increase that a seed head will be produced containing 30, 60, or 100 seeds, each having as much life as the first.

Life, by living, increases.

Life cannot live without increasing, and the fundamental impulse of life is to live. It is in response to this fundamental impulse that Original Substance works, and creates. God must live, and God cannot live except as God creates and increases. In multiplying forms, God is moving on to live more.

The universe is a Great Advancing Life, and the purpose of nature is the advancement of life toward perfection, toward perfect functioning. The purpose of nature is perfect health.

The purpose of Nature, so far as a human being is concerned, is that he should be continuously advancing into more life, and progressing toward perfect life; and that he should live the most complete life possible in his present sphere of action.

This must be so, because that which lives in a person is seeking more life.

Give a little child a pencil and paper, and he begins to draw crude figures. That which lives in him is trying to express Itself in art. Give him a set of blocks, and he will try to build something. That which lives in him is seeking expression in architecture. Seat him at a piano, and he will try to draw harmony from the keys. That which lives in him is trying to express Itself in music.

That which lives in a person is always seeking to live more, and since a person lives most when he is well, the Principle of Nature in him can seek only health. The natural state of a human being is a state of perfect health, and everything in him and in nature tends toward health.

Sickness can have no place in the thought of Original Substance, for it is by its own nature continually impelled toward the fullest and most perfect life" therefore, toward health. A human being, as he exists in the thought of the Formless Substance, has perfect health. Disease, which is abnormal or perverted function" motion imperfectly made, or made in the direction of imperfect life has no place in the thought of the Thinking Stuff.

The Supreme Mind never thinks of disease. Disease was not created or ordained by God, or sent forth from God. It is wholly a product of separate consciousness, of the individual thought of a person. God, the Formless Substance, does not see disease, think disease, know disease, or recognize disease. Disease is recognized only by the thought of humanity; God thinks nothing but health.

From all the foregoing, we see that health is a *fact* or **TRUTH** in the Original Substance from which we are all formed, and that disease is imperfect functioning, resulting from the imperfect thoughts of people, past and present. If a person's thoughts of himself had always been those of perfect health, a person could not possibly now be otherwise than perfectly healthy.

A human being in perfect health is the thought of Original Substance, and a human being in imperfect health is the result of his own failure to think perfect health, and to perform the voluntary functions of life in a healthy way. We will here arrange in a syllabus the basic truths of the Science of Being Well:

There is a Thinking Substance from which all things are made, and which, in its original state, permeates, penetrates, and fills the interspaces of the universe. It is the life of All.

The thought of a form in this Substance causes the form; the thought of a motion produces the motion. In relation to humanity, the thoughts of this Substance are always of perfect functioning and perfect health.

A person is a thinking center, capable of original thought; and his thought has power over his own functioning. By thinking imperfect thoughts he has caused imperfect and perverted functioning; and by performing the voluntary functions of life in a perverted manner, he has assisted in causing disease.

If a person will think only thoughts of perfect health, he can cause within himself the functioning of perfect health; all the Power of Life will be exerted to assist him. But this healthy functioning will not continue unless a person performs the external, or voluntary, functions of living in a healthy manner.

A person's first step must be to learn how to think perfect health; and his second step to learn how to eat, drink, breathe, and sleep in a perfectly healthy way. If a person takes these two steps, he will certainly become well, and remain so.

CHAPTER 3

Life and Its Organisms

The human body is the abiding place of energy which renews it when worn, which eliminates waste or poisonous matter, and which repairs the body when broken or injured. This energy we call life. Life is not generated or produced within the body; it produces the body.

The seed which has been kept in the storehouse for years will grow when planted in the soil; it will produce a plant. But the life in the plant is not generated by its growing; it is the life which makes the plant grow.

The performance of function does not cause life; it is life which causes function to be performed. Life is first; function afterward.

It is life which distinguishes organic from inorganic matter, but it is not produced after the organization of matter.

Life is the principle or force which causes organization; it builds organisms.

It is a principle or force inherent in Original Substance; all life is One.

This Life Principle of the All is the Principle of Health in a person, and becomes constructively active whenever a person thinks in a Certain Way. Whoever, therefore, thinks in this Certain Way will surely have perfect health if his external functioning is in conformity with his thought. But the external functioning must conform to the thought; a person cannot hope to be well by thinking health, if he eats, drinks, breathes, and sleeps like a sick person.

The universal Life Principle, then, is the Principle of Health in a human being. It is one with original substance. There is one Original Substance from which all things are made; this substance is alive, and its life is the Principle of Life of the universe. This Substance has created from itself all the forms of organic life by thinking them, or by thinking the motions and functions which produce them.

Original Substance thinks only health, because It knows all truth. There is no truth which is not known in the Formless, which is All, and in all. It not only knows all truth, but it has all power. Its vital power is the source of all the energy there is. A conscious life which knows all truth and which has all power cannot go wrong or perform function imperfectly. Knowing all, it knows too much to go wrong, and so the Formless cannot be diseased or think disease.

A human being is a form of this Original Substance, and has a separate consciousness of his own, but his consciousness is limited, and therefore imperfect. By reason of his limited knowledge a person can and does think wrongly, and so he causes perverted and imperfect functioning in his own body. A human being has not yet known enough not to go wrong. The diseased or imperfect functioning may not instantly result from an imperfect thought, but it is bound to come if the thought becomes habitual.

Any thought continuously held by a person tends to the establishment of the corresponding condition in his body.

Also, the human being has failed to learn how to perform the voluntary functions of his life in a healthy way. He does not know when, what, and how to eat. He knows little about breathing and less about sleep. He does all these things in a wrong way, and under wrong conditions; and this because he has neglected to follow the only sure guide to the knowledge of life. He has tried to live by logic rather than by instinct. He has made living a matter of art, and not of nature. And he has gone wrong.

His only remedy is to begin to go right, and this he can surely do. It is the work of this book to teach the whole truth, so that the person who reads it shall know too much to go wrong.

The thoughts of disease produce the forms of disease. A person must learn to think health; and being Original Substance which takes the form of its thoughts, he will become the form of health and manifest perfect health in all his functioning. The people who were healed by touching the bones of the saint were really healed by thinking in a Certain Way, and not by any power emanating from the relics. There is no healing power in the bones of dead men, whether they be those of saint or sinner.

The people who were healed by the doses of either the allopath or the homeopath were also really healed by thinking in a Certain Way; there is no drug which has within itself the power to heal disease.

The people who have been healed by prayers and affirmations were also healed by thinking in a certain way; there is no curative power in strings of words.

All the sick who have been healed, by whatsoever system, have thought in a Certain Way; and a little examination will show us what this way is.

The two essentials of the Way are Faith and a Personal Application of the Faith.

The people who touched the saint's bones had faith, and so great was their faith that in the instant they touched the relics they severed all mental relations with disease, and mentally unified themselves with health.

This change of mind was accompanied by an intense devotional **FEELING** which penetrated to the deepest recesses of their souls, and so aroused the Principle of Health to powerful action. By faith they claimed that they were healed, or appropriated health to themselves, and in full faith they ceased to think of themselves in connection with disease and thought of themselves only in connection with health.

These are the two essentials to thinking in the Certain Way which will make you well: first, claim or appropriate health by faith, and, second, sever all mental relations with disease and enter into mental relations with health.

That which we make ourselves, mentally, we become physically, and that with which we unite ourselves mentally we become unified with physically. If your thought always relates you to disease, then your thought becomes a fixed power to cause disease within you. And if your thought always relates you to health, then your thought becomes a fixed power exerted to keep you well.

In the case of the people who are healed by medicines, the result is obtained in the same way. They have, consciously or unconsciously, sufficient faith in the means used that they sever mental relations with disease and enter into mental relations with health.

Faith may be unconscious. It is possible for us to have a sub-conscious or inbred faith in things like medicine, in which we do not believe to any extent objectively, and this sub-conscious faith may be quite sufficient to quicken the Principle of Health into constructive activity. Many who have little conscious faith are healed in this way, while many others who have great faith in the means are not healed because they do not make the personal application to themselves. Their faith is general, but not specific for their own cases.

In the Science of Being Well we have two main points to consider: first, how to think with faith, and, second, how to so apply the thought to ourselves as to quicken the Principle of Health into constructive activity.

We begin by learning What to Think.

CHAPTER 4

What to Think

In order to sever all mental relations with disease, you must enter into mental relations with health, making the process positive, not negative one of assumption, not of rejection. You are to receive or appropriate health rather than to reject and deny disease. Denying disease accomplishes next to nothing; it does little good to cast out the devil and leave the house vacant, for he will presently return with others worse than himself. When you enter into full and constant mental relations with health, you must of necessity cease all relationship with disease.

The first step in the Science of Being Well, then, is to enter into complete thought connection with health.

The best way to do this is to form a mental image or picture of yourself as being well, imagining a perfectly strong and healthy body, and to spend sufficient time in contemplating this image to make it your habitual thought of yourself.

This is not so easy as it sounds. It necessitates the taking of considerable time for meditation, and not all persons have the imaging faculty well enough developed to form a distinct mental picture of themselves in a perfect or idealized body. It is much easier, as in *The Science of Getting Rich*, to form a mental image of the things one wants to have, for we have seen these things or their counterparts and know how they look. We can picture them very easily from memory. But if we have never seen ourselves in a perfect body, a clear mental image is hard to form.

It is not necessary or essential, however, to have a clear mental image of yourself as you wish to be; it is only essential to form a **CONCEPTION** of perfect health, and to relate yourself to it. This Conception of Health is not a mental picture of a particular thing. It is an understanding of health, and carries with it the idea of perfect functioning in every part and organ.

You may TRY to picture yourself as perfect in physique that helps and you MUST *think of yourself as doing everything in the manner of a perfectly strong and healthy person.*

You can picture yourself as walking down the street with an erect body and a vigorous stride. You can picture yourself as doing your day's work easily and with surplus vigor, never tired or weak. You can picture in your mind how all things would be done by a person full of health and power, and you can make yourself the central figure in the picture, doing things in just that way.

Never think of the ways in which weak or sickly people do things; always think of the way strong people do things. Spend your leisure time in thinking about the Strong Way, until you have a good conception of it, and always think of yourself in connection with the Strong Way of Doing Things. That is what I mean by having a Conception of Health.

In order to establish perfect functioning in every part, a person does not have to study anatomy or physiology so that he can form a mental image of each separate organ and address himself to it. He does not have to treat his liver, his kidneys, his stomach, or his heart. There is one Principle of Health in a human being, who has control over all the involuntary functions of his life, and the thought of perfect health, impressed upon this Principle, will reach each part and organ. A person's liver is not controlled by a liver-principle, his stomach by a digestive principle, and so on. The Principle of Health is One.

The less you go into the detailed study of physiology, the better for you. Our knowledge of this science is very imperfect, and leads to imperfect thought.

Imperfect thought causes imperfect functioning, which is disease.

Let me illustrate: Until quite recently, physiology fixed ten days as the extreme limit of a human being's endurance without food. It was considered that only in exceptional cases could a person survive a longer fast. So the impression became universally disseminated that one who was deprived of food must die in from five to ten days. And numbers of people, when cut off from food by shipwreck, accident, or famine, did die within this period.

But the performances of Dr. Tanner, the 40-day faster, and the writings of Dr. Dewey and others on the fasting cure, together with the experiments of numberless people who have fasted from 40 to 60 days, have shown that a human's ability to live without food is vastly greater than had been supposed. Any person, properly educated, can fast from 20 to 40 days with little loss in weight, and often with no apparent loss of strength at all.

The people who starved to death in ten days or less did so because they believed that death was inevitable. An erroneous physiology had given them a wrong thought about themselves. When a person is deprived of food he will die in from 10 to 50 days, according to the way he has been taught, or, in other words, according to the way he thinks about it. So you see that an erroneous physiology can work very mischievous results.

No Science of Being Well can be founded on current physiology; it is not sufficiently exact in its knowledge. With all its pretensions, comparatively little is really known as to the interior workings and processes of the body. It is not known just how food is digested. It is not known just what part food plays, if any, in the generation of force. It is not known exactly what the liver, spleen, and pancreas are for, or what part their secretions play in the chemistry of assimilation. On all these and most other points we theorize, but we do not really know.

When a person begins to study physiology, he enters the domain of theory and disputation. He comes among conflicting opinions, and he is bound to form mistaken ideas concerning himself. These mistaken ideas lead to the thinking of wrong thoughts, and this leads to perverted functioning and disease.

All that the most perfect knowledge of physiology could do for a person would be to enable him to think only thoughts of perfect health, and to eat, drink, breathe, and sleep in a perfectly healthy way. And this, as we shall show, he can do without studying physiology at all.

This, for the most part, is true of all hygiene. There are certain fundamental propositions which we should know, and these will be explained in later chapters, but aside from these propositions, ignore physiology and hygiene. They tend to fill your mind with thoughts of imperfect conditions, and these thoughts will produce the imperfect conditions in your own body. You cannot study any science which recognizes disease, if you are to think nothing but health.

Drop all investigation as to your present condition, its causes, or possible results, and set yourself to the work of forming a conception of health.

Think about health and the possibilities of health, of the work that may be done and the pleasures that may be enjoyed in a condition of perfect health. Then make this conception your guide in thinking of yourself. Refuse to entertain for an instant any thought of yourself which is not in harmony with it. When any idea of disease or imperfect functioning enters your mind, cast it out instantly by calling up a thought which is in harmony with the Conception of Health.

Think of yourself at all times as realizing this conception, as being a strong and perfectly healthy personage, and do not harbor a contrary thought.

KNOW that as you think of yourself in unity with this conception, the Original Substance which permeates and fills the tissues of your body is taking form according to the thought, and know that this Intelligent Substance or mind stuff will cause function to be performed in such a way that your body will be rebuilt with perfectly healthy cells.

The Intelligent Substance, from which all things are made, permeates and penetrates all things; and so it is in and through your body. It moves according to its thoughts, and so if you hold only the thoughts of perfectly healthy function, it will cause the movements of perfectly healthy function within you.

Hold with persistence to the thought of perfect health in relation to yourself. Do not permit yourself to think in any other way. Hold this thought with perfect faith that it is the fact, the truth. It is the truth so far as your mental body is concerned.

You have a mind-body and a physical body. The mind-body takes form just as you think of yourself, and any thought which you hold continuously is made visible by the transformation of the physical body into its image. Implanting the thought of perfect functioning in the mind-body will, in due time, cause perfect functioning in the physical body.

The transformation of the physical body into the image of the ideal held by the mind-body is not accomplished instantaneously we cannot transfigure our physical bodies at will as Jesus did. In the creation and recreation of forms, Substance moves along the fixed lines of growth it has established, and the impression upon it of the health thought causes the healthy body to be built cell by cell. Holding only thoughts of perfect health will ultimately cause perfect functioning, and perfect functioning will in due time produce a perfectly healthy body.

It may be as well to condense this chapter into a syllabus:

Your physical body is permeated and filled with an Intelligent Substance, which forms a body of mind-stuff. This mind-stuff controls the functioning of your physical body. A thought of disease or of imperfect function, impressed upon the mind-stuff, causes disease or imperfect functioning in the physical body.

If you are diseased, it is because wrong thoughts have made impressions on this mind-stuff. These may have been either your own thoughts or those of your parents, we begin life with many sub-conscious impressions, both right and wrong. But the natural tendency of all mind is toward health, and if no thoughts are held in the conscious mind save those of health, all internal functioning will come to be performed in a perfectly healthy manner.

The Power of Nature within you is sufficient to overcome all hereditary impressions, and if you will learn to control your thoughts, so that you shall think only those of health, and if you will perform the voluntary functions of life in a perfectly healthy way, you can certainly be well.

CHAPTER 5

Faith

The Principle of Health is moved by Faith. Nothing else can call it into action, and only faith can enable you to relate yourself to health, and sever your relation with disease, in your thoughts.

You will continue to think of disease unless you have faith in health. If you do not have faith, you will doubt. If you doubt, you will fear. And if you fear, you will relate yourself in mind to that which you fear.

If you fear disease, you will think of yourself in connection with disease, and that will produce within yourself the form and motions of disease. Just as Original Substance creates from itself the forms of its thoughts, so your mind-body, which is original substance, takes the form and motion of whatever you think about. If you fear disease, dread disease, have doubts about your safety from disease, or if you even contemplate disease, you will connect yourself with it and create its forms and motions within you.

Let me enlarge somewhat upon this point. The potency, or creative power, of a thought is given to it by the faith that is in it.

Thoughts which contain no faith create no forms.

The Formless Substance, which knows all truth and therefore thinks only truth, has perfect faith in every thought, because it thinks only truth, and so all its thoughts create.

But if you will imagine a thought in Formless Substance in which there was no faith, you will see that such a thought could not cause the Substance to move or take form.

Keep in mind the fact that only those thoughts which are conceived in faith have creative energy. Only those thoughts which have faith with them are able to change function, or to quicken the Principle of Health into activity.

If you do not have faith in health, you will certainly have faith in disease. If you do not have faith in health, it will do you no good to think about health, for your thoughts will have no potency, and will cause no change for the better in your conditions.

If you do not have faith in health, I repeat, you will have faith in disease. And if, under such conditions, you think about health for ten hours a day and think about disease for only a few minutes, the disease thought will control your condition because it will have the potency of faith, while the health thought will not. Your mind-body will take on the form and motions of disease and retain them, because your health thought will not have sufficient dynamic force to change form or motion.

In order to practice the Science of Being Well, you must have complete faith in health.

Faith begins in belief; and we now come to the question: *What must you believe in order to have faith in health?*

You must believe that there is more health-power than disease-power in both yourself and your environment; and you cannot help believing this if you consider the facts. These are the facts:

There is a Thinking Substance from which all things are made, and which, in its original state, permeates, penetrates, and fills the interspaces of the universe.

The thought of a form, in this Substance, produces the form; the thought of a motion institutes the motion. In relation to the human being, the thoughts of Original Substance are always of perfect health and perfect functioning. This Substance, within and without a human being, always exerts its power toward health.

A person is a thinking center, capable of original thought. He has a mind-body of Original Substance permeating a physical body, and the functioning of his physical body is determined by the **FAITH** of his mind-body. If a person thinks with faith of the functioning of health, he will cause his internal functions to be performed in a healthy manner, provided that he performs the external functions in a corresponding manner. But if a person thinks, with faith, of disease, or of the power of disease, he will cause his internal functioning to be the functioning of disease.

The Original Intelligent Substance is in a human being, moving toward health and it is pressing upon him from every side. The human being lives, moves, and has his being in a limitless ocean of health-power, and he uses this power according to his faith. If he appropriates it and applies it to himself it is all his, and if he unifies himself with it by unquestioning faith, he cannot fail to attain health, for the power of this Substance is all the power there is.

A belief in the above statements is a foundation for faith in health. If you believe them, you believe that health is the natural state of humanity, and that a human being lives in the midst of Universal Health that all the power of nature makes for health, and that health is possible to all, and can surely be attained by all.

You will believe that the power of health in the universe is 10,000 times greater than that of disease in fact, that disease has no power whatever, being only the result of perverted thought and faith. And if you believe that health is possible to you, and that it may surely be attained by you, and that you know exactly what to do in order to attain it, you will have faith in health. You will have this faith and knowledge if you read this book through with care and determine to believe in and practice its teachings.

It is not merely the possession of faith, but the personal application of faith which works healing. You must claim health in the beginning, and form a conception of health, and, as far as may be, of yourself as a perfectly healthy person. And then, by faith, you must claim that you **ARE REALIZING** this conception.

Do not assert with faith that you are going to get well; assert with faith that you are well. Having faith in health, and applying it to yourself, means having faith that you are healthy. *And the first step in this is to claim that it is the truth.*

Mentally take the attitude of being well, and do not say anything or do anything which contradicts this attitude. Never speak a word or assume a physical attitude which does not harmonize with the claim: I am perfectly well.

When you walk, go with a brisk step, and with your chest thrown out and your head held up. Watch that at all times your physical actions and attitudes are those of a healthy person.

When you find that you have relapsed into the attitude of weakness or disease, change instantly: straighten up, and think of health and power. Refuse to consider yourself as other than a perfectly healthy person.

One great aid, perhaps the greatest aid in applying your faith you will find in the exercise of gratitude.

Whenever you think of yourself, or of your advancing condition, give thanks to the Great Intelligent Substance for the perfect health you are enjoying.

Remember that there is a continual inflow of life from the Supreme, which is received by all created things according to their forms, and by every person according to his faith. Health from God is continually being urged upon you, and when you think of this, lift up your mind reverently, and give thanks that you have been led to the Truth and into perfect health of mind and body. Be, all the time, in a grateful frame of mind, and let gratitude be evident in your speech. Gratitude will help you to own and control your own field of thought.

Whenever the thought of disease is presented to you, instantly claim health, and thank God for the perfect health you have. Do this so that there shall be no room in your mind for a thought of ill. Every thought connected in any way with ill health is unwelcome, and you can close the door of your mind in its face by asserting that you are well, and by reverently thanking God that it is so. Soon the old thoughts will return no more.

Gratitude has a twofold effect: it strengthens your own faith, and it brings you into close and harmonious relations with the Supreme. You believe that there is one Intelligent Substance from which all life and all power come, you believe that you receive your own life from this substance, and you relate yourself closely to It by feeling continuous gratitude.

It is easy to see that the more closely you relate yourself to the Source of Life the more readily you may receive life from it. And it is easy also to see that your relation to It is a matter of mental attitude.

We cannot come into physical relationship with God, for God is mind-stuff and we also are mind-stuff. Our relation with God must therefore be a mind relation. It is plain, then, that the person who feels deep and hearty gratitude will live in closer touch with God than the person who never looks up to God in thankfulness.

The ungrateful or unthankful mind really denies that it receives at all, and so cuts its connection with the Supreme. The grateful mind is always looking toward the Supreme, is always open to receive from it, and it will receive continually.

The Principle of Health in a human being receives its vital power from the Principle of Life in the universe, and a person relates himself to the Principle of Life by faith in health, and by gratitude for the health he receives.

A person may cultivate both faith and gratitude by the proper use of his will.

CHAPTER 6

Use of the Will

In the practice of the Science of Being Well, the will is not used to compel yourself to go when you are not really able to go or to do things when you are not physically strong enough to do them. You do not direct your will upon your physical body or try to compel the proper performance of internal function by will power.

You direct the will upon the mind, and use it in determining what you shall believe, what you shall think, and to what you shall give your attention.

The will should never be used upon any person or thing external to you, and it should never be used upon your own body. The sole legitimate use of the will is in determining to what you shall give your attention and what you shall think about the things to which your attention is given.

All belief begins in the will to believe.

You cannot always and instantly believe what you will to believe; but you can always will to believe what you want to believe. You want to believe truth about health, and you can will to do so. The statements you have been reading in this book are the truth about health, and you can will to believe them. This must be your first step toward getting well.

These are the statements you must will to believe:

That there is a Thinking Substance from which all things are made, and that a human being receives the Principle of Health, which is his life, from this Substance.

That a human being himself is Thinking Substance a mind-body permeating a physical body, and that as a person' thoughts are, so will the functioning of his physical body be.

That if a person will think only thoughts of perfect health, he must and will cause the internal and involuntary functioning of his body to be the functioning of health, provided that his external and voluntary functioning and attitude are in accordance with his thoughts.

When you will to believe these statements, you must also begin to act upon them. You cannot long retain a belief unless you act upon it, you cannot increase a belief until it becomes faith unless you act upon it, and you certainly cannot expect to reap benefits in any way from a belief so long as you act as if the opposite were true.

You cannot long have faith in health if you continue to act like a sick person. If you continue to act like a sick person, you cannot help continuing to think of yourself as a sick person. And if you continue to think of yourself as a sick person, you will continue to be a sick person.

The first step toward acting externally like a well person is to begin to act internally like a well person. Form your conception of perfect health, and get into the way of thinking about perfect health until it begins to have a definite meaning to you. Picture yourself as doing the things a strong and healthy person would do, and have faith that you can and will do those things in that way. Continue this until you have a vivid **CONCEPTION** of health, and what it means to you.

When I speak in this book of a conception of health, I mean a conception that carries with it the idea of the way a healthy person looks and does things. Think of yourself in connection with health until you form a conception of how you would live, appear, act, and do things as a perfectly healthy person. Think about yourself in connection with health until you conceive of yourself, in imagination, as always doing everything in the manner of a well person â" until the thought of health conveys the idea of what health means to you. As I have said in a former chapter, you may not be able to form a clear mental image of yourself in perfect health, but you can form a conception of yourself as acting like a healthy person.

Form this conception, and then think only thoughts of perfect health in relation to yourself, and, so far as may be possible, in relation to others. When a thought of sickness or disease is presented to you, reject it. Do not let it get into your mind. Do not entertain or consider it at all. Meet it by thinking health, by thinking that you are well, and by being sincerely grateful for the health you are receiving.

Whenever suggestions of disease are coming thick and fast upon you, and you are in a tight place, fall back upon the exercise of gratitude. Connect yourself with the Supreme, give thanks to God for the perfect health God gives you, and you will soon find yourself able to control your thoughts, and to think what you want to think. In times of doubt, trial, and temptation, the exercise of gratitude is always a sheet anchor which will prevent you from being swept away.

Remember that the great essential thing is to **SEVER ALL MENTAL RELATIONS WITH DISEASE, AND TO ENTER INTO FULL MENTAL RELATIONSHIP WITH HEALTH.** This is the **KEY** to all mental healing; it is the whole thing.

Here we see the secret of the great success of Christian Science. More than any other formulated system of practice, it insists that its converts shall sever relations with disease, and relate themselves fully with health. The healing power of Christian Science is not in its theological formulae nor in its denial of matter, but in the fact that it induces the sick to ignore disease as an unreal thing and accept health by faith as a reality. Its failures are made because its practitioners, while thinking in the Certain Way, do not eat, drink, breathe, and sleep in the same way.

While there is no healing power in the repetition of strings of words, yet it is a very convenient thing to have the central thoughts so formulated that you can repeat them readily, and so that you can use them as affirmations whenever you are surrounded by an environment which gives you adverse suggestions. When those around you begin to talk of sickness and death, close your ears and mentally assert something like the following:

There is One Substance, and I am that Substance.

That Substance is eternal, and it is Life; I am that Substance, and I am Eternal Life.

That Substance knows no disease; I am that Substance, and I am Health.

Exercise your will power in choosing only those thoughts which are thoughts of health, and arrange your environment so that it shall suggest thoughts of health. Do not have about you books, pictures, or other things which suggest death, disease, deformity, weakness, or age. Have only those which convey the ideas of health, power, joy, vitality, and youth. When you are confronted with a book, or anything else which suggests disease, do not give it your attention.

Think of your conception of health, and your gratitude, and affirm as above. Use your will power to fix your attention upon thoughts of health. In a future chapter I shall touch upon this point again. What I wish to make plain here is that you must think only health, recognize only health, and give your attention only to health, and that you must control thought, recognition, and attention by the use of your will.

Do not try to use your will to compel the healthy performance of function within you. The Principle of Health will attend to that if you give your attention only to thoughts of health.

Do not try to exert your will upon the Formless to compel It to give you more vitality or power. It is already placing all the power there is at your service.

You do not have to use your will to conquer adverse conditions, or to subdue unfriendly forces. There are no unfriendly forces; there is only One Force, and that force is friendly to you. It is a force which makes for health.

Everything in the universe wants you to be well. You have absolutely nothing to overcome but your own habit of thinking in a certain way about disease, and you can do this only by forming a habit of thinking in another Certain Way about health.

A person can cause all the internal functions of his body to be performed in a perfectly healthy manner by continuously thinking in a Certain Way and by performing the external functions in a certain way. He can think in this Certain Way by controlling his attention, and he can control his attention by the use of his will.

He can decide what things he will think about.

CHAPTER 7

Health from God

I will give a chapter here to explain how a human being may receive health from the Supreme. By the Supreme I mean the Thinking Substance from which all things are made, and which is in all and through all, seeking more complete expression and fuller life. This Intelligent Substance, in a perfectly fluid state, permeates and penetrates all things, and is in touch with all minds. It is the source of all energy and power, and constitutes the inflow of life, vitalizing all things. It is working to one definite end and for the fulfillment of one purpose, and that purpose is the advancement of life toward the complete expression of Mind. When a person harmonizes himself with this Intelligence, it can and will give him health and wisdom. When a person holds steadily to the purpose to live more abundantly, he comes into harmony with this Supreme Intelligence.

The purpose of the Supreme Intelligence is the most Abundant Life for all. The purpose of this Supreme Intelligence for you is that you should live more abundantly. If, then, your own purpose is to live more abundantly, you are unified with the Supreme you are working with It, and it must work with you.

But as the Supreme Intelligence is in all, *if you harmonize with it you must harmonize with all, and you must desire more abundant life for all as well as for yourself.* Two great benefits come to you from being in harmony with the Supreme Intelligence.

First, you will receive wisdom.

By wisdom I do not mean knowledge of facts so much as ability to perceive and understand facts, and to judge soundly and act rightly in all matters relating to life. Wisdom is the power to perceive truth, and the ability to make the best use of the knowledge of truth. It is the power to perceive at once the best end to aim at, and the means best adapted to attain that end.

With wisdom comes poise, and the power to think rightly, to control and guide your thoughts, and to avoid the difficulties which come from wrong thinking.

With wisdom you will be able to select the right courses for your particular needs, and to so govern yourself in all ways as to secure the best results. You will know how to do what you want to do. You can readily see that wisdom must be an essential attribute of the Supreme Intelligence, since That which knows all truth must be wise, and you can also see that just in proportion as you harmonize and unify your mind with that Intelligence you will have wisdom.

But I repeat that since this Intelligence is All, and in all, you can enter into Its wisdom only by harmonizing with all. If there is anything in your desires or your purpose which will bring oppression to any, or work injustice to, or cause lack of life for any, you cannot receive wisdom from the Supreme. Furthermore, your purpose for your own self must be the best.

A person can live in three general ways: for the gratification of his body, for that of his intellect, or for that of his soul.

The first is accomplished by satisfying the desires for food, drink, and those other things which give enjoyable physical sensations. The second is accomplished by doing those things which cause pleasant mental sensations, such as gratifying the desire for knowledge or those for fine clothing, fame, power, and so on. The third is accomplished by giving way to the instincts of unselfish love and altruism.

A person lives most wisely and completely when he functions most perfectly along all of these lines, without excess in any of them. The person who lives swinishly, for the body alone, is unwise and out of harmony with God. That person who lives solely for the cold enjoyments of the intellect, though he be absolutely moral, is unwise and out of harmony with God. And the person who lives wholly for the practice of altruism, and who throws himself away for others, is as unwise and as far from harmony with God as those who go to excess in other ways.

To come into full harmony with the Supreme, you must purpose to **LIVE** to live to the utmost of your capabilities in body, mind, and soul. This must mean the full exercise of function in all the different ways, but without excess, for excess in one causes deficiency in the others. Behind your desire for health is your own desire for more abundant life, and behind that is the desire of the Formless Intelligence to live more fully in you.

So, as you advance toward perfect health, hold steadily to the purpose to attain complete life, physical, mental, and spiritual; to advance in all ways, and in every way to live more. If you hold this purpose you will be given wisdom. He that willeth to do the will of the Father shall KNOW, said Jesus. Wisdom is the most desirable gift that can come to a person, for it makes him rightly self-governing.

But wisdom is not all you may receive from the Supreme Intelligence. You may receive physical energy, vitality, life force. The energy of the Formless Substance is unlimited, and permeates everything. You are already receiving or appropriating to yourself this energy in an automatic and instinctive way, but you can do so to a far greater degree if you set about it intelligently. The measure of a person's strength is not what God is willing to give him, but what he, himself, has the will and the intelligence to appropriate to himself. God gives you all there is. Your only question is how much to take of the unlimited supply.

A noted scholar has pointed out that there is apparently no limit to the powers of the human being, and this is simply because the human being's power comes from the inexhaustible reservoir of the Supreme. The runner who has reached the stage of exhaustion, when his physical power seems entirely gone, by running on in a Certain Way may receive his second wind. His strength is renewed in a seemingly miraculous fashion, and he can go on indefinitely. And by continuing in the Certain Way, he may receive a third, fourth, and fifth wind. We do not know where the limit is, or how far it may be possible to extend it.

The conditions are that the runner must have absolute faith that the strength will come, that he must think steadily of strength and have perfect confidence that he has it, and that he must continue to run on. If he admits a doubt into his mind, he falls exhausted, and if he stops running to wait for the accession of strength, it will never come.

His faith in strength, his faith that he can keep on running, his unwavering purpose to keep on running, and his action in keeping on seem to connect him to the source of energy in such a way as to bring him a new supply.

In a very similar manner, the sick person who has unquestioning faith in health, whose purpose brings him into harmony with the source, and who performs the voluntary functions of life in a certain way, will receive vital energy sufficient for all his needs, and for the healing of all his diseases.

God, who seeks to live and express himself fully in humanity, delights to give human beings all that is needed for the most abundant life. Action and reaction are equal, and when you desire to live more, if you are in mental harmony with the Supreme, the forces which make for life begin to concentrate about you and upon you. The One Life begins to move toward you, and your environment becomes surcharged with it. Then, if you appropriate it by faith, it is yours.

Ye shall ask what ye will, and it shall be done unto you. Your Father doesn't give his spirit by measure; he delights to give good gifts to you.

CHAPTER 8

Summary of the Mental Actions

Let me now summarize the mental actions and attitudes necessary to the practice of the Science of Being Well: first, you believe that there is a Thinking Substance, from which all things are made, and which, in its original state, permeates, penetrates, and fills the interspaces of the universe. This Substance is the Life of All, and is seeking to express more life in all. It is the Principle of Life of the universe, and the Principle of Health in a human being. A human being is a form of this Substance, and draws his vitality from it. He is a mind-body of original substance, permeating a physical body, and the thoughts of his mind-body control the functioning of his physical body. If a person thinks no thoughts save those of perfect health, the functions of his physical body will be performed in a manner of perfect health.

In order to consciously relate yourself to the All-Health, your purpose must be to live fully on every plane of your being. You must want all that there is in life for body, mind, and soul, and this will bring you into harmony with all the life there is.

The person who is in conscious and intelligent harmony with All will receive a continuous inflow of vital power from the Supreme Life, and this inflow is prevented by angry, selfish or antagonistic mental attitudes. If you are against any part, you have severed relations with all you will receive life, but only instinctively and automatically, not intelligently and purposefully.

You can see that if you are mentally antagonistic to any part, you cannot be in complete harmony with the Whole. Therefore, as Jesus directed, be reconciled to everybody and everything before you offer worship.

Want for everybody all that you want for yourself.

The reader is recommended to read what we have said in a former work, ***The Science of Getting Rich***, concerning the Competitive mind and the Creative mind. It is very doubtful whether one who has lost health can completely regain it so long as he remains in the competitive mind.

Being on the Creative or Good-Will plane in mind, the next step is to form a conception of yourself as in perfect health, and to hold no thoughts which are not in full harmony with this conception. Have **FAITH** that if you think only thoughts of health you will establish in your physical body the functioning of health; and use your will to determine that you will think only thoughts of health.

Never think of yourself as sick, or as likely to be sick; never think of sickness in connection with yourself at all. And, as far as may be, shut out of your mind all thoughts of sickness in connection with others. Surround yourself as much as possible with the things which suggest the ideas of strength and health.

Have faith in health, and accept health as an actual present fact in your life. Claim health as a blessing bestowed upon you by the Supreme Life, and be deeply grateful at all times. Claim the blessing by faith, know that it is yours, and never admit a contrary thought to your mind.

Use your will-power to withhold your attention from every appearance of disease in yourself and others. Do not study disease, think about it, nor speak of it. At all times, when the thought of disease is thrust upon you, move forward into the mental position of prayerful gratitude for your perfect health.

The mental actions necessary to being well may now be summed up in a single sentence: Form a conception of yourself in perfect health, and think only those thoughts which are in harmony with that conception. That with faith and gratitude and the purpose to really live covers all the requirements.

It is not necessary to take mental exercises of any kind, except as described in Chapter 6, or to do wearying stunts in the way of affirmations, and so on. It is not necessary to concentrate the mind on the affected parts. It is far better not to think of any part as affected. It is not necessary to treat yourself by auto-suggestion, or to have others treat you in any way whatever. The power that heals is the Principle of Health within you, and to call this Principle into Constructive Action it is only necessary, having harmonized yourself with the All-Mind, to claim by **FAITH** the All-Health and to hold that claim until it is physically manifested in all the functions of your body.

In order to hold this mental attitude of faith, gratitude, and health, however, your external acts must be only those of health. You cannot long hold the internal attitude of a well person if you continue to perform the external acts of a sick person. It is essential not only that your every thought should be a thought of health, but that your every act should be an act of health, performed in a healthy manner. If you will make every thought a thought of health, and every conscious act an act of health, it must infallibly follow that every internal and unconscious function shall come to be healthy, for all the power of life is being continually exerted toward health.

We shall next consider how you may make every act an act of health.

CHAPTER 9

When to Eat

You cannot build and maintain a perfectly healthy body by mental action alone or by the performance of the unconscious or involuntary functions alone. There are certain actions, more or less voluntary, which have a direct and immediate relation with the continuance of life itself. These are eating, drinking, breathing, and sleeping.

No matter what a person's thought or mental attitude may be, he cannot live unless he eats, drinks, breathes, and sleeps, and, moreover, he cannot be well if he eats, drinks, breathes, and sleeps in an unnatural or wrong manner. It is therefore vitally important that you should learn the right way to perform these voluntary functions, and I shall proceed to show you this way, beginning with the matter of eating, which is most important.

There has been a vast amount of controversy as to when to eat, what to eat, how to eat, and how much to eat, and all this controversy is unnecessary, for the Right Way is very easy to find. You have only to consider the Law which governs all attainment, whether of health, wealth, power, or happiness; and that law is *that you must do what you can do now, where you are now; do every separate act in the most perfect manner possible, and put the power of faith into every action.*

The processes of digestion and assimilation are under the supervision and control of an inner division of a person's mentality, which is generally called the subconscious mind, and I shall use that term here in order to be understood. The subconscious mind is in charge of all the functions and processes of life, and when more food is needed by the body, it makes the fact known by causing a sensation called hunger.

Whenever food is needed and can be used, there is hunger, and whenever there is hunger it is time to eat. When there is no hunger it is unnatural and wrong to eat, no matter how great may **APPEAR** to be the need for food.

Even if you are in a condition of apparent starvation, with great emaciation, if there is no hunger you may know that **FOOD CANNOT BE USED**, and it will be unnatural and wrong for you to eat. Though you have not eaten for days or weeks, if you have no hunger you may be perfectly sure that food cannot be used, and will probably not be used if taken. Whenever food is needed, if there is power to digest and assimilate it, so that it can be normally used, the sub-conscious mind will announce the fact by a decided hunger.

Food, taken when there is no hunger, will sometimes be digested and as similated, because Nature makes a special effort to perform the task which is thrust upon her against her will, but if food is habitually taken when there is no hunger, the digestive power is at last destroyed, and numberless evils caused.

If the foregoing be true and it is indisputably so it is a self-evident proposition that the natural time (and the healthy time) to eat is when one is hungry, and that it is never a natural or a healthy action to eat when one is not hungry. You see, then, that it is an easy matter to scientifically settle the question when to eat. **ALWAYS** eat when you are hungry, and **NEVER** eat when you are not hungry. This is obedience to nature, which is obedience to God.

We must not fail, however, to make clear the distinction between hunger and appetite.

Hunger is the call of the sub-conscious mind for more material to be used in repairing and renewing the body, and in keeping up the internal heat. Hunger is never felt unless there is need for more material, and unless there is power to digest it when taken into the stomach.

Appetite is a desire for the gratification of sensation. The drunkard has an appetite for liquor, but he cannot have a hunger for it. A normally fed person cannot have a hunger for candy or sweets. The desire for these things is an appetite. You cannot hunger for tea, coffee, spiced foods, or for the various taste-tempting devices of the skilled cook. If you desire these things, it is with appetite, not with hunger.

Hunger is nature's call for material to be used in building new cells, and nature never calls for anything which may not be legitimately used for this purpose.

Appetite is often largely a matter of habit. If one eats or drinks at a certain hour, and especially if one takes sweetened or spiced and stimulating foods, the desire comes regularly at the same hour, but this habitual desire for food should never be mistaken for hunger.

Hunger does not appear at specified times. It only comes when work or exercise has used sufficient energy to make the taking in of new raw material a necessity.

For instance, if a person has been sufficiently fed on the preceding day, it is impossible that he should feel a genuine hunger on arising from refreshing sleep. In sleep the body is recharged with vital power, and the assimilation of the food which has been taken during the day is completed the system has no need for food immediately after sleep, unless the person went to his rest in a state of starvation. With a system of feeding which is even a reasonable approach to a natural one, no one can have a real hunger for an early morning breakfast. There is no such thing possible as a normal or genuine hunger immediately after arising from sound sleep.

The early morning breakfast is always taken to gratify appetite, never to satisfy hunger. No matter whom you are, or what your condition is; no matter how hard you work, or how much you are exposed, unless you go to your bed starved, you cannot arise from your bed hungry.

Hunger is not caused by sleep, but by work. And it does not matter who you are, or what your condition, or how hard or easy your work, the so-called no-breakfast plan is the right plan for you. It is the right plan for everybody, because it is based on the universal law that hunger never comes until it is **EARNED**. I am aware that a protest against this will come from the large number of people who enjoy their breakfasts, whose breakfast is their best meal who believe that their work is so hard that they cannot get through the forenoon on an empty stomach, and so on. But all their arguments fall down before the facts.

They enjoy their breakfast as the toper enjoys his morning dram, because it gratifies a habitual appetite and not because it supplies a natural want. It is their best meal for the same reason that his morning dram is the toper's best drink. And they **CAN** get along without it, because millions of people, of every trade and profession, **DO** get along without it, and are vastly better for doing so.

If you are to live according to the Science of Being Well, you must **NEVER EAT UNTIL YOU HAVE AN EARNED HUNGER.**

But if I do not eat on arising in the morning, when shall I take my first meal?

In 99 cases out of a 100, twelve o'clock noon is early enough, and it is generally the most convenient time. If you are doing heavy work, you will get by noon a hunger sufficient to justify a good-sized meal. And if your work is light, you will probably still have hunger enough for a moderate meal. The best general rule or law that can be laid down is that you should eat your first meal of the day at noon if you are hungry, and if you are not hungry, wait until you become so.

And when shall I eat my second meal?

Not at all, unless you are hungry for it and that with a genuine earned hunger. If you do get hungry for a second meal, eat at the most convenient time, but do not eat until you have a really earned hunger.

The reader who wishes to fully inform himself as to the reasons for this way of arranging the mealtimes will find the best books thereon cited in the preface to this work. From the foregoing, however, you can easily see that the Science of Being Well readily answers the question, When, and how often shall I eat?

The answer: Eat when you have an earned hunger, and never eat at any other time.

CHAPTER 10

What to Eat

The current sciences of medicine and hygiene have made no progress toward answering the question, what shall I eat? The contests between the vegetarians and the meat eaters, the cooked food advocates, raw food advocates, and various other schools of theorists, seem to be interminable. And from the mountains of evidence and argument piled up for and against each special theory, it is plain that if we depend on these scientists we shall never know what is the natural food of humans. Turning away from the whole controversy, then, we will ask the question of Nature herself, and we shall find that she has not left us without an answer.

On the question of what to eat, the answer is simple: Eat what Nature provides. The One Living Substance from which all things are made has made an abundance of perfect foods for every person in every place humans can live, and has given every person the physical and mental faculties to know what foods he should eat and how and when he should eat them.

Whenever people have attempted to improve on Nature, they go wrong. For humanity does not yet know enough not to go wrong. Nature is the physical form of the One Living Substance, operating according to the rules of the One Living Substance, with the energy of the One Living Substance. Nature provides every person exactly what is needed for perfect health.

The Great Intelligence, which is in and through all, has in reality practically settled the question as to what we shall eat. In ordering the affairs of nature, It has decided that a human being's food shall be according to the zone in which he lives. These are the foods best for the requirements of the climate. These are the foods which will be the freshest when a person eats them, and therefore most filled with the life force of the One Living Substance. In acquiring these foods a person can be in closest association with the Principle of Life that created them. Therefore, a person need only ask himself what food grows and lives where he lives.

How shall a person know which of these foods to eat, according to his age, gender, ancestry, condition of health, exposure to cold, physical and mental activity?

Again, we see that the Great Intelligence operating in Nature answers the question. It provides a variety of foods in every zone, and it provides a human being with hunger and taste.

A person needs food as a raw material for the Principle of Health in his own body to direct in providing energy, heat, defense, and tissue repair and growth. He needs protein, carbohydrates, fats, vitamins, and minerals. These are found in the flesh, milk, blood, eggs, bones, and organs of water and land creatures, and in the roots, stems, leaves, flowers, seeds, grains, nuts, and fruits of land and water plants. The Great Intelligence guides the masses of people to discover ways of procuring and preparing these foods in harmony with Nature. A person's own Principle of Health guides his hunger and taste to the particular foods that will fill its needs.

With all the various ways food is prepared, how shall a person know the proper way?

He should procure and prepare his food in ways that cooperate with Nature. It is only when people work against Nature that they go wrong. To illustrate this point let us compare the health of people working in cooperation with Nature with the health of these same people working against Nature.

In every climate there are tribes who have learned over thousands of years the wisdom of nature and the best ways to gather, prepare, and eat the foods of the region in perfect harmony with the seasons and cycles of Nature.

The perfect health of these people provides a shining example of what is possible in physical strength and endurance, perfect eyesight and teeth, longevity, skill and agility, mental development, morality, and overall well-being. Moreover, they have learned the secrets of healthy reproduction and child-rearing such that there are not only happy, healthy children, but the absence of unsociable behavior.

What secrets of eating are followed by these perfectly healthy people?

They eat only foods that occur in nature or that can be simply made from these.

They eat only the best foods, and parts of foods, with the greatest nutrient content.

They eat both animal and plant foods.

Many foods from both plant and animal sources are eaten raw.

From wild animals, bones, and organs are as important as (and often preferred over) muscle meat.

From domesticated animals, fresh milk (and in some cases, even blood) is drawn. When milk products are used, they are made from milk taken from vitally healthy animals after they have been well fed on newly growing spring grasses.

Cheese, butter, and other milk products that can be stored for later use are made from this milk. During other seasons, the animals are fed the highest quality hay.

For some groups, insects in both adult and immature forms are important food sources, even where other animal foods are available.

In zones near the sea, sea creatures are the source of animal food. Fish eggs are a rich source of nutrients. Where they are not available year-round, both the flesh and eggs of fish are dried for winter use in a way that preserves or increases nutrient content.

Plant foods are eaten liberally during the season in which they grow and are ripe. Where they are not growing year-round, some are preserved for winter use in ways that preserves their nutrients.

Sweet foods of all kinds are eaten only sparingly on special occasions. Refined sugar is avoided altogether, as are all foods made by adding refined sugar.

Land used for plant cultivation is fertilized liberally with natural substances, and allowed periods of rest.

Grains are eaten whole, or ground immediately before use. The entire grain is used.

Children are nursed, and then given high nutrient foods to help them grow. There are times of natural decrease in food supply, and ceremonial times, when the people eat less, or not at all.

The people actively participate in the physical pursuit of growing, gathering, hunting, and preparing their food. They have community ceremonies of gratitude and celebration.

These are the practices of the healthiest people on earth.

What happens when these same people abandon their way of living and eating and replace their foods with unnatural foods?

They develop disease, deformity, misery, and unsociable behavior.

What are the unnatural foods that cause these effects?

They are refined and preserved foods from which natural life has been removed or lost, or sugar and flavors added to hide the absence of nutrients. They are foods so old that no life force remains in them. They are foods from unhealthy plants and animals, containing life force that bears the impression of weakness or disease.

What is needed for perfect health is vital food, brimming with life force, eaten according to the practices of healthy people.

How shall the modern city dweller acquire this vital food and incorporate these practices into his life?

First is to remember that he is to eat the food Nature provides in the zone in which he lives.

He must align himself with the Principle of Life with gratitude that there is abundant food for all and with faith that he will be perfectly guided to the best sources available in his area. Perfect health requires a relationship with the Source of all food with faith, gratitude, and joy. Food must be gathered with the attitude of more life to all and less to none.

A person must either learn to grow and gather, raise animals, hunt and fish, or find those who do. If he does not procure his own food directly from Nature, he must form a friendly relationship with those who do. He can then knowingly choose to deal with those who operate in harmony with Nature, exercising gratitude and wisdom.

The person who does not know how to identify a farmer or hunter following the natural laws of producing and finding
food can be guided by these simple concepts:

Choosing your food providers

The food provider is healthy, happy, and of a generous spirit. He uses no poisons of any kind in the production of foods.

If he raises animals, they are healthy and treated with kindness, respect, and gratitude. They are fed only the best foods for their health, not for abnormal growth or food production. They are not confined in unhealthy conditions, but given freedom to move about normally, and only sheltered for their protection.

If he fishes or hunts, he catches or kills lake, river, land or sea creatures in their natural environment. He uses means that ensure the healthy survival of all the species caught, whether or not they are the ones to be eaten.

If he farms, he uses only healthy, living soil uncontaminated by previous poisons. He replenishes the life of the soil so that his crops are rich in natural nutrients. His crops and soil are so healthy that they do not attract pests, and he farms in such a way that birds and other creatures eating the insects on his farm are unharmed. Any water running off his land contains no chemicals that will harm any other part of life.

These are the characteristics of a person who knows the laws of Nature in the production and procurement of food.
You must also know how to determine the correct people with whom to associate in any other steps of obtaining your food.

Do not associate with anyone in the process of procuring food who speaks of disease, fear, or lack in any way. Associate only with those who gratefully and joyfully appreciate the life-giving qualities of food, are happy to grow it, harvest it, prepare it, serve it, eat it, and know that there is an abundance of the best food for all. This is important whether you are dealing with someone who is selling you land on which to farm, or a farmer, or butcher, or truck driver, or store clerk, or cook, or waiter in a restaurant.

You must not eat foods produced or transported carelessly, or treated in any other way than as precious, life-giving substances. This is easily accomplished when you are the one procuring the food from its natural source or if you are in direct and harmonious relationship with all those who are.

The city dweller who thinks it is too difficult or too expensive to obtain food in this way need only review **The Science of Getting Rich**. All his doubts will there be answered. He will be guided in the correct manner of acquiring all the money he wants, and in attracting to himself all other resources he desires.

Once a person is supplied with a variety of vital foods from which to choose, how shall he know what to eat at a given meal? Here is the only needed guideline: Eat what your *body* wants. Your body wants what the Principle of Health requires to create perfect health.

What your body wants is determined very simply. The thought of the food, when you are truly hungry, is appealing. The taste of the food while chewing it is pleasant. After eating, your body feels energized and satisfied. There is no sleepiness, irritability, congestion, pain, discomfort of any kind, from the moment you begin to eat until the next day. Over a period of days, weeks and months, you continue to feel well.

This is how you will know you are eating the correct foods. Then you will not need to give the least thought to what you should or should not eat. You will want the right foods. The Principle of Health in your own body will guide you to know what to eat just as surely as it will guide you to know when to eat.

If you do not eat until you have an **EARNED** hunger, you will not find your taste demanding unnatural or unhealthy foods. If you make an association with your source of food that brings joy and gratitude, you will further increase your desire to eat what is natural and healthy.

It is when a person becomes lazy and allows himself to be tempted by taste and convenience rather than following the Great Intelligence with which he is bestowed, that he pays the price of decreased health.

When you learn to cooperate with Nature you will want what is good for you, and you will eat what you want. This you can do with perfect results if you eat in the right way, and how to do this will be explained in the next chapter.

CHAPTER 11

How to Eat

It is a settled fact that a person naturally chews his food. The few faddists who maintain that we should bolt our nourishment, after the manner of the dog and others of the lower animals, can no longer get a hearing. We know that we should chew our food. And if it is natural that we should chew our food, the more thoroughly we chew it the more completely natural the process must be. If you will chew every mouthful to a liquid, you need not be in the least concerned as to whether you are getting enough nutrients, for you have already chosen the best foods according to Natural Law. Whether or not this chewing shall be an irksome and laborious task or a most enjoyable process depends upon the mental attitude in which you come to the table.

If your mind and attitude are on other things, or if you are anxious or worried about business or domestic affairs, you will find it almost impossible to eat without bolting more or less of your food. You must learn to live so scientifically that you will have no business or domestic cares to worry about. This you can do.

You must also arrange your life so that you are not in the presence of others who distract from the enjoyment of your meal. This way, you can learn to give your undivided attention to the act of eating while at the table.

The matter of eating only when in a peaceful state of mind must be emphasized. You must focus on gratitude before eating the food on your table and on the full enjoyment of each bite while eating. After eating, you must again focus on gratitude for the vital force from the food supplied to you through the One Living Substance. These mental actions will assist in the physical extraction of vital force from your food, and in bringing the Principle of Health within you into full Constructive Activity.

You must therefore eat with an eye single to the purpose of getting all the enjoyment you can from that meal. Dismiss everything else from your mind, and do not let anything take your attention from the food and its taste until your meal is finished. Be cheerfully confident, for if you follow these instructions you may **KNOW** that the food you eat is exactly the right food, and that it will agree with you to perfection.

Sit down to the table with confident cheerfulness, and take a moderate portion of the food. Take whatever thing looks most desirable to you. Do not select some food because you think it will be good for you select that which will taste good to you. If you are to get well and stay well, you must drop the idea of doing things because they are good for your health, and do things because you want to do them. Select the food you want most, gratefully give thanks to God that you have learned how to eat it in such a way that digestion shall be perfect, and take a moderate mouthful of it.

Do not fix your attention on the act of chewing; fix it on the **TASTE** of the food. And taste and enjoy it until it is reduced to a liquid state and passes down your throat by involuntary swallowing.

No matter how long it takes, do not think of the time. Think of the taste. Do not allow your eyes to wander over the table, speculating as to what you shall eat next. Do not worry for fear there is not enough, and that you will not get your share of everything. Do not anticipate the taste of the next thing. Keep your mind centered on the taste of what you have in your mouth.

And that is all of it.

Scientific and healthful eating is a delightful process after you have learned how to do it, and after you have overcome the bad old habit of gobbling down your food without chewing. It is best not to have too much conversation going on while eating. Be cheerful, but not talkative. Do the talking afterward.

In most cases, some use of the will is required to form the habit of correct eating. The bolting habit is an unnatural one, and is without doubt mostly the result of fear. Fear that we will be robbed of our food, fear that we will not get our share of the good things, fear that we will lose precious time, these are the causes of haste. Then there is anticipation of the dainties that are to come for dessert and the consequent desire to get at them as quickly as possible. And there is mental abstraction, or thinking of other matters while eating. All these must be overcome.

When you find that your mind is wandering, call a halt. Think for a moment of the food and of how good it tastes, of the perfect digestion and assimilation that are going to follow the meal, and begin again. Begin again and again, though you must do so 20 times in the course of a single meal. And again and again, though you must do so every meal for weeks and months. It is perfectly certain that you **CAN** form the Fletcher habit if you persevere, and when you have formed it, you will experience a healthful pleasure you have never known.

This is a vital point, and I must not leave it until I have thoroughly impressed it upon your mind. Given the right materials, perfectly prepared, the Principle of Health will positively build you a perfectly healthy body, and you cannot prepare the materials *perfectly* in any other way than the one I am describing.

If you are to have perfect health, you **MUST** eat in just this way. You can, and the doing of it is only a matter of a little perseverance. What use for you to talk of mental control unless you will govern yourself in so simple a matter as ceasing to bolt your food? What use to talk of concentration unless you can keep your mind on the act of eating for so short a space as 15 or 20 minutes, especially with all the pleasures of taste to help you?

Go on, and conquer. In a few weeks, or months, as the case may be, you will find the habit of scientific eating becoming fixed, and soon you will be in so splendid a condition, mentally and physically, that nothing would induce you to return to the bad old way.

We have seen that if a person will think only thoughts of perfect health, his internal functions will be performed in a healthy manner, and we have seen that in order to think thoughts of health, a person must perform the voluntary functions in a healthy manner. The most important of the voluntary functions is that of eating, and we see, so far, no special difficulty in eating in a perfectly healthy way.

I will here summarize the instructions as to when to eat, what to eat, and how to eat, with the reasons why:

NEVER eat until you have an **EARNED** hunger, no matter how long you go without food. This is based on the fact that whenever food is needed in the system, if there is power to digest it, the sub-conscious mind announces the need by the sensation of hunger.

Learn to distinguish between genuine hunger and the gnawing and craving sensations caused by unnatural appetite. Hunger is never a disagreeable feeling, accompanied by weakness, faintness, or gnawing feelings at the stomach. It is a pleasant, anticipatory desire for food. It does not come at certain hours or at stated intervals. It only comes when the body is ready to receive, digest, and assimilate food.

Eat whatever foods you want, making your selection from the full variety of the best foods found in the zone in which you live. The Supreme Intelligence has guided humanity to the selection of these foods, and they are the right ones. I am referring, of course, to the foods which are taken to satisfy hunger, not to those which have been contrived merely to gratify appetite or perverted taste. The instinct which has guided people to make use of the great staples of food to satisfy their hunger is a divine one. God has made no mistake; if you eat these foods you will not go wrong.

Eat your food with cheerful confidence in a pleasant atmosphere, and get all the pleasure that is to be had from the taste of every mouthful. Chew each morsel to a liquid, keeping your attention fixed on the enjoyment of the process. This is the only way to eat in a perfectly complete and successful manner; and when anything is done in a completely successful manner, the general result cannot be a failure.

In the attainment of health, the law is the same as in the attainment of riches: if you make each act a success in itself, the sum of all your acts must be a success. When you eat in the mental attitude I have described, and in the manner I have described, nothing can be added to the process it is done in a perfect manner, and it is successfully done. And if eating is successfully done, digestion, assimilation, and the building of a healthy body are successfully begun.

We next take up the question of the quantity of food required.

CHAPTER 12

Hunger and Appetites

It is very easy to find the correct answer to the question, How much shall I eat? You are never to eat until you have an earned hunger, and you are to stop eating the instant you **BEGIN** to feel that your hunger is abating. Never gorge yourself. Never eat to repletion. When you begin to feel that your hunger is satisfied, know that you have enough. For until you have enough, you will continue to feel the sensation of hunger.

If you eat as directed in the last chapter, it is probable that you will begin to feel satisfied before you have taken half your usual amount, but stop there, all the same. No matter how delightfully attractive the dessert, or how tempting the pie or pudding, do not eat a mouthful of it if you find that your hunger has been in the least degree assuaged by the other foods you have taken.

Whatever you eat after your hunger begins to abate is taken to gratify taste and appetite, not hunger and is not called for by nature at all. It is therefore excess, mere debauchery and it cannot fail to work mischief.

This is a point you will need to watch with nice discrimination, for the habit of eating purely for sensual gratification is very deeply rooted with most of us. The usual dessert of sweet and tempting foods is prepared solely with a view to inducing people to eat after hunger has been satisfied, and all the effects are evil. For the effect of eating these unwholesome foods is often an increase in appetite.

The same is true of alcohol taken before eating. Both will trick you to eat far more than you would otherwise want, and make it difficult to focus your attention on the satisfaction of your true hunger. You will find that if you eat as directed in the preceding chapters, the plainest food will soon come to taste like kingly fare to you, for your sense of taste, like all your other senses, will become so acute with the general improvement in your condition that you will find new delights in common things.

No glutton ever enjoyed a meal like the person who eats for hunger only, who gets the most out of every mouthful, and who stops on the instant that he feels the edge taken from his hunger. The first intimation that hunger is abating is the signal from the sub-conscious mind that it is time to quit.

The average person who takes up this plan of living will be greatly surprised to learn how little food is really required to keep the body in perfect condition.

The amount depends upon the work, upon how much muscular exercise is taken, and upon the extent to which the person is exposed to cold.

The woodchopper who goes into the forest in the winter time and swings his axe all day can eat two full meals, but the brain worker who sits all day on a chair, in a warm room, does not need one-third and often not one-tenth as much. Most woodchoppers eat two or three times as much, and most brain workers from three to ten times as much as nature calls for, and the elimination of this vast amount of surplus rubbish from their systems is a tax on vital power which in time depletes their energy and leaves them an easy prey to so-called disease.

Get all possible enjoyment out of the taste of your food, but never eat anything merely because it tastes good. And on the instant that you feel that your hunger is less keen, stop eating.

If you will consider for a moment, you will see that there is positively no other way for you to settle these various food questions than by adopting the plan here laid down for you. As to the proper time to eat, there is no other way to decide than to say that you should eat whenever you have an **EARNED HUNGER**. It is a self-evident proposition that that is the right time to eat, and that any other is a wrong time to eat.

As to what to eat, the Eternal Wisdom has decided that the people shall eat the best products of the zones in which they live. The staple foods of your particular zone are the right foods for you, and the Eternal Wisdom, working in and through the minds of people, has taught them how best to prepare these foods by cooking and otherwise.

And as to how to eat, you know that you must chew your food in a peaceful state of mind, and if food must be chewed, then reason tells us that the more thorough and perfect the operation the better.

I repeat that success in anything is attained by making each separate act a success in itself. If you make each action, however small and unimportant, a thoroughly successful action, your day's work as a whole cannot result in failure. If you make the actions of each day successful, the sum total of your life cannot be failure.

A great success is the result of doing a large number of little things, and doing each one in a perfectly successful way. If every thought is a healthy thought, and if every action of your life is performed in a healthy way, you must soon attain to perfect health. It is impossible to devise a way in which you can perform the act of eating more successfully, and in a manner more in accord with the laws of life, than by chewing every mouthful to a liquid, enjoying the taste fully, and keeping a cheerful confidence the while. Nothing can be added to make the process more successful, while if anything be subtracted, the process will not be a completely healthy one.

In the matter of how much to eat, you will also see that there could be no other guide so natural, so safe, and so reliable as the one I have prescribed to stop eating on the instant you feel that your hunger begins to abate. The subconscious mind may be trusted with implicit reliance to inform us when food is needed, and it may be trusted as implicitly to inform us when the need has been supplied. If **ALL** food is eaten for hunger, and **NO** food is taken merely to gratify taste, you will never eat too much, and if you eat whenever you have an **EARNED** hunger, you will always eat enough.

By reading carefully the summing up in the following chapter, you will see that the requirements for eating in a perfectly healthy way are really very few and simple.

The matter of drinking in a natural way may be dismissed here with a very few words. If you wish to be exactly and rigidly scientific, drink nothing but water, drink only when you are thirsty, drink whenever you are thirsty, and stop as soon as you feel that your thirst begins to abate.

But if you are living rightly in regard to eating, it will not be necessary to practice asceticism or great self-denial in the matter of drinking. You can take an occasional cup of weak coffee without harm. You can, to a reasonable extent, follow the customs of those around you.

Do not get the soda fountain habit. Do not drink merely to tickle your palate with sweet liquids.

Be sure that you take a drink of water whenever you feel thirst. Never be too lazy, too indifferent, or too busy to get a drink of water when you feel the least thirst. If you obey this rule, you will have little inclination to take strange and unnatural drinks. Drink only to satisfy thirst, drink whenever you feel thirst, and stop drinking as soon as you feel thirst abating. That is the perfectly healthy way to supply the body with the necessary fluid material for its internal processes.

CHAPTER 13

In a Nutshell

There is a Cosmic Life which permeates, penetrates, and fills the interspaces of the universe, being in and through all things. This Life is not merely a vibration, or form of energy it is a Living Substance. All things are made from it. It is All, and in all.

This Substance thinks, and it assumes the form of that which it thinks about. The thought of a form, in this substance, creates the form; the thought of a motion institutes the motion. The visible universe, with all its forms and motions, exists because it is in the thought of Original Substance.

A human being is a form of Original Substance and can think original thoughts, and within himself a person's thoughts have controlling or formative power. The thought of a condition produces that condition; the thought of a motion institutes that motion. So long as a person thinks of the conditions and motions of disease, so long will the conditions and motions of disease exist within him. If a person will think only of perfect health, the Principle of Health within him will maintain normal conditions.

To be well, a person must form a conception of perfect health, and hold thoughts harmonious with that conception as regards himself and all things. He must think only of healthy conditions and functioning. He must not permit a thought of unhealthy or abnormal conditions or functioning to find lodgment in his mind at any time.

In order to think only of healthy conditions and functioning, a person must perform the voluntary acts of life in a perfectly healthy way. He cannot think perfect health so long as he knows that he is living in a wrong or unhealthy way, or even so long as he has doubts as to whether or not he is living in a healthy way.

A person cannot think thoughts of perfect health while his voluntary functions are performed in the manner of one who is sick. The voluntary functions of life are eating, drinking, breathing, and sleeping. When a person thinks only of healthy conditions and functioning, and performs these externals in a perfectly healthy manner, he must have perfect health.

In eating, a person must learn to be guided by his hunger. He must distinguish between hunger and appetite, and between hunger and the cravings of habit. He must **NEVER** eat unless he feels an **EARNED HUNGER**.

He must learn that genuine hunger is never present after natural sleep and that the demand for an early morning meal is purely a matter of habit and appetite; and he must not begin his day by eating in violation of natural law. He must wait until he has an Earned Hunger, which, in most cases, will make his first meal come at about the noon hour.

No matter what his condition, vocation, or circumstances, he must make it his rule not to eat until he has an **EARNED HUNGER**, and he may remember that it is far better to fast for several hours after he has become hungry than to eat before he begins to feel hunger. It will not hurt you to go hungry for a few hours, even though you are working hard, but it will hurt you to fill your stomach when you are not hungry, whether you are working or not. If you never eat until you have an Earned Hunger, you may be certain that in so far as the time of eating is concerned, you are proceeding in a perfectly healthy way. This is a self-evident proposition.

As to what he shall eat, a person must be guided by that Intelligence which has arranged that the people of any given portion of the earth's surface must live on the staple products of the zone which they inhabit. Have faith in God, and trust God's ability to guide your taste to that which your body requires. Do not worry over the controversies as to the relative merits of cooked and raw foods, of vegetables and meats, or as to your need for carbohydrates and proteins.
Eat only when you have an earned hunger, and then take the best foods of the healthy people in the zone in which you live, and have perfect confidence that the results will be good. They will be.

Do not seek for luxuries, or for things imported or fixed up to tempt the taste. Stick to the plain foods, and when these do not taste good, fast until they do. Then you will be functioning in a perfectly healthy manner, so far as what to eat is concerned. I repeat, if you have no hunger or taste for the plain foods, do not eat at all. Wait until hunger comes. Go without eating until the plainest food tastes good to you, and then begin your meal with what you like best.

In deciding how to eat, a person must be guided by reason. We can see that the abnormal states of hurry and worry produced by wrong thinking about business and similar things have led us to form the habit of eating too fast, and chewing too little.

We know that an angry or distracting atmosphere upsets the process of digestion. Reason tells us that food should be chewed, and that the more thoroughly it is chewed the better it is prepared for the chemistry of digestion. Furthermore, we can see that the person who eats slowly and chews his food to a liquid, keeping his mind on the process and giving it his undivided attention, will enjoy more of the pleasure of taste than he who bolts his food with his mind on something else.

To eat in a perfectly healthy manner, a person must concentrate his attention on the act with cheerful enjoyment and confidence. He must taste his food, and he must reduce each mouthful to a liquid before swallowing it. The foregoing instructions, if followed, make the function of eating completely perfect. Nothing can be added as to what, when, and how.

In the matter of how much to eat, a person must be guided by the same inward intelligence, or Principle of Health, which tells him when food is wanted. He must stop eating in the moment that he feels hunger abating; he must not eat beyond this point to gratify taste. If he ceases to eat in the instant that the inward demand for food ceases he will never overeat, and the function of supplying the body with food will be performed in a perfectly healthy manner.

The matter of eating naturally is a very simple one; there is nothing in all the foregoing that cannot be easily practiced by anyone. This method, put into practice, will infallibly result in perfect digestion and assimilation, and all anxiety and careful thought concerning the matter can at once be dropped from the mind. Whenever you have an earned hunger, eat with thankfulness from the variety of natural foods before you, chewing each mouthful to a liquid, and stopping when you feel the edge taken from your hunger.

The importance of the mental attitude is sufficient to justify an additional word.

While you are eating, as at all other times, think only of healthy conditions and normal functioning. Enjoy what you eat. If you carry on a conversation at the table, talk of the goodness of the food, and of the pleasure it is giving you. Never mention that you dislike this or that. Speak only of those things which you like. Never discuss the wholesomeness or unwholesomeness of foods. Never mention or think of unwholesomeness at all.

If there is anything on the table for which you do not care, pass it by in silence, or with a word of commendation. Never criticize or object to anything. Eat your food with gladness and with singleness of heart, praising God and giving thanks. Let your watchword be perseverance. Whenever you fall into the old way of hasty eating, or of wrong thought and speech, bring yourself up short and begin again.

It is of the most vital importance to you that you should be a self-controlling and self-directing person, and you can never hope to become so unless you can master yourself in so simple and fundamental a matter as the manner and method of your eating.

If you cannot control yourself in this, you cannot control yourself in anything that will be worthwhile.

On the other hand, if you carry out the foregoing instructions, you may rest in the assurance that in so far as right thinking and right eating are concerned you are living in a perfectly scientific way, and you may also be assured that if you practice what is prescribed in the following chapters you will quickly build your body into a condition of perfect health.

CHAPTER 14

Breathing

The function of breathing is a vital one, and it immediately concerns the continuance of life. We can live many hours without sleeping, and many days without eating or drinking, but only a few minutes without breathing.

The act of breathing is involuntary, but the manner of it and the provision of the proper conditions for its healthy performance fall within the scope of volition. A person will continue to breathe involuntarily, but he can voluntarily determine *what* he shall breathe, and how deeply and thoroughly he shall breathe. And he can, of his own volition, keep the physical mechanism in condition for the perfect performance of the function.

It is essential, if you wish to breathe in a perfectly healthy way, that the physical machinery used in the act should be kept in good condition. You must keep your spine moderately straight, and the muscles of your chest must be flexible and free in action. You cannot breathe in the right way if your shoulders are greatly stooped forward and your chest hollow and rigid. Sitting or standing at work in a slightly stooping position tends to produce a hollow chest. So does lifting heavy weights or light weights.

The tendency of work, of almost all kinds, is to pull the shoulders forward, curve the spine, and flatten the chest, and if the chest is greatly flattened, full and deep breathing becomes impossible and perfect health is out of the question.

Various gymnastic exercises have been devised to counteract the effect of stooping while at work, such as hanging by the hands from a swing or trapeze bar, or sitting on a chair with the feet under some heavy article of furniture and bending backward until the head touches the floor, and so on. All these are good enough in their way, but very few people will follow them long enough and regularly enough to accomplish any real gain in physique. The taking of health exercises of any kind is burdensome and unnecessary.

There is a more natural, simpler, and much better way.

This better way is to keep yourself straight, and to breathe deeply. Let your mental conception of yourself be that you are a perfectly straight person, and whenever the matter comes to your mind, be sure that you instantly expand your chest, throw back your shoulders, and straighten up.

Whenever you do this, slowly draw in your breath until you fill your lungs to their utmost capacity. Crowd in all the air you possibly can, and while holding it for an instant in the lungs, throw your shoulders still further back, and stretch your chest. At the same time try to pull your spine forward between the shoulders. Then let the air go easily.

This is the one great exercise for keeping the chest full, flexible, and in good condition. Straighten up, fill your lungs **FULL**, stretch your chest and straighten your spine, and exhale easily. And this exercise you must repeat, in season and out of season, at all times and in all places, until you form a habit of doing it. You can easily do so.

Whenever you step out of doors into the fresh, pure air, **BREATHE.** When you are at work, and think of yourself and your position, **BREATHE.** When you are in company, and are reminded of the matter, **BREATHE.** When you are awake in the night, **BREATHE.** No matter where you are or what you are doing, whenever the idea comes to your mind, straighten up and **BREATHE.** If you walk to and from your work, take this exercise all the way. It will soon become a delight to you, and you will keep it up, not for the sake of health, but as a matter of pleasure.

Do not consider this a health exercise. *Never take health exercises or do gymnastics to make you well. To do so is to recognize sickness as a present fact or as a possibility, which is precisely what you must not do.* The people who are always taking exercises for their health are always thinking about being sick. It ought to be a matter of pride with you to keep your spine straight and strong as much so as it is to keep your face clean.

Keep your spine straight, and your chest full and flexible for the same reason that you keep your hands clean and your nails manicured because it is slovenly to do otherwise. Do it without a thought of sickness, present or possible. You must either be crooked and unsightly or you must be straight, and if you are straight your breathing will take care of itself. You will find the matter of health exercises referred to again in a future chapter.

It is essential, however, that you should breathe **AIR**. It appears to be the intention of nature that the lungs should receive air containing its regular percentage of oxygen and not greatly contaminated by other gases, or by filth of any kind.

Do not allow yourself to think that you are compelled to live or work where the air is not fit to breathe. If your house cannot be properly ventilated, move. And if you are employed where the air is bad, get another job you can, by practicing the methods given in the preceding volume of this series, *The Science of Getting Rich*.

If no one would consent to work in bad air, employers would speedily see to it that all work rooms were properly ventilated. The worst air is that filled with poisonous chemical gases. Next to that is air heavily charged with mold, asbestos, or factory dust particles. After that is air from which the oxygen has been exhausted by breathing as that of airplanes, churches and theaters where crowds of people congregate, and the outlet and supply of air are poor.

Then there is air containing other natural gases than oxygen and hydrogen sewer gas and the effluvium from decaying things. Air that contains household dust or pollen may be endured better than any of these. Small particles of organic matter other than food are more easily thrown off from the lungs than gases, which go into the blood.

I speak advisedly when I say other than food. Air is largely a food. It is the most thoroughly alive thing we take into the body. Every breath carries life. The odors from earth, grass, tree, flower, plant, and from cooking foods are foods in themselves. They are minute particles of the substances from which they come, and are often so attenuated that they pass directly from the lungs into the blood, and are assimilated without digestion. And the atmosphere is permeated with the One Original Substance, which is life itself.

Consciously recognize this whenever you think of your breathing, and think that you are breathing in life. You really are, and conscious recognition helps the process. See to it that you do not breathe air containing poisonous gases, and that you do not re-breathe the air which has been used by yourself or others.

That is all there is to the matter of breathing correctly. Keep your spine straight and your chest flexible, and breathe pure air, recognizing with thankfulness the fact that you breathe in the Eternal Life. That is not difficult, and beyond these things give little thought to your breathing except to thank God that you have learned how to do it perfectly.

CHAPTER 15

Sleep

Vital power is renewed in sleep. Every living thing sleeps. Humans, animals, reptiles, fish, and insects sleep, and even plants have regular periods of slumber. And this is because it is in sleep that we come into such contact with the Principle of Life in nature that our own lives may be renewed. It is in sleep that our brains are recharged with vital energy and the Principle of Health within us is given new strength. It is of the first importance, then, that we should sleep in a natural, normal, and perfectly healthy manner.

Studying sleep, we note that the breathing is much deeper and more forcible and rhythmic than in the waking state. Much more air is inspired when asleep than when awake, and this tells us that the Principle of Health requires large quantities of some element in the atmosphere for the process of renewal.

If you would surround sleep with natural conditions, then, the first step is to see that you have an unlimited supply of fresh and pure air to breathe. Physicians have found that sleeping in the pure air of out-of-doors is very effective in the treatment of pulmonary troubles and, taken in connection with the Way of Living and Thinking prescribed in this book, you will find that it is just as effective in curing every other sort of trouble.

Do not take any half-way measures in this matter of securing pure air while you sleep. Ventilate your bedroom thoroughly, so thoroughly that it will be practically the same as sleeping out of doors. Have a door or window open wide; have one open on each side of the room, if possible. If you cannot have a good draught of air across the room, pull the head of your bed close to the open window, so that the air from without may come fully into your face. No matter how cold or unpleasant the weather, have a window open, and open wide, and try to get a circulation of pure air through the room. Pile on the bedclothes, if necessary, to keep you warm, but have an unlimited supply of fresh air from out of doors. This is the first great requisite for healthy sleep.

The brain and nerve centers cannot be thoroughly vitalized if you sleep in dead or stagnant air. You must have the living atmosphere, vital with nature's Principle of Life. I repeat, do not make any compromise in this matter. Ventilate your sleeping room completely, and see that there is a circulation of outdoor air through it while you sleep. You are not sleeping in a perfectly healthy way if you shut the doors and windows of your sleeping room, whether in winter or summer.

Have fresh air. If you are where there is no fresh air, move. If your bedroom cannot be ventilated, get into another house.

Next in importance is the mental attitude in which you go to sleep. It is well to sleep intelligently, purposefully, knowing what you do it for. Lie down thinking that sleep is an infallible revitalizer, and go to sleep with a confident faith that your strength is to be renewed, that you will awake full of vitality and health. Put purpose into your sleep as you do into your eating. Give the matter your attention for a few minutes, as you go to rest.

Do not go to bed with a discouraged or depressed feeling; go there joyously, to be made whole. Do not forget the exercise of gratitude in going to sleep. Before you close your eyes, give thanks to God for having shown you the way to perfect health, and go to sleep with this grateful thought uppermost in your mind.

A bedtime prayer of thanksgiving is a mighty good thing. It puts the Principle of Health within you into communication with its source, from which it is to receive new power while you are in the silence of unconsciousness.

You may see that the requirements for perfectly healthy sleep are not difficult. First, to see that you breathe pure air from out of doors while you sleep, and, second, to put the Within into touch with the Living Substance by a few minutes of grateful meditation as you go to bed. Observe these requirements, go to sleep in a thankful and confident frame of mind, and all will be well.

If you have insomnia, do not let it worry you. While you lie awake, form your conception of health. Meditate with thankfulness on the abundant life which is yours. Breathe, and feel perfectly confident that you will sleep in due time and you will. Insomnia, like every other ailment, must give way before the Principle of Health aroused to full constructive activity by the course of thought and action herein described.

The reader will now comprehend that it is not at all burdensome or disagreeable to perform the voluntary functions of life in a perfectly healthy way. The perfectly healthy way is the easiest, simplest, most natural and most pleasant way. The cultivation of health is not a work of art, difficulty, or strenuous labor. You have only to lay aside artificial observances of every kind and eat, drink, breathe, and sleep in the most natural and delightful way, and if you do this, thinking health and only health, you will certainly be well.

CHAPTER 16

Supplementary Instructions

In forming a conception of health, it is necessary to think of the manner in which you would live and work if you were perfectly well and very strong to imagine yourself doing things in the way of a perfectly well and very strong person, until you have a fairly good conception of what you would be if you were well.

Then take a mental and physical attitude in harmony with this conception, and do not depart from this attitude. You must unify yourself in thought with the thing you desire, and whatever state or condition you unify with yourself in thought will soon become unified with you in body. The scientific way is to sever relations with everything you do not want, and to enter into relations with everything you do want. Form a conception of perfect health, and relate yourself to this conception in word, act, and attitude.

Guard your speech. Make every word harmonize with the conception of perfect health. Never complain. Never say things like these: I did not sleep well last night, I have a pain in my side, I do not feel at all well today, and so on. Say: I am looking forward to a good night's sleep tonight, I can see that I progress rapidly and things of similar meaning. As far as everything which is connected with disease is concerned, your way is to forget it; and as far as everything which is connected with health is concerned, your way is to unify yourself with it in thought and speech.

This is the whole thing in a nutshell: *make yourself one with Health in thought, word, and action, and do not connect yourself with sickness either by thought, word, or action.*

Do not read doctor books or medical literature, or the literature of those whose theories conflict with those herein set forth. To do so will certainly undermine your faith in the Way of Living upon which you have entered and cause you to again come into mental relations with disease. This book really gives you all that is required; nothing essential has been omitted, and practically all the superfluous has been eliminated.

The Science of Being Well is an exact science, like arithmetic. Nothing can be added to the fundamental principles, and if anything be taken from them, a failure will result. If you follow strictly the way of living prescribed in this book, you will be well. And you certainly **CAN** follow this way, both in thought and action.

Relate not only yourself, but so far as possible all others, in your thoughts, to perfect health. Do not sympathize with people when they complain, or even when they are sick and suffering. Turn their thoughts into a constructive channel if you can. Do all you can for their relief, but do it with the health thought in your mind.

Do not let people tell their woes and catalogue their symptoms to you. Turn the conversation to some other subject, or excuse yourself and go. Better be considered an unfeeling person than to have the disease thought forced upon you.

When you are in company of people whose conversational stock-in-trade is sickness and kindred matters, ignore what they say and fall to offering a mental prayer of gratitude for your perfect health. And if that does not enable you to shut out their thoughts, say good-by and leave them.

No matter what they think or say, politeness does not require you to permit yourself to be poisoned by diseased or perverted thought. When we have a few more hundreds of thousands of enlightened thinkers who will not stay where people complain and talk sickness, the world will advance rapidly toward health.

When you let people talk to you of sickness, you assist them to increase and multiply sickness.

What shall I do when I am in pain? Can one be in actual physical suffering and still think only thoughts of *health*?

Yes. Do not resist pain; recognize that it is a good thing. Pain is caused by an effort of the Principle of Health to overcome some unnatural condition. This you must know and feel.

When you have a pain, think that a process of healing is going on in the affected part, and mentally assist and cooperate with it. Put yourself in full mental harmony with the power which is causing the pain assist it, help it along. Do not hesitate, when necessary, to use hot fomentations and similar means to further the good work which is going on. If the pain is severe, lie down and give your mind to the work of quietly and easily cooperating with the force which is at work for your good.

This is the time to exercise gratitude and faith. Be thankful for the power of health which is causing the pain, and be certain that the pain will cease as soon as the good work is done. Fix your thoughts, with confidence, on the Principle of Health which is making such conditions within you that pain will soon be unnecessary. You will be surprised to find how easily you can conquer pain, and after you have lived for a time in this Scientific Way, pains and aches will be things unknown to you.

What shall I do when I am too weak for my work? Shall I drive myself beyond my strength, trusting in God to support me? Shall I go on, like the runner, expecting a second wind?

No; better not. When you begin to live in this Way, you will probably not be of normal strength, and you will gradually pass from a low physical condition to a higher one. If you relate yourself mentally with health and strength, and perform the voluntary functions of life in a perfectly healthy manner, your strength will increase from day to day, but for a time you may have days when your strength is insufficient for the work you would like to do.

At such times rest, and exercise gratitude. Recognize the fact that your strength is growing rapidly, and feel a deep thankfulness to the Living One from whom it comes. Spend an hour of weakness in thanksgiving and rest, with full faith that great strength is at hand, and then get up and go on again. While you rest do not think of your present weakness; *think of the strength that is coming.*

Never, at any time, allow yourself to think that you are giving way to weakness. When you rest, as when you go to sleep, fix your mind on the Principle of Health which is building you into complete strength.

What shall I do about that great bugaboo which scares millions of people to death every year, constipation?

Do not worry. Read Horace Fletcher on The *A.B Z. of Our Own Nutrition*, and get the full force of his explanation of the fact that when you live on this scientific plan there will be much less matter to eliminate. The material from the plant foods you are naturally guided to eat will take care of the matter. The gross feeders that eat from three to ten times as much fat, meat, and starch as can be utilized in their systems have a great amount of waste to eliminate and not the plant materials to assist, but if you live in the manner we have described it will be otherwise with you.

If you eat only when you have an **EARNED HUNGER**, and chew every mouthful to a liquid, and if you stop eating the instant you **BEGIN** to be conscious of an abatement of your hunger, you will so perfectly prepare your food for digestion and assimilation that practically all of it will be taken up by the absorbents, and there will be little remaining in the bowels to be excreted. If you are able to entirely banish from your memory all that you have read in doctor books and patent medicine advertisements concerning constipation, you need give the matter no further thought at all. The Principle of Health will take care of it.

But if your mind has been filled with fear-thought in regard to constipation, it may be well in the beginning for you to occasionally flush the colon with warm water. There is not the least need of doing it, except to make the process of your mental emancipation from fear a little easier; it may be worth while for that. And as soon as you see that you are making good progress, and that you have cut down your quantity of food, and are really eating in the Scientific Way, dismiss constipation from your mind forever; you have nothing more to do with it. Put your trust in that Principle within you this has the power to give you perfect health. Relate to It by your reverent gratitude to the Principle of Life which is All Power, and go on your way rejoicing.

What about exercise?

Everyone is the better for a little all-round use of the muscles every day, and the best way to get this is to do it by engaging in some form of play or amusement. Get your exercise in the natural way as recreation, not as a forced stunt for health's sake alone. Ride a stationary bike or a bicycle, play tennis or go bowling, or just play catch with your children. Have some avocation like gardening in which you can spend an hour every day with pleasure and profit.

There are a thousand ways in which you can get exercise enough to keep your body supple and your circulation good, and yet not fall into the rut of exercising for your health. Exercise for fun or profit. Exercise because you are too healthy to sit still, and not because you wish to become healthy, or to remain so.

Are long continued fasts necessary?

Seldom, if ever. The Principle of Health does not often require 20, 30, or 40 days to get ready for action. Under normal conditions, hunger will come in much less time. In most long fasts, the reason hunger does not come sooner is because it has been inhibited by the patient himself. He begins the fast with the **FEAR** if not actually with the hope that it will be many days before hunger comes. The literature he has read on the subject has prepared him to expect a long fast, and he is grimly determined to go to a finish, let the time be as long as it will. And the sub-conscious mind, under the influence of powerful and positive suggestion, suspends hunger.

When, for any reason, nature takes away your hunger, go cheerfully on with your usual work, and do not eat until she gives it back. No matter if it is two, three, ten days, or longer, you may be perfectly sure that when it is time for you to eat you will be hungry. And if you are cheerfully confident and keep your faith in health, you will suffer from no weakness or discomfort caused by abstinence.

When you are not hungry, you will feel stronger, happier, and more comfortable if you do not eat than you will if you do eat, no matter how long the fast. And if you live in the scientific way described in this book, you will never have to take long fasts, you will seldom miss a meal, and you will enjoy your meals more than ever before in your life. Get an earned hunger before you eat, and whenever you get an earned hunger, eat.

CHAPTER 17

A Summary of the Science of Living Well

Health is perfectly natural functioning, normal living. There is a Principle of Life in the universe; it is the Living Substance, from which all things are made. This Living Substance permeates, penetrates, and fills the interspaces of the universe. In its invisible state it is in and through all forms, and yet all forms are made of it.

To illustrate: Suppose that a very fine and highly diffusible aqueous vapor should permeate and penetrate a block of ice. The ice is formed from living water and is living water in form, while the vapor is also living water, unformed, permeating a form made from itself. This illustration will explain how Living Substance permeates all forms made from It. All life comes from It. It is all the life there is.

This Universal Substance is a thinking substance, and takes the form of its thought. The thought of a form, held by it, creates the form; and the thought of a motion causes the motion. It cannot help thinking, and so is forever creating. And it must move on toward fuller and more complete expression of itself. This means toward more complete life and more perfect functioning and that means toward perfect health.

The power of the living substance must always be exerted toward perfect health. It is a force in all things making for perfect functioning.

All things are permeated by a power which makes for health.

A human being can relate himself to this power, and ally himself with it. He can also separate himself from it in his thoughts.

A human being is a form of this Living Substance, and has within him a Principle of Health. This Principle of Health, when in full constructive activity, causes all the involuntary functions of the human body to be perfectly performed.

A human being is a thinking substance, permeating a visible body, and the processes of his body are controlled by his thought.

When a person thinks only thoughts of perfect health, the internal processes of his body will be those of perfect health. A person's first step toward perfect health must be to form a conception of himself as perfectly healthy and as doing all things in the way and manner of a perfectly healthy person. Having formed this conception, he must relate himself to it in all his thoughts, and sever all thought relations with disease and weakness.

If he does this, and thinks his thoughts of health with positive **FAITH**, a person will cause the Principle of Health within him to become constructively active, and to heal all his diseases. He can receive additional power from the universal Principle of Life by faith, and he can acquire faith by looking to this Principle of Life with reverent gratitude for the health it gives him. If a person will consciously accept the health which is being continually given to him by the Living Substance, and if he will be duly grateful for it, he will develop faith.

A person cannot think only thoughts of perfect health unless he performs the voluntary functions of life in a perfectly healthy manner. These voluntary functions are eating, drinking, breathing, and sleeping. If a person thinks only thoughts of health, has faith in health, and eats, drinks, breathes, and sleeps in a perfectly healthy way, he must have perfect health.

Health is the result of thinking and acting in a Certain Way, and if a sick person begins to think and act in this Way, the Principle of Health within him will come into constructive activity and heal all his diseases. This Principle of Heath is the same in all, and is related to the Life Principle of the universe. It is able to heal every disease, and will come into activity whenever a person thinks and acts in accordance with the Science of Being Well. Therefore, every person can attain perfect health.

Please Study the Science of Getting Rich first.

The Science of Being Great

By

Wallace D. Wattles

CHAPTER 1

Any Person May Become Great

There is a Principle of Power in every person. By the intelligent use and direction of this principle, man can develop his own mental faculties. Man has an inherent power by which he may grow in whatsoever direction he pleases, and there does not appear to be any limit to the possibilities of his growth. No man has yet become so great in any faculty but that it is possible for some one else to become greater. The possibility is in the Original Substance from which man is made. Genius is Omniscience flowing into man.

Genius is more than talent. Talent may merely be one faculty developed out of proportion to other faculties, but genius is the union of man and God in the acts of the soul. Great men are always greater than their deeds. They are in connection with a reserve of power that is without limit. We do not know where the boundary of the mental powers of man is; we do not even know that there is a boundary.

The power of conscious growth is not given to the lower animals; it is mans alone and may be developed and increased by him. The lower animals can, to a great extent, be trained and developed by man; but man can train and develop himself. He alone has this power, and he has it to an apparently unlimited extent.

The purpose of life for man is growth, just as the purpose of life for trees and plants is growth. Trees and plants grow automatically and along fixed lines; man can grow, as he will. Trees and plants can only develop certain possibilities and characteristics; man can develop any power, which is or has been shown by any person, anywhere. Nothing that is possible in spirit is impossible in flesh and blood. Nothing that man can think is impossible-in action. Nothing that man can imagine is impossible of realization.

Man is formed for growth, and he is under the necessity of growing. It is essential to his happiness that he should continuously advance. Life without progress becomes unendurable, and the person who ceases from growth must either become imbecile or insane. The greater and more harmonious and well rounded his growth, the happier man will be.

There is no possibility in any man that is not in every man; but if they proceed naturally, no two men will grow into the same thing, or be alike. Every man comes into the world with a predisposition to grow along certain lines, and growth is easier for him along those lines than in any other way. This is a wise provision, for it gives endless variety. It is as if a gardener should throw all his bulbs into one basket; to the superficial observer they would look alike, but growth reveals a tremendous difference. So of men and women, they are like a basket of bulbs. One may be a rose and add brightness and color to some dark corner of the world; one may be a lily and teach a lesson of love and purity to every eye that sees; one may be a climbing vine and hide the rugged outlines of some dark rock; one may be a great oak among whose boughs the birds shall nest and sing, and beneath whose shade the flocks shall rest at noon, but every one will be something worthwhile, something rare, something perfect.

There ere are undreamed of possibilities in the common lives all around us in a large sense, there are no "common" people. In times of national stress and peril the cracker-box loafer of the corner store and the village drunkard become heroes and statesmen through the quickening of the Principle of Power within them. There is a genius in every man and woman, waiting to be brought forth. Every village has its great man or woman; someone to whom all go for advice in time of trouble; some one who is instinctively recognized as being great in wisdom and insight. To such a one the minds of the whole community turn in times of local crisis; he is tacitly recognized as being great. He does small things in a great way. He could do great things as well if he did but undertake them; so can any man; so can you. The Principle of Power gives us just what we ask of it; if we only undertake little things, it only gives us power for little things; but if we try to do great things in a great way it gives us all the power there is.

But beware of undertaking great things in a small way: of that we shall speak farther on.

There are two mental attitudes a man may take. One makes him like a football. It has resilience and reacts strongly when force is applied to it, but it originates nothing; it never acts of itself. There is no power within it. Men of this type are controlled by circumstances and environment; their destinies are decided by things external to themselves. The Principle of Power within them is never really active at all. They never speak or act from within. The other attitude makes man like a flowing spring. Power comes out from the center of him. He has within him a well of water springing up into everlasting life, he radiates force; heist felt by his environment. The Principle of Power in him is in constant action. He is self-active. "He hath life in himself."

No greater good can come to any man or woman than to become self-active. All the experiences of life are designed by Providence to force men and women into self-activity; to compel them to cease being creatures of circumstances and master their environment. In his lowest stage, man is the child of chance and circumstance and the slave of fear. His acts are all reactions resulting from the impingement upon him of forces in his environment. He acts only as he is acted upon; he originates nothing. But the lowest savage has within him a Principle of Power sufficient to master all that he fears; and if he learns this and becomes self-active, he becomes as one of the gods.

The awakening of the Principle of Power in man is the real conversion; the passing from death to life. It is when the dead hear the voice of the Son of Man and come forth and live. It is the resurrection and the life. When it is awakened, man becomes a son of the Highest and all power is given to him in heaven and on earth.

Nothing was ever in any man that is not in you; no man ever had more spiritual or mental power than you can attain, or did greater things than you can accomplish. You can become what you want to be.

CHAPTER 2

Heredity and Opportunity

You are not barred from attaining greatness by heredity. No matter who or what your ancestors may have been or how unlearned or lowly their station, the upward way is open for you. There is no such thing as inheriting a fixed mental position; no matter how small the mental capital we receive from our parents, it may be increased; no man is born incapable of growth.

Heredity counts for something. We are born with subconscious mental tendencies; as, for instance, a tendency to melancholy, or cowardice, or to ill temper; but all these subconscious tendencies may be overcome. When the real man awakens and comes forth he can throw them off very easily. Nothing of this kind need keep you down; if you have inherited undesirable mental tendencies, you can eliminate them and put desirable tendencies in their places. An inherited mental trait is a habit of thought of your father or mother impressed upon your subconscious mind; you can substitute the opposite impression by forming the opposite habit of thought. You can substitute a habit of cheerfulness for a tendency to despondency; you can overcome cowardice or ill temper.

Heredity may count for something, too, in an inherited conformation of the skull. There is something in phrenology, if not as much as its exponents claim; it is true that the different faculties are localized in the brain, and that the power of a faculty depends upon the number of active brain cells in its area. A faculty whose brain area is large is likely to act with more power than one whose cranial section is small; hence persons with certain conformations of the skull show talent as musicians, orators, mechanics, and so on. It has been argued from this that a man's cranial formation must, to a great extent, decide his station in life, but this is an error. It has been found that a small brain section, with many fine and active cells, gives as powerful expression to faculty as a larger brain with coarser cells; and it has been found that by turning the Principle of Power into any section of the brain, with the will and purpose to develop a particular talent, the brain cells may be multiplied indefinitely. Any faculty, power, or talent you possess, no matter how small or rudimentary, may be increased; you can multiply the brain cells in this particular area until it acts as powerfully as you wish. It is true that

you can act most easily through those faculties that are now most largely developed; you can do, with the least effort, the things which "come naturally"; but it is also true that if you will make the necessary effort you can develop any talent. You can do what you desire to do and become what you want to be. When you fix upon some ideal and proceed as hereinafter directed, all the power of your being is turned into the faculties required in the realization of that ideal; more blood and nerve force go to the corresponding sections of the brain, and the cells are quickened, increased, and multiplied in number. The proper use of the mind of man will build a brain capable of doing what the mind wants to do.
The brain does not make the man; the man makes the brain.

Your place in life is not fixed by heredity.

Nor are you condemned to the lower levels by circumstances or lack of opportunity. The Principle of Power in man is sufficient for all the requirements of his soul. No possible combination of circumstances can keep him down, if he makes his personal attitude right and determines to rise. The power, which formed man and purposed him for growth, also controls the circumstances of society, industry, and government; and this power is never divided against itself. The power which is in you is in the things around you, and when you begin to move forward, the things will arrange themselves for your advantage, as described in later chapters of this book. Man was formed for growth, and all things external were designed to promote his growth. No sooner does a man awaken his soul and enter on the advancing way than he finds that not only is God for him, but nature, society, and his fellow men are for him also; and all things work together for his good if he obeys the law. Poverty is no bar to greatness, for poverty can always be removed. Martin Luther, as a child, sang in the streets for bread. Linnaeus the naturalist had only forty dollars with which to educate himself; he mended his own shoes and often had to beg meals from his friends. Hugh Miller, apprenticed to a stonemason, began to study geology in a quarry. George Stephenson, inventor of the locomotive engine, and one of the greatest of civil engineers, was a coal miner, working in a mine, when he awakened and began to think. James Watt was a sickly child, and was not strong enough to be sent to school. Abraham Lincoln was a poor boy. In each of these cases we see a Principle of Power in the man that lifts him above all opposition and adversity.

There is a Principle of Power in you; if you use it and apply it in a certain way you can overcome all heredity, and master all circumstances and conditions and become a great and powerful personality.

CHAPTER 3

The Source of Power

Man's brain, body, mind, faculties, and talents are the mere instruments he uses in demonstrating greatness; in themselves they do not make him great. A man may have a large brain and a good mind, strong faculties, and brilliant talents, and yet he is not a great man unless he uses all these in a great way. That quality which enables man to use his abilities in a great way makes him great; and to that quality we give the name of wisdom. Wisdom is the essential basis of greatness.

Wisdom is the power to perceive the best ends to aim at and the best means for reaching those ends. It is the power to perceive the right thing to do. The man who is wise enough to know the right thing to do, who is good enough to wish to do only the right thing, and who is able and strong enough to do the right thing is a truly great man. He will instantly become marked as a personality of power in any community and men will delight to do him honor.

Wisdom is dependent upon knowledge. Where there is complete ignorance there can be no wisdom, no knowledge of the right thing to do. Man's knowledge is comparatively limited and so his wisdom must be small, unless he can connect his mind with knowledge greater than his own and draw from it, by inspiration, the wisdom that his own limitations deny him. This he can do; this is what the really great men and women have done. Man's knowledge is limited and uncertain; therefore he cannot have wisdom in himself.

Only God knows all truth; therefore only God can have real wisdom or the right thing to do at all times, and man can receive wisdom from God. I proceed to give an illustration: Abraham Lincoln had limited education; but he had the power to perceive truth. In Lincoln we see pre-eminently apparent the fact that real wisdom consists in knowing the right thing to do at all times and under all circumstances; in having the will to do the right thing, and in having talent and ability enough to be competent and able to do the right thing. Back in the days of the abolition agitation, and during the compromise period, when all other men were more or less confused as to what was right or as to what ought to be done, Lincoln was never uncertain. He saw through the superficial arguments of the pro-slavery men; he saw, also, the impracticability and fanaticism of the abolitionists; he saw the right ends to aim at and he saw the best means to attain those ends. It was because men recognized that he perceived truth and knew the right thing to do that they made him president. Any man who develops the power to perceive truth, and who can show that he always knows the right thing to do and that he can be trusted to do the right thing, will be honored and advanced; the whole world is looking eagerly for such men.

When Lincoln became president he was surrounded by a multitude of so-called able advisers, hardly any two of whom were agreed. At times they were all opposed to his policies; at times almost the whole North was opposed to what he proposed to do. But he saw the truth when others were misled by appearances; his judgment was seldom or never wrong. He was at once the ablest statesman and the best soldier of the period. Where did he, a comparatively unlearned man, get this wisdom? It was not due to some peculiar formation of his skull or to some fineness of texture of his brain. It was not due to some physical characteristic. It was not even a quality of mind due to superior reasoning power.

Processes of reason do not often reach knowledge of truth.

It was due to a spiritual insight. He perceived truth, but where did he perceive it and whence did the perception come? We see something similar in Washington, whose faith and courage, due to his perception of truth, held the colonies together during the long and often apparently hopeless struggle of the Revolution. We see something of the same thing in the phenomenal genius of Napoleon, who always knew, in military matters, the best means to adopt. We see that the greatness of Napoleon was in nature rather than in Napoleon, and we discover back of Washington and Lincoln something greater than either Washington or Lincoln. We see the same thing in all great men and women. They perceive truth; but truth cannot be perceived until it exists; and there can be no truth until there is a mind to perceive it. Truth does not exist apart from mind. Washington and Lincoln were in touch and communication with a mind that knew all knowledge and contained all truth. The same is true of all who manifest wisdom. Wisdom is obtained by reading the mind of God.

CHAPTER 4

The Mind of God

There is a Cosmic Intelligence that is in all things and through all things. This is the one real substance. From it all things proceed. It is Intelligent Substance or Mind Stuff. It is God. Where there is no substance there can be no intelligence; for where there is no substance there is nothing. Where there is thought there must be a substance which thinks. Thought cannot be a function; for function is motion, and it is inconceivable that mere motion should think. Thought cannot be vibration, for vibration is motion, and that motion should be intelligent is not thinkable. Motion is nothing but the moving of substance; if there be intelligence shown it must be in the substance and not in the motion. Thought cannot be the result of motions in the brain; if thought is in the brain it must be in the brain's substance and not in the motions which brain substance makes.

But thought is not in the brain substance, for brain substance, without life, is quite unintelligent and dead. Thought is in the life-principle that animates the brain, in the spirit substance, which is the real man. The brain does not think, the man thinks and expresses his thought through the brain.

There is a spirit substance that thinks. Just as the spirit substance of man permeates his body, and thinks and knows in the body, so the Original Spirit Substance, God, permeates all nature and thinks and knows in nature. Nature is as intelligent as man, and knows more than man; nature knows all things. The All-Mind has been in touch with all things from the beginning; and it contains all knowledge. Man's experience covers a few things, and these things man knows; but God's experience covers all the things that have happened since the creation, from the wreck of a planet or the passing of a comet to the fall of a sparrow. All that is and all that has been are present in the Intelligence that is wrapped about us and enfolds us and presses upon us from every side.

All the encyclopedias men have written are but trivial affairs compared to the vast knowledge held by the mind in which men live, move, and have their being.

The truths men perceive by inspiration are thoughts held in this mind. If they were not thoughts men could not perceive them, for they would have no existence; and they could not exist as thoughts unless there is a mind for them to exist in; and a mind can be nothing else than a substance which thinks.

Man is thinking substance, a portion of the Cosmic Substance; but man is limited, while the Cosmic Intelligence from which he sprang, which Jesus calls the Father, is unlimited. All intelligence, power, and force come from the Father. Jesus recognized this and stated it very plainly. Over and over again he ascribed all his wisdom and power to his unity with the Father, and to his perceiving the thoughts of God. "My Father and I are one."

This was the foundation of his knowledge and power. He showed the people the necessity of becoming spiritually awakened; of hearing his voice and becoming like him. He compared the unthinking man who is the prey and sport of circumstances to the dead man in a tomb, and besought him to hear and come forth.

"God is spirit," he said; "be born again, become spiritually awake, and you may see his kingdom. Hear my voice; see what I am and what I do, and come forth and live. The words I speak are spirit and life; accept them and they will cause a well of water to spring up within you. Then you will have life within yourself."
"I do what I see the Father do," he said, meaning that he read the thoughts of God. "The Father shows all things to the son." "If any man has the will to do the will of God, he shall know truth." "My teaching is not my own, but his that sent me." "You shall know the truth and the truth shall make you free." "The spirit shall guide you into all truth."

We are immersed in mind and that mind contains all knowledge and all truth. It is seeking to give us this knowledge, for our Father delights to give good gifts to his children. The prophets and seers and great men and women, past and present, were made great by what they received from God, not by what they were taught by men. This limitless reservoir of wisdom and power is open to you; you can draw upon it, as you will, according to your needs. You can make yourself what you desire to be; you can do what you wish to do; you can have what you want. To accomplish this you must learn to become one with the Father so that you may perceive truth; so that you may have wisdom and know the right ends to seek and the right means to use to attain those ends, and so that you may secure power and ability to use the means. In closing this chapter resolve that you will now lay aside all else and concentrate upon the attainment of conscious unity with God.

"Oh, when I am safe in my sylvan home, I tread on the pride of Greece and Rome, and when I am stretched beneath the pines, where the evenings tar so holy shines, I laugh at the lore and pride of man, at the Sophist schools and the learned clan, for what are they all in their high conceit, when man in the bush with God may meet?"

CHAPTER 5

Preparation

If you become like God you can read his thoughts; and if you do not you will find the inspirational perception of truth impossible.

You can never become a great man or woman until you have overcome anxiety, worry, and fear. It is impossible for an anxious person, a worried one, or a fearful one to perceive truth; all things are distorted and thrown out of their proper relations by such mental states, and those who are in them cannot read the thoughts of God.

If you are poor, or if you are anxious about business or financial matters, you are recommended to study carefully the first volume of this series, "***The Science of Getting Rich***." That will present to you a solution for your problems of this nature, no matter how large or how complicated they may seem to be. There is not the least cause for worry about financial affairs; every person who wills to do so may rise above want, have all he needs, and become rich. The same source upon which you propose to draw for mental unfolding and spiritual power is at your service for the supply of all your material wants. Study this truth until it is fixed in your thoughts and until anxiety is banished from your mind; enter the Certain Way, which leads to material riches.

Again, if you are anxious or worried about your health, realize it is possible for you to attain perfect health so that you may have strength sufficient for all that you wish to do and more. That Intelligence which stands ready to give you wealth and mental and spiritual power will rejoice to give you health also. Perfect health is yours for the asking, if you will only obey the simple laws of life and live aright. Conquer ill health and cast out fear. But it is not enough to rise above financial and physical anxiety and worry; you must rise above moral evil-doing as well. Sound your inner consciousness now for the motives that actuate you and make sure they are right. You must cast out lust, and cease to be ruled by appetite, and you must begin to govern appetite. You must eat only to satisfy hunger, never for gluttonous pleasure, and in all things you must make the flesh obey the spirit.

You must lay aside greed; have no unworthy motive in your desire to become rich and powerful. It is legitimate and right to desire riches, if you want them for the sake of the soul, but not if you desire them for the lusts of the flesh. Cast out pride and vanity; have no thought of trying to rule over others or of outdoing them. This is a vital point; there is no temptation so insidious as the selfish desire to rule over others.

Nothing so appeals to the average man or woman as to sit in the uppermost places at feasts, to be respectfully saluted in the market place, and to be called Rabbi, Master. To exercise some sort of control over others is the secret motive of every selfish person. The struggle for power over others is the battle of the competitive world, and you must rise above that world and its motives and aspirations and seek only for life. Cast out envy; you can have all that you want, and you need not envy any man what he has. Above all things see to it that you do not hold malice or enmity toward any one; to do so cuts you off from the mind whose treasures you seek to make your own. "He that loves not his brother loves not God."

Lay aside all narrow personal ambition and determine to seek the highest good and to be swayed by no unworthy selfishness.

Go over all the foregoing and set these moral temptations out of your heart one by one; determine to keep them out. Then resolve that you will not only abandon all evil thought but that you will forsake all deeds, habits, an d courses of action which do not commend themselves to your noblest ideals. This is supremely important, make this resolution with all the power of your soul, and you are ready for the next step toward greatness, which is explained in the following chapter.

"DRAW nigh to God and He will draw nigh to you."

CHAPTER 6

The Social Point of View

Without faith it is impossible to please God, and without faith it is impossible for you to become great. The distinguishing characteristic of all really great men and women is an unwavering faith. We see this in Lincoln during the dark days of the war; we see it in Washington at Valley Forge; we see it in Livingstone, the crippled missionary, threading the mazes of the dark continent, his soul aflame with the determination to let in the light upon the accursed slave trade, which his soul abhorred; we see it in Luther, and in Frances Willard, in every man and woman who has attained a place on the muster roll of the great ones of the world. Faith-not a faith in one's self or in one s own powers but faith in principle; in the Something Great which upholds right, and which may be relied upon to give us the victory in due time. Without this faith it is not possible for any one to rise to real greatness. The man who has no faith in principle will always be a small man. Whether you have this faith or not depends upon your point of view. You must learn to see the world as being produced by evolution, as a something that is evolving and becoming, not as a finished work. Millions of years ago God worked with very low and crude forms of life, low and crude, yet each perfect after its kind. Higher and more complex organisms, animal and vegetable, appeared through the successive ages; the earth passed through stage after stage in its unfolding, each stage perfect in itself, and to be succeeded by a higher one. What I wish you to note is that the so-called "lower organisms" are as perfect after their kind as the higher ones; that the world in the Eocene period was perfect for that period; it was perfect, but God's work was not finished. This is true of the world today. Physically, socially, and industrially it is all good, and it is all perfect. It is not complete anywhere or in any part, but, so far as the handiwork of God has gone, it is perfect.

This must be your point of view that the world and all it contains is perfect, though not completed.

"All's right with the world." That is the great fact. There is nothing wrong with anything; there is nothing wrong with anybody.

All the facts of life you must contemplate from this standpoint.

There is nothing wrong with nature. Nature is a great advancing presence working beneficently for the happiness of all. All things in Nature are good; she has no evil. She is not completed; for creation is still unfinished, but she is going on to give to man even more bountifully than she has given to him in the past. Nature is a partial expression of God, and God is love. She is perfect but not complete.

So it is of human society and government. What though there are trusts and combinations of capital and strikes and lockouts and so on. All these things are part of the forward movement; they are incidental to the evolutionary process of completing society. When it is complete there will be harmony; but it cannot be completed without them. J. P. Morgan is as necessary to the coming social order as the strange animals of the age of reptiles were to the life of the succeeding period, and just as these animals were perfect after their kind, so Morgan is perfect after his kind.

Behold it is all very good. See government, and industry as being perfect now, and as advancing rapidly toward being complete; then you will understand that there is nothing to fear, no cause for anxiety, nothing to worry about. Never complain of any of these things. They are perfect; this is the very best possible world for the stage of development man has reached.

This will sound like rank folly to many, perhaps to most people. "What!" they will say, "are not child labor and the exploitation of men and women in filthy and unsanitary factories evil things? Aren't saloons evil? Do you mean to say that we shall accept all these and call them good?"

Child labor and similar things are no more evil than the way of living and the habits and practices of the cave dweller were evil. His ways were those of the savage stage of man's growth, and for that stage they were perfect. Our Industrial practices are those of the savage stage of industrial development, and they are also perfect.

Nothing better is possible until we cease to be mental savages in industry and business, and become men and women. This can only come about by the rise of the whole race to a higher viewpoint. And this can only come about by the rise of such individuals here and there as are ready for the higher viewpoint. The cure for all this inharmoniousness lies not with the masters or employers but with the workers themselves. Whenever they reach a higher viewpoint, whenever they shall desire to do so, they can establish complete brotherhood and harmony in Industry; they have the numbers and the power. They are getting now what they desire. Whenever they desire more in the way of a higher, purer, more harmonious life, they will receive more. True, they want more now, but they only want more of the things that make for animal enjoyment, and so industry remains in the savage, brutal, animal stage; when the workers begin to rise to the mental plane of living and ask for more of the things that make for the life of the mind and soul, industry will at once be raised above the plane of savagery and brutality. But it is perfect now upon its plane, behold, in fact it is all very good. So it is true of saloons and dens of vice. If the majority of the people desire these things, it is right and necessary that they should have them. When the majority desires a world without such discords, they will create such a world. So long as men and women are on the plane of bestial thought, so long the social order will be in part disorder, and will show bestial manifestations. The people make society what it is, and as the people rise above the bestial thought, society will rise above the beastly in its manifestations. But a society which thinks in a bestial way must have saloons and dives; it is perfect after its kind, as the world was in the Eocene period, and very good.

All this does not prevent you from working for better things.

You can work to complete an unfinished society, instead of to renovate a decaying one; and you can work with a better heart and a more hopeful spirit. It will make an immense difference with your faith and spirit whether you look upon civilization as a good thing that is becoming better or as a bad and evil thing that is decaying. One viewpoint gives you an advancing and expanding mind and the other gives you a descending and decreasing mind.

One viewpoint will make you grow greater and the other will inevitably cause you to grow smaller. One will enable you to work for the eternal things; to do large works in a great way toward the completing of all that is incomplete and inharmonious; and the other will make you a mere patchwork reformer, working almost without hope to save a few lost souls from what you will grow to consider a lost and doomed world. So you see it makes a vast difference to you, this matter of the social viewpoint. "All's right with the world. Nothing can possibly be wrong but my personal attitude, and I will make that right. I will see the facts of nature and all the events, circumstances, and conditions of society, politics, government, and industry from the highest viewpoint. It is all perfect, though incomplete. It is all the handiwork of God; behold, it is all very good."

CHAPTER 7

The Individual Point of View

Important as the matter of your point of view for the facts of social life is, it is of less moment than your viewpoint for your fellow men, for your acquaintances, friends, relatives, your immediate family, and, most of all, yourself. You must learn not to look upon the world as a lost and decaying thing but as a something perfect and glorious which is going on to a most beautiful completeness; and you must learn to see men and women not as lost and accursed things, but as perfect beings advancing to become complete. There are no "bad" or "evil" people. An engine, which is on the rails pulling a heavy train, is perfect after its kind, and it is good. The power of steam, which drives it, is good. Let a broken rail throw the engine into the ditch, and it does not become bad or evil by being so displaced; it is a perfectly good engine, but off the track.

The power of steam that drives it into the ditch and wrecks it is not evil, but a perfectly good power. So that which is misplaced or applied in an incomplete or partial way is not evil. There are no evil people; there are perfectly good people who are off the track, but they do not need condemnation or punishment; they only need to get upon the rails again.

That which is undeveloped or incomplete often appears to us as evil because of the way we have trained ourselves to think. The root of a bulb that shall produce a white lily is an unsightly thing; one might look upon it with disgust. But how foolish we should be to condemn the bulb for its appearance when we know the lily is within it. The root is perfect after its kind; it is a perfect but incomplete lily, and so we must learn to look upon every man and woman, no matter how unlovely in outward manifestation; they are perfect in their stage of being and they are becoming complete.

Behold, it is all very good.

Once we come into a comprehension of this fact and arrive at this point of view, we lose all desire to find fault with people, to judge them, criticize them, or condemn them. We no longer work as those who are saving lost souls, but as those who are among the angels, working out the completion of a glorious heaven. We are born of the spirit and we see the kingdom of God. We no longer see men as trees walking, but our vision is complete. We have nothing but good words to say. It is all good; a great and glorious humanity coming to completeness. And in our association with men this puts us into an expansive and enlarging attitude of mind; we see them as great beings and we begin to deal with them and their affairs in a great way. But if we fall to the other point of view and see a lost and degenerate race we shrink into the contracting mind; and our dealings with men and their affairs will be in a small and contracted way. Remember to hold steadily to this point of view; if you do you cannot fail to begin at once to deal with your acquaintances and neighbors and with your own family as a great personality deals with men. This same viewpoint must be the one from which you regard yourself. You must always see yourself as a great advancing soul. Learn to say: "There is **THAT** in me of whom I am made, which knows no imperfection, weakness, or sickness. The world is incomplete, but God in my own consciousness is both perfect and complete. Nothing can be wrong but my own personal attitude, and my own personal attitude can be wrong only when I disobey **THAT** which is within. I am a perfect manifestation of God so far as I have gone, and I will press on to be complete. I will trust and not be afraid." When you are able to say this understandingly you will have lost all fear and you will be far advanced upon the road to the development of a great and powerful personality.

CHAPTER 8

Consecration

Having attained to the viewpoint that puts you into the right relations with the world and with your fellow men, the next step is consecration; and consecration in its true sense simply means obedience to the soul. You have that within you that which is always impelling you toward the upward and advancing way; and that impelling something is the divine Principle of Power; you must obey it without question. No one will deny the statement that if you are to be great, the greatness must be a manifestation of something within; nor can you question that this something must be the very greatest and highest that is within. It is not the mind, or the intellect, or the reason. You cannot be great if you go no farther back for principle than to your reasoning power. Reason knows neither principle nor morality. Your reason is like a lawyer in that it will argue for either side. The intellect of a thief will plan robbery and murder as readily as the intellect of a saint will plan a great philanthropy. Intellect helps us to see the best means and manner of doing the right thing, but intellect never shows us the right thing. Intellect and reason serve the selfish man for his selfish ends as readily as they serve the unselfish man for his unselfish ends. Use intellect and reason without regard to principle, and you may become known as a very able person, but you will never become known as a person whose life shows the power of real greatness.

There is too much training of the intellect and reasoning powers and too little training in obedience to the soul. This is the only thing that can be wrong with your person al attitude-when it fails to be one of obedience to the Principle of Power.

By going back to your own center you can always find the pure idea of right for every relationship. To be great and to have power it is only necessary to conform your life to the pure idea as you find it in the **GREAT WITHIN**. Every compromise on this point is made at the expense of a loss of power. This you must remember. There are many ideas in your mind that you have outgrown, and which, from force of habit you still permit to dictate the actions of your life. Cease all this; abandon everything you have outgrown. There are many ignoble customs, social and other, which you still follow, although you know they tend to dwarf and belittle you and keep you acting in a small way. Rise above all this. I do not say that you should absolutely disregard conventionalities, or the commonly accepted standards of right and wrong. You cannot do this; but you can deliver your soul from most of the narrow restrictions that bind the majority of your fellow men. Do not give your time and strength to the support of obsolete institutions, religious or otherwise; do not be bound by creeds in which you do not believe. Be free. You have perhaps formed some sensual habits of mind or body; abandon them. You still indulge in distrustful fears that things will go wrong, or that people will betray you, or mistreat you; get above all of them. You still act selfishly in many ways and on many occasions; cease to do so. Abandon all these, and in place of them put the best actions you can form a conception of in your mind. If you desire to advance, and you are not doing so, remember that it can be only because your thought is better than your practice. You must do as well as you think.

Let your thoughts be ruled by principle, and then live up to your thoughts.

Let your attitude in business, in politics, in neighborhood affairs, and in your own home be the expression of the best thoughts you can think. Let your manner toward all men and women, great and small, and especially to your own family circle, always be the most kindly, gracious, and courteous you can picture in your imagination. Remember your viewpoint; you are a god in the company of gods and must conduct yourself accordingly.

The steps to complete consecration are few and simple. You cannot be ruled from below if you are to be great; you must rule from above. Therefore you cannot be governed by physical impulses; you must bring your body into subjection to the mind; but your mind, without principle, may lead you into selfishness and immoral ways; you must put the mind into subjection to the soul, and your soul is limited by the boundaries of your knowledge; you must put it into subjection to that Our soul which needs no searching of the understanding but before whose eye all things are spread. That constitutes consecration. Say: "I surrender my body to be ruled by my mind; I surrender my mind to be governed by my soul, and I surrender my soul to the guidance of God." Make this consecration complete and thorough, and you have taken the second great step in the way of greatness and power.

CHAPTER 9

Identification

Having recognized God as the advancing presence in nature, society, and your fellow men, and harmonized yourself with all these, and having consecrated your self to that within you which impels you toward the greatest and the highest, the next step is to become aware of and recognize fully the fact that the Principle of Power within you is God Himself. You must consciously identify yourself with the Highest. This is not some false or untrue position to be assumed; it is a fact to be recognized. You are already one with God; you want to become consciously aware of it. There is one substance, the source of all things, and this substance has within itself the power that creates all things; all power is inherent in it. This substance is conscious and thinks; it works with perfect understanding and intelligence. You know that this is so, because you know that substance exists and that consciousness exists; and that it must be substance that is conscious.

Man is conscious and thinks; man is substance, he must be substance, else he is nothing and does not exist at all. If man is substance and thinks, and is conscious, then he is Conscious Substance. It is not conceivable that there should be more than one Conscious Substance; so man is the original substance, the source of all life and power embodied in a physical form. Man cannot be something different from God. Intelligence is one and the same everywhere, and must be everywhere an attribute of the same substance. There cannot be one kind of intelligence in God and another kind of intelligence in man; intelligence can only be in intelligent substance, and Intelligent Substance is God. Man is of one and the same stuff with God, and so all the talents, powers, and possibilities that are in God are in man, not just in a few exceptional men but in everyone. "All power is given to man, in heaven and on earth." "Is it not written, ye are gods?" The Principle of Power in man is man himself, and man himself is God. But while man is original substance, and has within him all power and possibilities, his consciousness is limited. He does not know all there is to know, and so he is liable to error and mistake. To save himself from these he must unite his mind to that outside him which does know all; he must become consciously one with God. There is a Mind surrounding him on every side, closer than breathing, nearer than hands and feet, and in this mind is the memory of all that has ever happened, from the greatest convulsions of nature in prehistoric days to the fall of a sparrow in this present time; and all that is in existence now as well. Held in this Mind is the great purpose that is behind all nature, and so it knows what is going to be. Man is surrounded by a Mind that knows all there is to know, past, present, and to come. Everything that men have said or done or written is present there. Man is of the same one identical stuff with this Mind; he proceeded from it; and he can so identify himself with it that he may know what it knows. "My Father is greater than I," said Jesus, "I come from him." "I and my Father are one. He shows the Son all things." "The spirit shall guide you into all truth."

Your identification of yourself with the Infinite must be accomplished by conscious recognition on your part. Recognizing it as a fact, that there is only God, and that all intelligence is in the one substance, you must affirm some what after this wise: "There is only one and that one is everywhere. I surrender myself to conscious unity with the highest. Not I, but the Father. I will to be one with the Supreme and to lead the divine life. I am one with infinite consciousness; there is but one mind, and I am that mind. I that speak unto you am he."

If you have been thorough in the work as outlined in the preceding chapters; if you have attained to the true viewpoint, and if your consecration is complete, you will not find conscious identification hard to attain; and once it is attained, the power you seek is yours, for you have made yourself one with all the power there is.

CHAPTER 10

Idealization

You are a thinking center in original substance, and the thoughts of original substance have creative power; whatever is formed in its thought and held as a thought-form must come into existence as a visible and so-called material form, and a thought-form held in thinking substance is a reality; it is a real thing, whether it has yet become visible to mortal eye or not. This is a fact that you should impress upon your understanding-that a thought held in thinking substance is a real thing; a form, and has actual existence, although it is not visible to you. You internally take the form in which you think of your self; and you surround yourself with the invisible forms of those things with which you associate in your thoughts.

If you desire a thing, picture it clearly and hold the picture steadily in mind until it becomes a definite thought-form; and if your practices are not such as to separate you from God, the thing you want will come to you in material form. It must do so in obedience to the law by which the universe was created.

Make no thought-form of your self in connection with disease or sickness, but form a conception of health. Make a thought-form of yourself as strong and hearty and perfectly well; impress this thought-form on creative intelligence, and if your practices are not in violation of the laws by which the physical body is built, your thought-form will become manifest in your flesh. This also is certain; it comes by obedience to law.

Make a thought-form of yourself, as you desire to be, and set your ideal as near to perfection as your imagination is capable of forming the conception. Let me illustrate: If a young law student wishes to become great, let him picture himself (while attending to the viewpoint, consecration, and identification, as previously directed) as a great lawyer, pleading his case with matchless eloquence and power before the judge and jury; as having an unlimited command of truth, of knowledge and of wisdom. Let him picture himself as the great lawyer in every possible situation and contingency; while he is still only the student in all circumstances let him never forget or fail to he the great lawyer in his thought-form of himself. As the thought-form grows more definite and habitual in his mind, the creative energies, both within and without, are set at work, he begins to manifest the form from within and all the essentials without, which go into the picture, begin to be impelled toward him. He makes himself into the image and God works with him; nothing can prevent him from becoming what he wishes to be.

In the same general way the musical student pictures himself as performing perfect harmonies, and as delighting vast audiences; the actor forms the highest conception he is capable of in regard to his art, and applies this conception to himself. The farmer and the mechanic do exactly the same thing. Fix upon your ideal of what you wish to make of yourself; consider well and be sure that you make the right choice; that is, the one that will be the most satisfactory to you in a general way. Do not pay too much attention to the advice or suggestions of those around you: do not believe that any one can know, better than yourself, what is right for you. Listen to what others have to say, but always form your own conclusions.

Do not let people decide what you are to be, what you feel that you want to be.

Do not be misled by a false notion of obligation or duty. You can owe no possible obligation or duty to others that should prevent you from making the most of yourself. Be true to yourself, and you cannot then be false to any man. When you have fully decided what thing you want to be, form the highest conception of that thing that you are capable of imagining, and make that conception a thought-form. Hold that thought-form as a fact, as the real truth about yourself, and believe in it.

Close your ears to all adverse suggestions. Never mind if people call you a fool and a dreamer. Dream on. Remember that Bonaparte, the half-starved lieutenant, always saw himself as the general of armies and the master of France, and he became, in outward realization, what he held himself to be in mind. So likewise will you. Attend carefully to all that has been said in the preceding chapters, and act as directed in the following ones, and you will become what you want to be.

CHAPTER 11

Realization

If you were to stop with the close of the last chapter, however, you would never become great; you would be indeed a mere dreamer of dreams, a castle-builder. Too many do stop there; they do not understand the necessity for present action in realizing the vision and bringing the thought-form into manifestation.

Two things are necessary; firstly, the making of the thought-form and secondly, the actual appropriation to yourself of all that goes into, and around, the thought-form. We have discussed the first, now we will proceed to give directions for the second. When you have made your thought-form, you are already, in your interior, what you want to be; next you must become externally what you want to be. You are already great within, but you are not yet doing the great things without. You cannot begin, on the instant, to do the great things; you cannot be before the world the great actor, or lawyer, or musician, or personality you know yourself to be; no one will entrust great things to you as yet for you have not made yourself known. But you can always begin to do small things in a great way.

Here lies the whole secret. You can begin to be great today in your own home, in your store or office, on the street, everywhere; you can begin to make yourself known as great, and you can do this by doing everything you do in a great way. You must put the whole power of your great soul in to every act, however small and commonplace, and so reveal to your family, your friends, and neighbors what you really are. Do not brag or boast of yourself; do not go about telling people what a great personage you are, simply live in a great way. No one will believe you if you tell him you are a great man, but no one can doubt your greatness if you show it in your actions. In your domestic circle be so just, so generous, so courteous, and kindly that your family, your wife, husband, children, brothers, and sisters shall know that you are a great and noble soul. In all your relations with men, be great, just, generous, courteous, and kindly. The great are never otherwise. This is your attitude.

Next, and most important, you must have absolute faith in your own perceptions of truth. Never act in haste or hurry; be deliberate in everything; wait until you feel that you know the true way. And when you do feel that you know the true way, be guided by your own faith though the entire world shall disagree with you. If you do not believe what God tells you in little things, you will never draw upon his wisdom and knowledge in larger things. When you feel deeply that a certain act is the right act, do it and have perfect faith that the consequences will be good. When you are deeply impressed that a certain thing is true, no matter what the appearances to the contrary may be, accept that thing as true and act accordingly. The one way to develop a perception of truth in large things is to trust absolutely to your present perception of Truth in small things. Remember that you are seeking to develop this very power or faculty - the perception of truth; you are learning to read the thoughts of God. Nothing is great and nothing is small in the sight of Omnipotence; he holds the sun in its place, but he also notes a sparrow's fall, and numbers the hairs of your head.

God is as much interested in the little matters of everyday life as he is in the affairs of nations. You can perceive truth about family and neighborhood affairs as well as about matters of statecraft. And the way to begin is to have perfect faith in the truth in these small matters, as it is revealed to you from day to day. When you feel deeply impelled to take a course that seems contrary to all reason and worldly judgment, take that course. Listen to the suggestions and advice of others, but always do what you feel deeply in the within to be the true thing to do. Rely with absolute faith, at all times, on your own perception of truth; but be sure that you listen to God - that you do not act in haste, fear, or anxiety.

Rely upon your perception of truth in all the facts and circumstances of life. If you deeply feel that a certain man will be in a certain place on a certain day, go there with perfect faith to meet him; he will be there, no matter how unlikely it may seem. If you feel sure that certain people are making certain combinations, or doing certain things, act in the faith that they are doing those things. If you feel sure of the truth of any circumstance or happening, near or distant, past, present, or to come, trust in your perception.

You may make occasion al mistakes at first because of your imperfect understanding of the within; but you will soon be guided almost invariably right. Soon your family and friends will begin to defer, more and more, to your judgment and to be guided by you. Soon your neighbors and townsmen will be coming to you for counsel and advice; soon you will be recognized as one who is great in small things, and you will be called upon more and more to take charge of larger things.

All that is necessary is to be guided absolutely, in all things, by your inner light, your perception of truth. Obey your soul, have perfect faith in yourself. Never think of yourself with doubt or distrust, or as one who makes mistakes. "If I judge, my judgment is just, for I seek not honor from men, but from the Father only."

CHAPTER 12

Hurry and Habit

No doubt you have many problems, domestic, social, physical, and financial, which seem to you to be pressing for instant solution.

You have debts that must be paid, or other obligations that must be met; you are unhappily or inharmoniously placed, and feel that something must be done at once. Do not get into a hurry and act from superficial impulses. You can trust God for the solution of all your personal riddles. There is no hurry. There is only God, and all is well with the world.

There is an invincible power in you, and the same power is in the things you want. It is bringing them to you and bringing you to them. This is a thought that you must grasp, and hold continuously that the same intelligence that is in you is in the things you desire. They are impelled toward you as strongly and decidedly as your desire impels you toward them. The tendency, therefore, of a steadily held thought must be to bring the things you desire to you and to group them around you. So long as you hold your thought and your faith right all must go well. Nothing can be wrong but your own personal attitude, and that will not be wrong if you trust and are not afraid. Hurry is a manifestation of fear; he who fears not has plenty of time. If you act with perfect faith in your own perceptions of truth, you will n ever be too late or too early; and nothing will go wrong. If things appear to be going wrong, do not get disturbed in mind; it is only in appearance. Nothing can go wrong in this world but yourself; and you can go wrong only by getting into the wrong mental attitude. Whenever you find yourself getting excited, worried, or into the mental attitude of hurry, sit down and think it over, play a game of some kind, or take a vacation. Go on a trip, and all will be right when you return. So surely as you find yourself in the mental attitude of haste, just so surely may you know that you are out of the mental attitude of greatness. Hurry and fear will instantly cut your connection with the universal mind; you will get no power, no wisdom, and no information until you are calm. And to fall into the attitude of hurry will check the action of the Principle of Power within you. Fear turns strength to weakness.

Remember that poise and power are inseparably associated.

The calm and balanced mind is the strong and great mind; the hurried and agitated mind is the weak one. Whenever you fall into the mental state of hurry you may know that you have lost the right viewpoint; you are beginning to look upon the world, or some part of it, as going wrong. At such times read Chapter Six of this book; consider the fact that this work is perfect, now, with all that it contains. Nothing is going wrong; nothing can be wrong; be poised, be calm, be cheerful; have faith in God.

Next as to habit, it is probable that your greatest difficulty will be to overcome your old habitual ways of thought, and to form new habits. The world is ruled by habit. Kings, tyrants, masters, and plutocrats hold their positions solely because the people have come to habitually accept them. Things are as they are only because people have formed the habit of accepting them as they are. When the people change their habitual thought about governmental, social, and industrial institutions, they will change the institutions.

You have formed, perhaps, the habit of thinking of yourself as a common person, as one of a limited ability, or as being more or less of a failure. Whatever you habitually think yourself to be, that you are. You must form, now, a greater and better habit; you must form a conception of yourself as a being of limitless power, and habitually think that you are that being. It is the habitual, not the periodical thought that decides your destiny. It will avail you nothing to sit apart for a few moments several times a day to affirm that you are great, if during all the balance of the day, while you are about your regular vocation, you think of yourself as not great. No amount of praying or affirmation will make you great if you still habitually regard yourself as being small.

The use of prayer and affirmation is to change your habit of thought. Any act, mental or physical, often repeated, becomes a habit. The purpose of mental exercises is to repeat certain thoughts over and over until the thinking of those thoughts becomes constant and habitual. The thoughts we continually repeat become convictions. What you must do is to repeat the new thought of yourself until it is the only way in which you think of yourself. Habitual thought, and not environment or circumstance, has made you what you are. Every person has some central idea or thought- form of himself, and by this idea he classifies and arranges all his facts and external relationships. You are classifying your facts either according to the idea that you are a great and strong personality, or according to the idea that you are limited, common, or weak. If the latter is the case you must change your central idea.

Get a new mental picture of yourself. Do not try to become great by repeating mere strings of words or superficial formulas; but repeat over and over the **THOUGHT** of your own power and ability until you classify external facts, and decide your place everywhere by this idea. In another chapter will be found an illustrative mental exercise and further directions on this point.

CHAPTER 13

Thought

Greatness is only attained by the constant thinking of great thoughts. No man can become great in outward personality until he is great internally; and no man can be great internally until he **THINKS**. No amount of education, reading, or study can make you great without thought; but thought can make you great with very little study. There are altogether too many people who are trying to make something of themselves, by reading books without thinking; all such will fail. You are not mentally developed by what you read, but by what you think about what you read.

Thinking is the hardest and most exhausting of all labor; and hence many people shrink from it. God has so formed us that we are continuously impelled to thought; we must either think or engage in some activity to escape thought. The headlong, continuous chase for pleasure in which most people spend all their leisure time is only an effort to escape thought. If they are alone, or if they have nothing amusing to take their attention, as a novel to read or a show to see, they must think; and to escape from thinking they resort to novels, shows, and all the endless devices of the purveyors of amusement. Most people spend the greater part of their leisure time running away from thought, hence they are where they are. We never move forward until we begin to think.

Read less and think more. Read about great things and think about great questions and issues. We have at the present time few really great figures in the political life of our country; our politicians are a petty lot. There is no Lincoln, no Webster, no Clay, Calhoun, or Jackson. Why? Because our present statesmen deal only with sordid and petty issues - questions of dollars and cents, of expediency and party success, of material prosperity without regard to ethical right. Thinking along these lines does not call forth great souls. The statesmen of Lincoln's time and previous times dealt with questions of eternal truth, of human rights and justice. Men thought upon great themes; they thought great thoughts, and they became great men.

Thinking, not mere knowledge or information, makes personality. Thinking is growth; you cannot think without growing.

Every thought engenders another thought. Write one idea and others will follow until you have written a page. You cannot fathom your own mind; it has neither bottom nor boundaries. Your first thoughts may be crude; but as you go on thinking you will use more and more of yourself; you will quicken new brain cells into activity and you will develop new faculties. Heredity, environment, circumstances, all things must give way before you if you practice sustained and continuous thought. But, on the other hand, if you neglect to think for yourself and only use other people's thought, you will never know what you are capable of; and you will end by being incapable of anything.

There can be no real greatness without original thought. All that a man does outwardly is the expression and completion of his inward thinking. No action is possible without thought, and no great action is possible until a great thought has preceded it. Action is the second form of thought, and personality is the materialization of thought. Environment is the result of thought; things group themselves or arrange themselves around you according to your thought. There is, as Emerson says, some central idea or conception of yourself by which all the facts of your life are arranged and classified. Change this central idea and you change the arrangement or classification of all the facts and circumstances of your life. You are what you are because you think as you do; you are where you are because you think as you do.

You see then the immense importance of thinking about the great essentials set forth in the preceding chapters. You must not accept them in any superficial way; you must think about them until they are a part of your central idea. Go back to the matter of the point of view and consider, in all its bearings, the tremendous thought that you live in a perfect world among perfect people, and that nothing can possibly be wrong with you but your own personal attitude. Think about all this until you fully realize all that it means to you. Consider that this is God's world and that it is the best of all possible worlds; that he has brought it thus far toward completion by the processes of organic, social, and industrial evolution, and that it is going on to greater completeness and harmony. Consider that there is one great, perfect, intelligent Principle of Life and Power, causing all the changing phenomena of the cosmos. Think about all this until you see that it is true, and until you comprehend how you should live and act as a citizen of such a perfect whole.

Next, think of the wonderful truth that this great Intelligence is in you; it is your own intelligence. It is an Inner Light impelling you toward the right thing and the best thing, the greatest act, and the highest happiness. It is a Principle of Power in you, giving you all the ability and genius there is. It will infallibly guide you to the best if you will submit to it and walk in the light. Consider what is meant by your consecration of yourself when you say: "I will obey my soul." This is a sentence of tremendous meaning; it must revolutionize the attitude and behavior of the average person. Then think of your identification with this Great Supreme; that all its knowledge is yours, and all its wisdom is yours, for the asking. You are a god if you think like a god. If you think like a god you cannot fail to act like a god. Divine thoughts will surely externalize themselves in a divine life. Thoughts of power will end in a life of power. Great thoughts will manifest in a great personality.

Think well of all this, and then you are ready to act.

CHAPTER 14

Action at Home

Do not merely think that you are going to become great; think that you are great now. Do not think that you will begin to act in a great way at some future time; begin now. Do not think that you will act in a great way when you reach a different environment; act in a great way where you are now. Do not think that you will begin to act in a great way when you begin to deal with great things; begin to deal in a great way with small things. Do not think that you will begin to be great when you get among more intelligent people, or among people who understand you better; begin now to deal in a great way with the people around you.

If you are not in an environment where there is scope for your best powers and talents you can move in due time; but meanwhile you can be great where you are. Lincoln was as great when he was a backwoods lawyer as when he was President; as a backwoods lawyer he did common things in a great way, and that made him President. Had he waited until he reached Washington to begin to be great, he would have remained unknown. You are not made great by the location in which you happen to be nor by the things with which you may surround your self. You are not made great by what you receive from others, and you can never manifest greatness so long as you depend on others. You will manifest greatness only when you begin to stand alone. Dismiss all thought of reliance on externals, whether things, books, or people.

As Emerson said, "Shakespeare will never be made by the study of Shakespeare." Shakespeare will be made by the thinking of Shakespearean thoughts.

Never mind how the people around you, including those of your own household, may treat you. That has nothing at all to do with your being great; that is, it cannot hinder you from being great. People may neglect you and be unthankful and unkind in their attitude toward you; does that prevent you from being great in your manner and attitude toward them? "Your Father," said Jesus, "is kind to the unthankful and the evil." Would God be great if he should go away and sulk because people were unthankful and did not appreciate him? Treat the unthankful and the evil in a great and perfectly kind way, just as God does. Do not talk about your greatness; you are really, in essential nature, no greater than those around you. You may have entered upon a way of living and thinking which they have not yet found, but they are perfect on their own plane of thought and action. You are entitled to no special honor or consideration for your greatness.

You are a god, but you are among gods. You will fall into the boastful attitude if you see other people's shortcomings and failures and compare them with your own virtues and successes; and if you fall into the boastful attitude of mind, you will cease to be great, and become small. Think of yourself as a perfect being among perfect beings, and meet every person as an equal, not as either superior or an inferior. Give your self no airs; great people never do.

Ask no honors and seek for no recognition, honors and recognition will come fast enough if you are entitled to them.

Begin at home. It is a great person who can always be poised, assured, calm, and perfectly kind and considerate at home. If your manner and attitude in your own family are always the best you can think, you will soon become the one on whom all the others will rely. You will be a tower of strength and a support in time of trouble. You will be loved and appreciated. At the same time do not make the mistake of throwing your self away in the service of others. The great person respects himself; he serves and helps, but he is never slavishly servile. You cannot help your family by being a slave to them, or by doing for them those things that by right they should do for themselves. You do a person an injury when you wait on him too much. The selfish and exacting are a great deal better off if their exactions are denied. The ideal world is not one where there are a lot of people being waited on by other people; it is a world where everybody waits on himself. Meet all demands, selfish and otherwise, with perfect kindness and consideration; but do not allow yourself to be made a slave to the whims, caprices, exactions, or slavish desires of any member of your family. To do so is not great, and it works an injury to the other party.

Do not become uneasy over the failures or mistakes of any member of your family, and feel that you must interfere. Do not be disturbed if others seem to be going wrong, and feel that you must step in and set them right. Remember that every person is perfect on his own plane; you cannot improve on the work of God. Do not meddle with the personal habits and practices of others, though they are your nearest and dearest; these things are none of your business. Nothing can be wrong but your own personal attitude; make that right and you will know that all else is right. You are a truly great soul when you can live with those who do things that you do not do, and yet refrain from either criticism or interference.

Do the things that are right for you to do, and believe that every member of your family is doing the things that are right for him.

Nothing is wrong with anybody or anything, behold, it is all very good. Do not be enslaved by any one else, but be just as careful that you do not enslave any one else to your own notions of what is right. Think, and think deeply and continuously; be perfect in your kindness and consideration; let your attitude be that of a god among gods, and not that of a god among inferior beings. This is the way to be great in your own home.

CHAPTER 15

Action Abroad

The rules that apply to your action at home must apply to your action everywhere. Never forget for an instant that this is a perfect world, and that you are a god among gods. You are as great as the greatest, but all are your equals.

Rely absolutely on your perception of truth. Trust to the inner light rather than to reason, but be sure that your perception comes from the inner light; act in poise and calmness; be still and attend on God. Your identification of yourself with the All-Mind will give you all the knowledge you need for guidance in any contingency that may arise in your own life or in the lives of others. It is only necessary that you should be supremely calm, and rely upon the eternal wisdom that is within you. If you act in poise and faith, your judgment will always be right, and you will always know exactly what to do. Do not hurry or worry; remember Lincoln in the dark days of the war. James Freeman Clarke relates that after the battle of Fredericksburg, Lincoln alone furnished a supply of faith and hope for the nation. Hundreds of leading men, from all parts of the country, went sadly into his room and came out cheerful and hopeful. They had stood face to face with the Highest, and had seen God in this lank, ungainly, patient man, although they knew it not.

Have perfect faith in yourself and in your own ability to cope with any combination of circumstances that may arise. Do not be disturbed if you are alone; if you need friends they will be brought to you at the right time. Do not be disturbed if you feel that you are ignorant, the information that you need will be furnished you when it is time for you to have it. That which is in you impelling you forward is in the things and people you need, impelling them toward you. If there is a particular man you need to know, he will be introduced to you; if there is a particular book you need to read it will be placed in your hands at the right time. All the knowledge you need is coming to you from both external and internal sources. Your information and your talents will always be equal to the requirements of the occasion. Remember that Jesus told his disciples not to worry as to what they should say when brought before the judges; he knew that the power in them would be sufficient for the needs of the h our. As soon as you awaken and begin to use your faculties in a great way you will apply power to the development of your brain; new cells will be created and dormant cells quickened into activity, and your brain will be qualified as a perfect instrument for your mind.

Do not try to do great things until you are ready to go about them in a great way. If you undertake to deal with great matters in a small way- that is, from a low viewpoint or with incomplete consecration and wavering faith and courage-you will fail. Do not be in a hurry to get to the great things. Doing great things will not make you great, but becoming great will certainly lead you to the doing of great things. Begin to be great where you are and in the things you do every day. Do not be in haste to be found out or recognized as a great personality. Do not be disappointed if men do not nominate you for office within a month after you begin to practice what you read in this book. Great people never seek for recognition or applause; they are not great because they want to be paid for being so. Greatness is reward enough for itself; the joy of being something and of knowing that you are advancing is the greatest of all joys possible to man.

If you begin in your own family, as described in the preceding chapter, and then assume the same mental attitude with your neighbors, friends, and those you meet in business, you will soon find that people are beginning to depend on you. Your advice will be sought, and a constantly increasing number of people will look to you for strength and inspiration, and rely upon your judgment.

Here, as in the home, you must avoid meddling with other people's affairs. Help all who come to you, but do not go about officiously endeavoring to set other people right. Mind your own business. It is no part of your mission in life to correct people's morals, habits, or practices. Lead a great life, doing all things with a great spirit and in a great way; give to him that asks of you as freely as you have received, but do not force your help or your opinions upon any man. If your neighbor wishes to smoke or drink, it is his business; it is none of yours until he consults you about it. If you lead a great life and do no preaching, you will save a thousand times as many souls as one who leads a small life and preaches continuously.

If you hold the right viewpoint of the world, others will find it out and be impressed by it through your daily conversation and practice. Do not try to convert others to your point of view, except by holding it and living accordingly. If your consecration is perfect you do not need to tell any one; it will speedily become apparent to all that you are guided by a higher principle than the average man or woman. If your identification with God is complete, you do not need to explain the fact to others; it will become self-evident. To become known as a great personality, you have nothing to do but to live. Do not imagine that you must go charging about the world like Don Quixote, tilting at windmills, and overturning things in general, in order to demonstrate that you are somebody. Do not go hunting for big things to do. Live a great life where you are, and in the daily work you have to do, and greater works will surely find you out. Big things will come to you, asking to be done.

Be so impressed with the value of a man that you treat even a beggar or the tramp with the most distinguished consideration. All is God. Every man and woman is perfect. Let your manner be that of a god addressing other gods. Do not save all your consideration for the poor; the millionaire is as good as the tramp. This is a perfectly good world, and there is not a person or thing in it but is exactly right; be sure that you keep this in mind in dealing with things and men.

Form your mental vision of yourself with care. Make the thought-form of yourself as you wish to be, and hold this with the faith that it is being realized, and with the purpose to realize it completely. Do every common act as a god should do it; speak every word as a god should speak it; meet men and women of both low and high estate as a god meets other divine beings. Begin thus and continue thus, and your unfolding in ability and power will be great and rapid.

CHAPTER 16

Some Further Explanations

We go back here to the matter of the point of view, for, besides being vitally important, it is the one that is likely to give the student the most trouble. We have been trained, partly by mistaken religious teachers, to look upon the world as being like a wrecked ship, storm-driven upon a rocky coast; utter destruction is inevitable at the end, and the most that can be done is to rescue, perhaps, a few of the crew. This view teaches us to consider the world as essentially bad and growing worse; and to believe that existing discords and inharmoniousness must continue and intensify until the end. It robs us of hope for society, government, and humanity, and gives us a decreasing outlook and contracting mind.

This is all wrong. The world is not wrecked. It is like a magnificent steamer with the engines in place and the machinery in perfect order. The bunkers are full of coal, and the ship is amply provisioned for the cruise; there is no lack of any good thing. Every provision Omniscience could devise has been made for the safety, comfort, and happiness of the crew; the steamer is out on the high seas tacking hither and thither because no one has yet learned the right course to steer. We are learning to steer, and in due time will come grandly into the harbor of perfect harmony.

The world is good, and growing better. Existing discords and inharmoniousness are but the pitching of the ship incidental to our own imperfect steering; they will all be removed in due time. This view gives us an increasing outlook and an expanding mind; it enables us to think largely of society and of ourselves, and to do things in a great way.

Furthermore, we see that nothing can be wrong with such a world or with any part of it, including our own affairs. If it is all moving on toward completion, then it is not going wrong; and as our own personal affairs are a part of the whole, they are not going wrong. You and all that you are concerned with are moving on toward completeness. Nothing can check this forward movement but yourself; and you can only check it by assuming a mental attitude that is at cross-purposes with the mind of God. You have nothing to keep right but yourself; if you keep yourself right, nothing can possibly go wrong with you, and you can have nothing to fear. No business or other disaster can come upon you if your personal attitude is right, for you are a part of that which is increasing and advancing, and you must increase and advance with it.

Moreover your thought-form will be mostly shaped according to your viewpoint of the cosmos. If you see the world as a lost and ruined thing you will see yourself as a part of it, and as partaking of its sins and weaknesses. If your outlook for the world as a whole is hopeless, your outlook for yourself cannot be hopeful. If you see the world as declining toward its end, you cannot see yourself as advancing. Unless you think well of all the works of God you cannot really think well of yourself, and unless you think well of yourself you can never become great.

I repeat that your place in life, including your material environment, is determined by the thought-form you habitually hold of yourself. When you make a thought-form of yourself you can hardly fail to form in your mind a corresponding environment. If you think of yourself as an incapable, inefficient person, you will think of yourself with poor or cheap surroundings. Unless you think well of yourself you will be sure to picture yourself in a more or less poverty stricken environment. These thoughts, habitually held, become invisible forms in the surrounding mind-stuff, and are with you continually. In due time, by the regular action of the eternal creative energy, the invisible thought-forms are produced in material stuff, and you are surrounded by your own thoughts made into material things.

See nature as a great living and advancing presence, and see human society in exactly the same way. It is all one, coming from one source, and it is all good. You yourself are made of the same stuff as God. All the constituents of God are parts of you; every power that God has is a constituent of man. You can move forward as you see God doing. You have within yourself the source of every power.

CHAPTER 17

More About Thought

Give place here to some further consideration of thought. You will never become great until your own thoughts make you great, and therefore it is of the first importance that you should **THINK**.

You will never do great things in the external world until you think great things in the internal world; and you will never think great things until you think about truth; about the verities. To think great things you must be absolutely sincere; and to be sincere you must know that your intentions are right. Insincere or false thinking is never great, however logical and brilliant it may be.

The first and most important step is to seek the truth about human relations, to know what you ought to be to other men, and what they ought to be to you. This brings you back to the search for a right viewpoint. You should study organic and social evolution.

Read Darwin and Walter Thomas Mills, and when you read, **THINK**; think the whole matter over until you see the world of things and men in the right way. **THINK** about what God is doing until you can **SEE** what He is doing.

Your next step is to think yourself into the right personal attitude. Your viewpoint tells you what the right attitude is, and obedience to the soul puts you into it. It is only by making a complete consecration of yourself to the highest that is within you that you can attain to sincere thinking. So long as you know you are selfish in your aims, or dishonest or crooked in any way in your intentions or practices, your thinking will be false and your thoughts will have no power. **THINK** about the way you are doing things; about all your intentions, purposes, and practices, until you know that they are right.

The fact of his own complete unity with God is one that no person can grasp without deep and sustained thinking. Anyone can accept the proposition in a superficial way, but to feel and realize a vital comprehension of it is another matter. It is easy to think of going outside of yourself to meet God, but it is not so easy to think of going inside yourself to meet God. But God is there, and in the holy of holies of your own soul you may meet him face to face. It is a tremendous thing; this fact that all you need is already within you; that you do not have to consider how to get the power to do what you want to do or to make yourself what you want to be.

You have only to consider how to use the power you have in the right way. And there is nothing to do but to begin. Use your perception of truth; you can see so me truth today; live fully up to that and you will see more truth tomorrow.

To rid yourself of the old false ideas you will have to think a great deal about the value of men-the greatness and worth of a human soul. You must cease from looking at human mistakes and look at successes; cease from seeing faults and see virtues. You can no longer look upon men and women as lost and ruined beings that are descending into hell; you must come to regard them as shining souls who are ascending toward heaven. It will require some exercise of will power to do this, but this is the legitimate use of the will-to decide what you will thin k about and how you will think.

The function of the will is to direct thought. Think about the good side of men; the lovely, attractive part, and exert your will in refusing to think of anything else in connection with them.

I know of no one who has attained to so much on this one point as Eugene V. Debs, twice the Liberal candidate for president of the United States. Mr. Debs reverences humanity. No appeal for help is ever made to him in vain. No one receives from him an unkind or censorious word. You cannot come into his presence without being made sensible of his deep and kindly personal interest in you. Every person, be he millionaire, grimy workingman, or toil worn woman, receives the radiant warmth of a brotherly affection that is sincere and true. No ragged child speaks to him on the street without receiving instant and tender recognition. Debs loves men. This has made him the leading figure in a great movement, the beloved hero of a million hearts, and will give him a deathless name. It is a great thing to love men so and it is only achieved by thought. No thing can make you great but thought.

"We may divide thinkers into those who think for themselves and those who think through others. The latter are the rule and the former the exception. The first are original thinkers in a double sense, and egotists in the noblest meaning of the word." -Sehopenhauer.

"The key to every man is his thought. Sturdy and defiant though he look he has a helm which he obeys, which is the idea after which all his facts are classified. He can only be reformed by showing him a new idea which commands his own." -Emerson.

"All truly wise thoughts have been thought already thousands of times; but to make them really ours we must think them over again honestly till they take root in our personal expression." -Goethe.

"All that a man is outwardly is but the expression and completion of his inward thought. To work effectively he must think clearly. To act nobly he must think nobly." -Channing.

"Great men are they who see that spirituality is stronger than any material force; that thoughts rule the world." -Emerson.

"Some people study all their lives, and at their death they have learned everything except to think." -Domergue.

"It is the habitual thought that frames itself into our life. It affects us even more than our intimate social relations do. Our confidential friends have not so much to do in shaping our lives as the thoughts have which we harbor?' -J. W. Teal.
"When God lets loose a great thinker on this planet, then all things are at risk. There is not a piece of science but its flank may be turned tomorrow; nor any literary reputation or the so-called eternal names of fame that may not be refused and condemned." -Emerson.

Think! Think!! THINK!!!

CHAPTER 18

Jesus' Idea of Greatness

In the twenty-third chapter of Matthew Jesus makes a very plain distinction between true and false greatness; and also points out the one great danger to all who wish to become great; the most insidious of temptations which all must avoid and fight unceasingly who desire to really climb in the world. Speaking to the multitude and to his disciples he bids them be ware of adopting the principle of the Pharisees. He points out that while the Pharisees are just and righteous men, honorable judges, true lawgivers and upright in their dealings with men, they "love the uppermost seats at feasts and greetings in the market place, and to be called Master, Master"; and in comparison with this principle, he says: "He that will be great among you let him serve."

The average person's idea of a great man, rather than of one who serves, is of one who succeeds in getting himself served. He gets himself in a position to command men; to exercise power over them, making them obey his will. The exercise of dominion over other people, to most persons, is a great thing. Nothing seems to be sweeter to the selfish soul than this. You will always find every selfish and undeveloped person trying to domineer over others, to exercise control over other men. Savage men were no sooner placed upon the earth than they began to enslave one another. For ages the struggle in war, diplomacy, politics, and government has been aimed at the securing of control over other men. Kings and princes have drenched the soil of the earth in blood and tears in the effort to extend their dominions and their power to rule more people.

The struggle of the business world today is the same as that on the battlefields of Europe a century ago so far as the ruling principle is concerned. Robert 0. Ingersoll could not understand why men like Rockefeller and Carnegie seek for more money and make themselves slaves to the business struggle when they already have more than they can possibly use. He thought it a kind of madness and illustrated it as follows: "Suppose a man had fifty thousand pairs of pants, seventy-five thousand vests, one hundred thousand coats, and one hundred and fifty thousand neckties, what would you think of him if he arose in the morning before light and worked until after it was dark every day, rain or shine, in all kinds of weather, merely to get another necktie?"

But it is not a good simile. The possession of neckties gives a man no power over other men, while the possession of dollars does. Rockefeller, Carnegie, and their kind are not after dollars but power. It is the principle of the Pharisee; it is the struggle for the high place. It develops able men, cunning men, resourceful men, but not great men.

I want you to contrast these two ideas of greatness sharply in your minds. "He that will be great among you let him serve." Let me stand before the average American audience and ask the name of the greatest American and the majority will think of Abraham Lincoln; and is this not because in Lincoln above all the other men who have served us in public life we recognize the spirit of service? Not servility, but service. Lincoln was a great man because he knew how to be a great servant. Napoleon, able, cold, selfish, seeking the high places, was a brilliant man. Lincoln was great; Napoleon was not. The very moment you begin to advance and are recognized as one who is doing things in a great way you will find yourself in danger. The temptation to patronize, advice, or take upon yourself the direction of other people's affairs is sometimes almost irresistible. Avoid, however, the opposite danger of falling into servility, or of completely throwing yourself away in the service of others. To do this has been the ideal of a great many people. The completely self-sacrificing life has been thought to be the Christ-like life, because, as I think, of a complete misconception of the character and teachings of Jesus. I have explained this misconception in a little book that I hope you may all sometime read, "A New Christ". Thousands of people imitating Jesus, as they suppose, have belittled themselves and given up all else to go about doing good; practicing an altruism that is really as morbid and as far from great as the rankest selfishness. The finer instincts which respond to the cry of trouble or distress are not by any means all of you; they are not necessarily the best part of you.

There are other things you must do besides helping the unfortunate, although it is true that a large part of the life and activities of every great person must be given to helping other people. As you begin to advance they will come to you. Do not turn them away. But do not make the fatal error of supposing that the life of complete self-abnegation is the way of greatness.

To make another point here, let me refer to the fact that Swedenborg's classification of fundamental motives is exactly the same as that of Jesus. He divides all men into two groups: those who live in pure love, and those who live in what he calls the love of ruling for the love of self. It will be seen that this is exactly the same as the lust for place and power of the Pharisees. Swedenborg saw this selfish love of power as the cause of all sin. It was the only evil desire of the human heart, from which all other evil desires sprang.

Over against this he places pure love. He does not say love of God or love of man, but merely love. Nearly all religionists make more of love and service to God than they do of love and service to man. But it is a fact that love to God is not sufficient to save a man from the lust for power, for some of the most ardent lovers of the Deity have been the worst of tyrants. Lovers of God are often tyrants, and lovers of men are often meddlesome and officious.

CHAPTER 19

A View of Evolution

But how shall we avoid throwing ourselves into selfless work if we are surrounded by poverty, ignorance, suffering, and every appearance of misery as very many people are? Those who live where the withered hand of want is thrust upon them from every side appealingly for aid must find it hard to refrain from continuous giving. Again, there are social and other irregularities, injustices done to the weak, which fire generous souls with an almost irresistible desire to set things right. We want to start a crusade; we feel that the wrongs will never be righted until we give ourselves wholly to the task. In all this we must fall back upon the point of view. We must remember that this is not a bad world but a good world in the process of becoming.

Beyond all doubt there was a time when there was no life upon this earth. The testimony of geology to the fact that the globe was once a ball of burning gas and molten rock, clothed about with boiling vapors, is indisputable. And we do not know how life could have existed under such conditions; that seems impossible. Geology tells us that later on a crust formed, the globe cooled and hardened, the vapors condensed and became mist or fell in rain. The cooled surface crumbled into soil; moisture accumulated, ponds and seas were gathered together, and at last somewhere in the water or on the land appeared something that was alive.

It is reasonable to suppose that this first life was in single-celled organisms, but behind these cells was the insistent urge of Spirit, the Great One Life seeking expression. And soon organisms having too much life to express themselves with one cell had two cells and then many, and still more life was poured into them.

Multiple-celled organisms were formed; plants, trees, vertebrates, and mammals, many of them with strange shapes, but all were perfect after their kind as everything is that God makes. No doubt there were crude and almost monstrous forms of both animal and plant life; but everything filled its purpose in its day and it was all very good. Then another day came, the great day of the evolutionary process, a day when the morning stars sang together and the sons of God shouted for joy to behold the beginning of the end, for man, the object aimed at from the be ginning, had appeared upon the scene. An ape-like being, little different from the beasts around him in appearance, but infinitely different capacity for growth and thought. Art and beauty, architecture and song, poetry and music, all these were unrealized possibilities in that ape man's soul. And for his time and kind he was very good.

"It is God that works in you to will and to do of his good pleasure," says St. Paul. From the day the first man appeared God began to work **IN** men, putting more and more of himself into each succeeding generation, urging them on to larger achievements and to better conditions, social, governmental, and domestic. Those who looking back into ancient history see the awful conditions which existed, the barbarities, idolatries, and sufferings, and reading about God in connection with these things are disposed to feel that he was cruel and unjust to man, should pause to think. From the ape-man to the coming Christ man the race has had to rise. And it could only be accomplished by the successive unfolding of the various powers and possibilities latent in the human brain.

God desired to express himself, to live in form, and not only that, but to live in a form through which he could express himself on the highest moral and spiritual plane. God wanted to evolve a form in which he could live as a god and manifest himself as a god. This was the aim of the evolutionary force. The ages of warfare, bloodshed, suffering, injustice, and cruelty were tempered in many ways with love and justice as time advanced. And this was developing the brain of man to a point where it should be capable of giving full expression to the love and justice of God. The end is not yet; God aims not at the perfection of a few choice specimens for exhibition, like the large berries at the top of the box, but at the glorification of the race. The time will come when the Kingdom of God shall be established on earth; the time foreseen by the dreamer of the Isle of Patmos, when there shall be no more crying, neither shall there be any more pain, for the former things are all passed away, and there shall be no night there.

CHAPTER 20

Serving God

I have brought you thus far through the two preceding chapters with a view to finally settling the question of duty. This is one that puzzles and perplexes very many people who are earnest and sincere, and gives them a great deal of difficulty in its solution.

When they start out to make something of themselves and to practice the science of being great, they find themselves necessarily compelled to rearrange many of their relationships. There are friends who perhaps must be alienated, there are relatives who misunderstand and who feel that they are in some way being slighted; the really great man is often considered selfish by a large circle of people who are connected with him and who feel that he might bestow upon them more benefits than he does. The question at the outset is: Is it my duty to make the most of myself regardless of everything else? Or shall I wait until I can do so without any friction or without causing loss to any one? This is the question of duty to self vs. duty to others.

One's duty to the world has been thoroughly discussed in the preceding pages and I give some consideration now to the idea of duty to God. An immense number of people have a great deal of uncertainty, not to say anxiety, as to what they ought to do for God.

The amount of work and service that is done for him in these United States in the way of church work and so on is enormous. An immense amount of human energy is expended in what is called serving God. I propose to consider briefly what serving God is and how a man may serve God best, and I think I shall be able to make plain that the conventional idea as to what constitutes service to God is all wrong.

When Moses went down into Egypt to bring out the Hebrews from bondage, his demand upon Pharaoh, in the name of the Deity, was, "Let the people go that they may serve me." He led them out into the wilderness and there instituted a new form of worship which has led many people to suppose that worship constitutes the service of God, although later God himself distinctly declared that he cared nothing for ceremonies, burned offerings, or oblation, and the teaching of Jesus if rightly understood, would do away with organized temple worship altogether. God does not lack anything that men may do for him with their hands or bodies or voices. Saint Paul points out that man can do no thing for God, for God does not need anything.

The view of evolution that we have taken shows God seeking expression through man. Through all the successive ages in which his spirit has urged man up the height, God has gone on seeking expression. Every generation of men is more Godlike than the preceding generation. Every generation of men demands more in the way of fine homes, pleasant surroundings, congenial work, rest, travel, and opportunity for study than the preceding generation.

I have heard some shortsighted economists argue that the working people of today ought surely to be fully contented because their condition is so much better than that of the workingman two hundred years ago who slept in a windowless hut on a floor covered with rushes in company with his pigs. If that man had all that he was able to use for the living of all the life he knew how to live, he was perfectly content, and if he had lack he was not contented. The man of today has a comfortable home and very many things, indeed, which were unknown a short period back in the past, and if he has all that he can use for the living of all the life he can imagine, he will be content. But he is not content. God has lifted the race so far that any common ma n can picture a better and more desirable life than he is able to live under existing conditions. And so long as this is true, so long as a man can think and clearly picture to himself a more desirable life, he will be discontented with the life he has to live, and rightly so. That discontent is the Spirit of God urging men on to more desirable conditions. It is God who seeks expression in the race. "He works in us to will and to do."

The only service you can render God is to give expression to what he is trying to give the world, through you. The only service you can render God is to make the very most of yourself in order that God may live in you to the utmost of your possibilities. In a former work of this series (*The Science of Getting Rich*) I refer to the little boy at the piano, the music in whose soul could not find expression through his untrained hands. This is a good illustration of the way the Spirit of God is over, about, around, and in all of us, seeking to do great things with us so we will train our hands and feet, our minds, brains, and bodies to do his service.

Your first duty to God, to yourself, and to the world is to make yourself as great a personality, in every way, as you possibly can. And that, it seems to me, disposes of the question of duty. There are one or two other things that might be disposed of in closing this chapter. I have written of opportunity in a preceding chapter. I have said, in a general way, that it is within the power of every man to become great, just as in "*The Science of Getting Rich*" I declared that it is within the power of every man to become rich. But these sweeping generalizations need qualifying. There are men who have such materialistic minds that they are absolutely incapable of comprehending the philosophy set forth in these books. There is a great mass of men and women who have lived and worked until they are practically incapable of thought along these lines; and they cannot receive the message. Something may be done for them by demonstration, that is, by living the life before them. But that is the only way they can be aroused. The world needs demonstration more than it needs teaching. For this mass of people our duty is to become as great in personality as possible in order that they may see and desire to do likewise. It is our duty to make ourselves great for their sakes; so that we may help prepare the world that the next generation shall have better conditions for thought.

One other point; I am frequently written to by people who wish to make something of themselves and to move out into the world, but who are hampered by home ties, having others more or less dependent upon them, whom they fear would suffer if left alone. In general I advise such people to move out fearlessly, and to make the most of themselves. If there is a loss at home it will be only temporary and apparent, for in a little while, if you follow the leading of Spirit, you will be able to take better care of your dependents than you have ever done before.

CHAPTER 21

A Mental Exercise

The purpose of mental exercises must not be misunderstood. There is no virtue in charms or formulated strings of words; there is no short cut to development by repeating prayers or incantations. A mental exercise is an exercise, not in repeating words, but in the thinking of certain thoughts. The phrases that we repeatedly hear become convictions, as Goethe says; and the thoughts that we repeatedly think become habitual, and make us what we are. The purpose in taking a mental exercise is that you may think certain thoughts repeatedly until you form a habit of thinking them; then they will be your thoughts all the time. Taken in the right way and with an understanding of their purpose, mental exercises are of great value; but taken as most people take them they are worse than useless.

The thoughts embodied in the following exercise are the ones you want to think. You should take the exercise once or twice daily, but you should think the thoughts continuously. That is, do not think them twice a day for a stated time and then forget them until it is time to take the exercise again. The exercise is to impress you with the material for continuous thought.

Take a time when you can have from twenty minutes to half an hour secure from interruption, and proceed first to make yourself physically comfortable. Lie at ease in a Morris chair, or on a couch, or in bed; it is best to lie flat on your back. If you have no other time, take the exercise on going to bed at night and before rising in the morning.

First let your attention travel over your body from the crown of your head to the soles of your feet, relaxing every muscle as you go.

Relax completely. And next, get physical and other ills off your mind. Let the attentions pass down the spinal cord and out over the nerves to the extremities, and as you do so think: - "My nerves are in perfect order all over my body. They obey my will, and I have great nerve force." Next bring your attention to the lungs and think: - "I am breathing deeply and quietly, and the air goes into every cell of my lungs, which are in perfect condition. My blood is purified and made clean." Next, to the heart: - "My heart is beating strongly and steadily, and my circulation is perfect, even to the extremities.' Next, to the digestive system: - "My stomach and bowels perform their work perfectly. My food is digested and assimilated and my body rebuilt and nourished. My liver, kidneys, and bladder each perform their several functions without pain or strain; I am perfectly well. My body is resting, my mind is quiet, and my soul is at peace.

"I have no anxiety about financial or other matters. God, who is within me, is also in all things I want, impelling them toward me; all that I want is already given to me. I have no anxiety about my health, for I am perfectly well. I have no worry or fear whatever.

"I rise above all temptation to moral evil. I cast out all greed, selfishness, and narrow personal ambition; I do not hold envy, malice, or enmity toward any living soul. I will follow no course of action which is not in accord 'with my highest ideals. I am right and I will do right."

VIEWPOINT

All is right with the world. It is perfect and advancing to completion. I will contemplate the facts of social, political, and industrial life only from this high viewpoint. Behold, it is all very good. I will see all human beings, all my acquaintances, friends, neighbors, and the members of my own household in the same way. They are all good. Nothing is wrong with the universe; nothing can be wrong but my own personal attitude, and henceforth I keep that right. My whole trust is in God.

CONSECRATION

I will obey my soul and be true to that within me that is highest. I will search within for the pure idea of right in all things, and when I find it I will express it in my outward life. I will abandon everything I have outgrown for the best I can think. I will have the highest thoughts concerning all my relationships, and my manner and action shall express these thought s. I surrender my body to be ruled by my mind; I yield my mind to the dominion of my soul, and I give my soul to the guidance of God.

IDENTIFICATION

There is but one substance and source, and of that I am made and with it I am one. It is my Father; I proceeded forth and came from it. My Father and I are one, and my Father is greater than I, and I do His will. I surrender myself to conscious unity with Pure Spirit; there is but one and that one is everywhere. I am one with the Eternal Consciousness.

IDEALIZATION

Form a mental picture of your self as you want to be, and at the greatest height your imagination can picture. Dwell upon this for some little time, holding the thought: "This is what I really am; it is a picture of my own perfect and advancing to completion. I will contemplate the facts of social, political, and industrial life only from this high viewpoint. Behold, it is all very good. I will see all human beings, all my acquaintances, friends, neighbors, and the members of my own household in the same way. They are all good.

Nothing is wrong with the universe, nothing can he wrong but my own personal attitude, and henceforth I keep that right. My whole trust is in God.

REALIZATION

I appropriate to myself the power to become what I want to be, and to do what I want to do. I exercise creative energy; all the power there is, is mine. I will arise and go forth with power and perfect confidence; I will do mighty works in the strength of the Lord, my God. I will trust and not fear, for God is with me.

CHAPTER 22

A Summary of The Science of Being Great

All men are made of the one intelligent substance, and therefore all contain the same essential powers and possibilities. Greatness is equally inherent in all, and may be manifested by all. Every person may become great. Every constituent of God is a constituent of man.

Man may overcome both heredity and circumstances by exercising the inherent creative power of the soul. If he is to become great, the soul must act, and must rule the mind and the body.

Man's knowledge is limited, and he falls into error through ignorance; to avoid this he must connect his soul with Universal Spirit. Universal Spirit is the intelligent substance from which all things come; it is in and through all things. All things are known to this universal mind, and man can so unite himself with it as to enter into all knowledge.

To do this man must cast out of himself everything that separates him from God. He must will to live the divine life, and he must rise above all moral temptations; he must forsake every course of action that is not in accord with his highest ideals.

He must reach the right viewpoint, recognizing that God is all, in all, and that there is nothing wrong. He must see that nature, society, government, and industry are perfect in their present stage, and advancing toward completion; and that all men and women everywhere are good and perfect. He must know that all is right with the world, and unite with God for the completion of the perfect work. It is only as man sees God as the Great Advancing Presence in all, and good in all that he can rise to real greatness.

He must consecrate himself to the service of the highest that is within himself, obeying the voice of the soul. There is an Inner Light in every man that continuously impels him toward the highest, and he must be guided by this light if he would become great.

He must recognize the fact that he is one with the Father, and consciously affirm this unity for himself and for all others. He must know himself to be a god among gods, and act accordingly. He must have absolute faith in his own perceptions of truth, and begin at home to act upon these perceptions. As he sees the true and right course in small things, he must take that course. He must cease to act unthinkingly, and begin to think; and he must be sincere in his thought.

He must form a mental conception of himself at the highest, and hold this conception until it is his habitual thought-form of himself. This thought-form he must keep continuously in view. He must outwardly realize and express that thought-form in his actions. He must do everything that he does in a great way. In dealing with his family, his neighbors, acquaintances, and friends, he must make every act an expression of his ideal. The man who reaches the right viewpoint and makes full consecration, and who fully idealizes himself as great, and who makes every act, however trivial, an expression of the ideal, has already attained to greatness. Everything he does will be done in a great way. He will make himself known, and will be recognized as a personality of power. He will receive knowledge by inspiration, and will know all that he needs to know. He will receive all the material wealth he forms in his thoughts, and will not lack for any good thing. He will be given ability to deal with any combination of circumstances that may arise, and his growth and progress will be continuous and rapid.

Great works will seek him out, and all men will delight to do him honor. Because of its peculiar value to the student of the Science of Being Great, I close this book by giving a portion of Emerson's essay on the "Oversoul." This great essay is fundamental, showing the foundation principles of monism and the science of greatness. I recommend the student to study it most carefully in connection with this book.

What is the universal sense of want and ignorance, but the fine innuendo by which the great soul makes its enormous claim? Why do men feel that the natural history of man has never been written, but always he is leaving behind what you have said of him, and it becomes old, and books of metaphysics worthless? The philosophy of six thousand years has not searched the chambers and magazines of the soul. In its experiments there has always remained, in the last analysis, a residuum it could not resolve. Man is a stream whose source is hidden. Always our being is descending into us from we know not whence. The most exact calculator has no prescience that somewhat incalculable may not balk the very next moment. I am constrained every moment to acknowledge a higher origin for events than the will I call mine.

As with events, so it is with thoughts. When I watch that flowing river, which, out of regions I see not, pours for a season its streams into me, -I see that I am a pensioner, -not a cause, but a surprised spectator of this ethereal water; that I desire and look up, and put myself in the attitude for reception, but from some alien energy the visions come.

The Supreme Critic on all the errors of the past and present, and the only prophet of that which must be, is that great nature in which we rest, as the earth lies in the soft arms of the atmosphere; that Unity, that Oversoul, with which every man's particular being is contained and made one with all other; that common heart, of which all sincere conversation is the worship, to which all right action is submission; that overpowering reality which confutes our tricks and talents, and constrains every one to pass for what he is, and to speak from his character and not from his tongue; and which evermore tends and aims to pass into our thought and hand, and become wisdom, and virtue, and power, and beauty. We live in succession, in division, in parts, in particles.

Meantime within man is the soul of the whole; the wise silence; the universal beauty, to which every part and particle is equally related, the eternal One. And this deep power in which we exist, and whose beatitude is all-accessible to us, is not only self- sufficing and perfect in every hour, but the act of seeing, and the thing seen, the seer and the spectacle, the subject and the object, are one. We see the world piece by piece, as the sun, the moon, the animal, the tree; but the whole, of which these are the shining parts, is the soul. It is only by the vision of that Wisdom, that the horoscope of the ages can be read, and it is only by falling back on our better thoughts, by yielding to the spirit of prophecy which is innate in every man, that we know what it says. Every mans' words, who speak from that life, must sound vain to those who do not dwell in the same thought on their own part. I dare not speak for it. My words do not carry its august sense; they fall short and cold. Only itself can inspire whom it will, and behold! Their speech shall he lyrical and sweet, and universal as the rising of the wind.

Yet I desire, even by profane words, if sacred I may not use, to indicate the heaven of this deity, and to report what hints I have collected of the transcendent simplicity and energy of the Highest Law.

If we consider what happens in conversation, in reveries, in remorse, in times of passion, in surprises, in the instruction of dreams wherein often we see ourselves in masquerade, -the droll disguises only magnifying and enhancing a real element, and forcing it on our distinct notice, -we shall catch many hints that will broaden and lighten into knowledge of the secret of nature. All goes to show that the soul in man is not an organ, but animates and exercises all the organs; is not a function, like the power of memory, of calculation, of comparison, -but uses these as hands and feet; is not a faculty, but a light; is not the intellect or the will, but the master of the intellect an d the will; - is the vast background of our being, in which they lie,-an immensity not possessed and that cannot be possessed. From within or from behind, a light shines through us upon things, and makes us aware that we are nothing, but the light is all. A man is the facade of a temple wherein all wisdom and all good abide. What we commonly call man, the eating, drinking, planting, counting man, does not, as we know him, represent himself, but misrepresents himself. Him we do not respect, but the soul, whose organ he is, would he let it appear through his action, would make our knees bend. When it breathes through his intellect, it is genius; when it flows through his affection it is love.

After its own law and not by arithmetic is the rate of its progress to be computed. The soul's advances are not made by gradation, such as can be represented by motion in a straight line; but rather by ascension of state, such as can be represented by metamorphosis,-from the egg to the worm, from the worm to the fly. The growths of genius are of a certain total character, that does not advance the elect individual first over John, then Adam, then Richard, and give to each the pain of discovered inferiority, but by every throe of growth the man expands there where he works, passing, at each pulsation, classes, populations of men. With each divine impulse the mind rends the thin rinds of the visible and finite, and comes out into eternity, and inspires and expires its air.

This is the law of moral and of mental gain. The simple rise, as by specific levity, not into a particular virtue, but into the region of all the virtues. They are in the spirit that contains them all. The soul is superior to all the particulars of merit. The soul requires purity, but purity is not it; requires justice, but justice is not that; requires beneficence, but is somewhat better; so that there is a kind of descent and accommodation felt when we leave speaking of moral nature, to urge a virtue which it en joins. For, to the soul in her pure action, all the virtues are natural, and not painfully acquired. Speak to his heart and the man becomes suddenly virtuous. Within the same sentiment is the germ of intellectual growth, which obeys the same law. Those who are capable of humility, of justice, of love, of aspiration, are already on a platform that commands the sciences and arts, speech and poetry, action and grace. For whoso dwells in this mortal beatitude, does already anticipate those special powers which men prize so highly; just as love does justice to all the gifts of the object beloved. The lover has no talent, no skill, which passes for quite nothing with his enamored maiden, however little she may possess of related faculty. And the heart that abandons itself to the Supreme Mind finds itself related to all its works and w ill travel a royal road to particular knowledge and powers. For, in ascending to this primary and aboriginal sentiment, we have come from our remote station on the circumference instantaneously to the center of the world, where, as in the closet of God, we see causes, and anticipate the universe, which is but a slow effect

About Wallace D. Wattles

Who is Wallace Wattles and why is he so popular again?

While it is difficult to discover much about Wallace Delois Wattles' life, it is known that he was born in the United States in 1860. And that he initially lived a life consisting of failure, defeat and poverty.

But then later in his life, after studying, practicing and applying the principles that he writes about in his books he turns his life completely around.

In the preface to ***The Science of Getting Rich***, perhaps one of the greatest books ever written, Wallace Wattles advises us to limit our study, as he must have himself, to "the monistic theory of the universe, the theory that One is All, and that All is One; that one Substance manifests itself as the seeming many elements of the material world.

This theory is of Hindu origin, and has been gradually winning its way into the thought of western world for three hundred years. It is the foundation of all the Oriental philosophies, and those of Descartes, Spinoza, Leibnitz, Schopenhauer, Hegel and Emerson."

He continues, "The reader who would dig to the philosophical foundations is advised to read Hegel and Emerson for himself."

Wallace Wattles wrote several books including *The Science of Getting Rich*,
The Science of Being Great, The Science of Being Well, Making of the Man Who Can, Health Through New Thought and Fasting, several shorter manuscripts, plus a novel, Hellfire Harrison.

However, it is for his prosperity classic, ***The Science of Getting Rich*** that he is best known.

Through his tireless study and application of New Thought Principles, Wallace was able to turn his life from poverty and failure in a prosperous way of living.

Having discovered these secrets, Wallace began to write books to share these principles and Universal Laws with the world.

His daughter Florence has been quoted as saying, "He wrote almost constantly. It was then that he formed his mental picture. He saw himself as a successful writer, a personality of power, an advancing man, and he began to work toward the realization of this vision. He lived every page ... His life was truly the powerful life."

Wattles died in 1911, not long after the 1910 publication of **The Science of Getting Rich**. His books, although known and used by the "lucky few, are finally being re-released to the public and are once again assisting millions of people to live a more complete life.

Supplemental Material

A Selection from the Essays of Prentice Mulford Published by
WILLIAM RIDER & SON, LTD, LONDON, 1918

The God in You

INTRODUCTION

There is a gospel older than Christianity, older than Buddhism, older than Brahmanism, older than the classic religions of Greece and Rome, older than the worship of idols and the worship of ancestors. This gospel has been preached under varying forms and names, and with stress laid upon different aspects of its truth and its applicability to differing conditions of civilization and to the different characters of the peoples to whom the message has been addressed. It is probably as old as the earliest traditions of civilized man, and the preaching of it becomes a periodical necessity through the very evolution and growth of civilization itself. It acts as an alternative medicine, a corrective of the tendency inherent in civilization to drift insensibly into channels of artificiality, to substitute the letter for the spirit, the creed for the life, the formula for the thing signified, habit for deliberate conscious action, the cant catchword for the life-giving principle, the spurious imitation for the genuine product. The Gospel to which I allude is the Gospel of the Return to Nature.

In every generation of the world's history since man was civilized, the realization of this state has been the dream of a few idealists who saw it existing in the far distant past of the world's history in an allegorical form as the fabled Golden Age sung of by the poets. If it is older than all the religions, it yet takes its place as an essential element of all of them in the first stages of their existence. Jesus Christ struck the keynote in his preaching when he bade his disciples "suffer the little children to come unto me, for of such is the Kingdom of Heaven," and again when he said, "Except ye be born again as a little child ye cannot enter into the Kingdom of Heaven." And the refrain of very many of his injunctions to his disciples was the adoption of what we should now call the Simple Life so much talked about but so little lived in these days of the twentieth century. Buddha gave expression to the same thought and practiced it in his renunciation of his princely life and his adoption of the life of the wondering preacher, of the begging friar. The same truth was inculcated in China by Lao-tsze and again to a later age, in France, by Jean Jacques Rousseau in his *Social Contract and his Discourse on the Origin of Inequality among Men.*"

Man is born free, and yet everywhere he is in chains." Such were the opening words of this inspiring message to the Peoples of the Earth. Man is born natural and civilization makes him artificial. He is born in touch with Nature and life under the open sky and in the green fields. Civilization draws him to courts and towns. Mankind is born to liberty and equality: civilization makes him either a tyrant on the one hand or a slave on the other. The thought underlying this gospel, whether preached by Christ or by Rousseau, or today by Edward Carpenter in his *Civilization, its Cause and Cure*, contrasted as the characters of the preachers will appear, is essentially the same.

Why were the Scribes and Pharisees hypocrites? Why, except because they had turned from the spirit to the letter, from Nature to artificiality? What was the crime of the French Monarchy but that it fostered and perpetuated unnatural conditions and artificial restrictions which froze the life-blood of the French people? What were the faults which Prentice Mulford saw in American civilization, if they were not the faults which arise directly from the too rapid growth of the luxuries and so-called advantages which civilization and commercial development bring in their train, and from the neglect of those forces which are inherent in Nature itself and without which the life-blood of a nation of necessity becomes contaminated and impoverished?

"You are fortunate if you love trees, and especially the wild ones growing where the great Creative Force placed them and independent of man's care. For all things that we call wild or natural are nearer the Infinite Mind than those which have been enslaved, artificialized and hampered by man. Being nearer the Infinite, they have in them the more perfect infinite force and thought. That is why, when you are in the midst of what is wild and natural, where every trace of man's works is left behind, you feel an indescribable exhilaration and freedom that you do not realize elsewhere."

This sentence seems to me to strike a note of the greatest importance in connection with all these "Return to Nature" movements in whatever period of the world's history they may have occurred. It is especially noteworthy how each movement of the kind has been followed by a great uprising of the life forces of the nation or nations to whom it was preached. It acts on the generation which listens to its preaching like the winds of spring on the sap of winter trees. It is the great revivals consequent on such preaching that let loose the pent-up energies of the human race and in doing so make the great epochs of history. Christianity was the result of one such great movement. The French Revolution was the result of such another.

The gospel of Rousseau was preached not to the French nation only. It was preached in France, it is true, but it was preached to mankind at large, and the fact that it was listened to by many nations outside France is more than half the explanation of the triumphs of Napoleon, the heir of the new French Democracy. In the early days of his triumph Napoleon came to the peoples of the other countries of Europe as much in the guise of a deliverer as of a conqueror. The soldiers that fought in the armies against him had heard the message of freedom and equality and were in no mood to contend with its conquering arm. The gospel according to Jean Jacques Rousseau was this life-giving force. Like a tonic breath from the sea, like a draught of champagne, it was at the same time invigorating and intoxicating to its hearers. Prentice Mulford was right, the Gospel of Nature, wherever preached, "has ever made man feel an indescribable exhilaration and freedom."

Where Mulford differed from Rousseau was in seeing more clearly, more spiritually, what the Return to Nature really signified. That it signified the getting in touch once more is: with "the Infinite Force and Mind as expressed by all natural things." This Spirit of Nature, "this Force of the Infinite Mind," was given out, he maintained, by every wild tree, bird, or animal. It was a literal element and force, going to man from tree and from living creature. If you loved Nature, if you loved the trees, you would find them, declared Mulford, responsive to such love.

"You are fortunate (he says) when you grow to a live, tender, earnest love for the wild trees, animals, and birds, and recognize them all as coming from and built of the same mind and spirit as your own, and able also to give you something very valuable in return for the love which you give them. The wild tree is not irresponsive or regardless of a love like that. Such love is not a myth or mere sentiment. It is a literal element and force going from you to the tree. It is felt by the spirit of the tree. You represent a part and belonging of the Infinite Mind. The tree represents another part and belonging of the Infinite Mind. It has its share of life, thought, and intelligence. You have a far greater share, which is to be greater still--and then still greater."

And again: "As the Great Spirit has made all things, is not that All-pervading mind and wisdom in all things? If then we love the trees, the rocks and all things, as the Infinite made them, shall they not in response to our love give us each of their peculiar thought and wisdom? Shall we not draw nearer to God through a love for these expressions of God in the rocks and trees, birds and animals?"

Poets have told us the same story. Sir Walter Scott did so, for instance, in his beautiful line in" The Lay of the Last Minstrel":

> "Call it not vain. They do not err. Who say that, when the poet dies, Mute Nature mourns her worshipper And celebrates his obsequies; That say mute crag and cavern lone For the departed hard make moan, And rivers teach their rushing wave To murmur dirges o'er his grave."

Wordsworth, too, understood the communion with Nature, as is shown by many of his verses, and most of all by his lines on the vision of the daffodils. The sight of the daffodils dancing by the lake was to him like the midnight dance of fairies or elves on the greensward, instinct with conscious vitality, and the impulse of contagious motion. This picture of the 'daffodils' delight in their own life and beauty recalled itself automatically to the poet's mind, and bade him join them in their fairy revels. No poet could have put the mood of communion with Nature in lines of greater felicity. They are, indeed, well known, but to the lover of Nature they will bear quoting again and again. The poet exclaims:

> "I gazed and gazed, but little thought What joy the show to me had brought. For oft, when on my couch I lie In vacant or in pensive mood. They flash upon that inward eye Which is the bliss of solitude; And then my heart with pleasure fills, And dances with the daffodils."

Other poets have voiced the same sense of communion with Nature in varying forms and degrees of intensity. A lesser known one of the present day has claimed poetry as Nature's mouthpiece, and condemned its neglect as a refusal to be brought into touch with Nature's many voices by the most articulate means at its disposal. Take the following verses as an example:-

> "If thou disdain the sacred Muse, Beware lest Nature, past recall, Indignant at that crime,

> refuse Thee entrance to her audience hall. Beware lest sea and sky and all that bears reflection of her face Be blotted with a hue less pall Of unillumined commonplace. Ah! Desolate hour when that shall be, When dew and sunlight, rain and wind Shall seem but trivial things to thee, Unloved, unheeded, undivined! Nay, rather let that morning find Thy molten soul exhaled and gone, than in a living death resigned So darkly still to labor on."

We see that poets galore have voiced this sentiment and have even expressed it like Sir Waiter Scott in the form of a belief in the conscious Life of Nature. Poets live in a world of fancy and imagination. We do not take their statements too literally. It is different when we come to a man who writes essays, which he would have us take as a guide in life, who, in his wildest flights, expects to be taken as intending to convey the full force of what he says, in however spiritual a sense.

You cannot say of the lines of Scott what the great Earl of Chatham said in quite a different connection, that " though poetry they are no fiction." * You feel that Scott was by way of expressing a poetic mood, the literal truth of which he would never dream of substantiating over the dinner table, Prentice Mulford, on the other hand, preached this doctrine as an actual truth to be accepted and acted upon, to be made a basis upon which to erect a practical manual on the subject of how to live most intensely, of how, in short, to be most alive while living. Prentice Mulford, in preaching his gospel, echoed in other words the message proclaimed by the Founder of Christianity: "I have come that ye might have life, and that ye might have it more abundantly."

To Mulford every man is an unconscious psychometrist. The infection of good or evil is all-pervasive.

"Everything (he tells us) from a stone to a human being sends out to you as you look upon it a certain amount of force affecting you beneficially or injuriously according to the quality of life or animation which it possesses. Take any article of furniture, a chair or a bedstead, for instance. It contains not only the thought of those who first planned and molded it on its construction, but it is also permeated with the thought and varying moods of all who have sat on it or slept in it. So also are the walls and every article of furniture in any room permeated with the thought of those who have dwelt in it, and if it has been long lived in by people whose lives were narrow, whose occupation varied little from year to year, whose moods were dismal and cheerless, the walls and furniture will be saturated with this gloomy and sickly order of thought.

"If you are very sensitive, and stay in such a room but for a single day, you will feel in some way the depressing effect of such thought, unless you keep very positive to it, and to keep sufficiently positive for twenty-four hours at a time to resist it would be extremely difficult. If you are in any degree weak or ailing you are then most negative or open to the nearest thought-element about you, and will be affected by it, in addition to the wearying mental effect (first mentioned) of any object kept constantly before the eyes.

"It is injurious, then, to be sick, or even wearied, in a room where other people have been sick, or where they have died, because in thought-element all the misery and depression, not only of the sick and dying but of such as gathered there and sympathized with the patient, will be still left in the room, and this is a powerful unseen agent for acting injuriously on the living."

The above quotation is from an essay on "Spells, or the Law of Change"; but our author develops the same idea to a fuller extent in another essay, that on "Positive and Negative Thought," in which he enlarges on the importance of being positive and not negative when surrounded by those who are emitting poisonous thought atmosphere, such as envy, jealousy, cynicism, or despondency. This, he tells us, is as real as a noxious gas and infinitely more dangerous. If you are then in a negative or receptive state you are to all intents and purposes a sponge, absorbing evil influences, the full harm of which may not be realized till days afterwards.

You must know, then, when to be in a positive and when in a negative frame of mind. As a rule you must be positive when you have dealings with the world and negative when you retire within yourself. These conditions inevitably alternate one with another, and the exercise of much positive force will bring about a natural reaction after a certain time. Why, asks Prentice Mulford, did the Christ so often withdraw from the multitude? It was, he avers, because after exercising in some way the immense power of concentrated thought, either by healing or talking, or by giving some proofs of his command over the physical elements, at which times he was positive and expending his forces, he, feeling the negative state coming upon him, left the crowd so that he should not absorb their lower thought.

Prentice Mulford lays great stress on the reality, indeed, substantiality of thought. "*As a man thinketh, so is he.*" "Your spirit," says Mulford, "is a bundle of thought." What you think most of that is your spirit. "Thought," he says again, "is a substance as much as air or any other unseen element of which chemistry makes us aware. Strong thought is the same as strong will. Every thought, spoken or unspoken, is a thing as real, though invisible, as water or metal. When you think you work. Every thought represents an outlay of force. If a man thinks murder he actually puts out an element of murder in the air. He sends from him a plan of murder as real as if drawn on paper. If the thought is absorbed by others, it inclines them towards violence, if not murder. If a person is ever thinking of sickness he sends from him the element of sickness. If he thinks of health, strength, and cheerfulness, he sends from him constructions of thought helping others towards health and strength, as well as himself."

In thought every man should look forward and cast the past behind him. "Nature buries its dead as quickly as possible, and gets them out of sight. It is better, however, to say that Nature changes what it has no further use for into other forms of life. The tree produces the new leaf with each return of spring. It will have nothing to do with its dead ones. It treasures up no withered rose leaves to bring back sad remembrance." . . . "Nothing in Nature is at a standstill. A gigantic incomprehensible Wisdom moves all things forward towards greater and higher powers and possibilities. You are included in and are part of this force."

If then, argues Mulford, you do not move forward with the rest of Nature, you will inevitably sink, and rightly sink, into decrepitude and decay. Why are outworn creeds outworn? Simply because they have not changed with the changing thought of man, they have not evolved with the evolution of the race. They have remained behind on a lower plane while man has moved forward to a higher. If you cling to them you cling to what will draw you back and draw you downward. It is the same in business. The business methods of one generation must be changed and modified in order to adapt the business to the conditions and demands of the uprising generation. The "good old times" may have been good in their way, though their goodness is generally exaggerated; but to attempt to revive their ways of thought for the use of later generations is like putting new wine into old bottles.

Prentice Mulford had absorbed among his other ideas the eastern doctrine of metempsychosis. The race had evolved, he held, from the lowest forms. It could, therefore, evolve indefinitely higher. Man, as at present constituted, was not its ultimate aim. The possibilities of human evolution were infinite.

"It is a grand mistake, he writes, that of supposing that any man or woman is the result of that one short life which we live here. We have all lived possibly in various forms as animal, bird, snake, insect, plant. Our starting-point of matter in existence has been dragged on the sea's bottom, embedded in icebergs, and vomited out of volcanoes amid fire, smoke and ashes. It has been tossed about on the ocean and has lain maybe for centuries and centuries embedded in the heart of some Pliocene mountain. We have crept up and up, now in one form, now in another, always gaining something more in intelligence, something more of force, by each change, until at last here we are, nor have we got far along yet."

If man's power of developing is indefinite it follows, thinks Mulford, that his power of prolonging life is also limitless; i.e. not merely prolonging life under other conditions outside the physical body, but even of prolonging life within the physical body itself. Hence his essay dealing with Immortality in the Flesh--an essay which more than any other has led to Mulford being dubbed a crank and a mad dreamer. " We believe," he writes, "that immortality in the flesh is a possibility, or in other words, that a physical body can be retained so long as the spirit desires its use, and that this body instead of decreasing in strength and vigor as the years go on, will increase and its youth will be perpetual."

There is a Law, says Mulford, of Silent Demand, and silent continuous demand made with concentration of will and thought can obtain whatever it asks for-- whatever it claims as its own, in view of the fact that each human being is part of the Infinite Life and has inalienable relationship to the Supreme Power. "There will be built," our author predicts, "in time, an edifice partaking of the nature of a church where all persons of whatever condition, age, nationality, or creed may come to lay their needs before the great Supreme Power and demand of that Power help to supply those needs. It should be a church without sect or creed. It should be open every day during the week and every evening until a reasonable hour. It should be a place of silence for the purpose of silent demand or prayer. It should be a place of earnest demand for permanent good, yet not a place of gloom. A church should be held as a sanctuary for the concentration of the strongest thought power. The strongest thought power is where the motive is the highest. You can get such power by unceasing silent demand of the Supreme Power of which you are a part."

This power of silent demand can be utilized, then, for all purposes. It can be utilized, for instance, to keep the body in health, to make good the wearing away of the tissues, to prevent the ageing and final perishing of the physical body. "The body is continually changing its elements in accordance with the condition of the mind. If it is in certain mental conditions, it is conveying to itself elements of decay, weakness, and physical death. If in another mental condition, it is adding to itself elements of strength and life. That which the spirit takes on in either case is thought or belief. Thoughts and beliefs materialize themselves in flesh and blood. Belief in inevitable decay and death brings from the spirit to the body the elements of decay and death. Belief in the possibility of a constant inflowing to the spirit of life brings life."

These ideas, as I have already suggested, seem fairly far-fetched. But it is a curious fact that science does not appear to reject them quite as decisively as one would have expected. Messrs. Carrington & Meader, in their book on *Death, its Causes and Phenomena*, which bears very directly on this interesting question, quote the observation of a physician, Dr. William A. Hammond: "There is no physiological reason why man should die," and also Dr. Monroe in his statement that the "human body as a machine is perfect. It is apparently intended to go on forever." And again, they cite the observation of Dr. Thomas J. Allen, who states that "the body is self-renewing and should not therefore wear out by constant disintegration."

The point is not so much perhaps that *natural death*, as we call it, is unnatural, as that the reason why mankind die after a certain age has never been satisfactorily explained from a medical point of view, and the medical evidence points to the fact not so much that man might conceivably be immortal as that the process of decay might be indefinitely retarded. That, in short, man might live to a far greater age than he does at present.

There is a great deal in Prentice Mulford which seems commonplace enough today. Men of the twentieth century are familiar with his doctrines and his teachings. They have been put forward with a great air of originality by many of his followers, and they have been repeated in various forms and with varying degrees of exaggeration. I doubt, however, if they have ever been put forward so freshly and so forcibly as they were by the pioneer of what we now call the New

Thought Movement--Prentice Mulford. There is in no other leader of this New Thought Movement such a sense of the communion with Nature, so fresh and full a recognition of the possibility of utilizing Nature's forces for the benefit of body and spirit. For, as I have already explained, Prentice Mulford was not only the first and greatest of the New Thought teachers, but also par excellence an apostle of the Return to Nature.

```
Ralph Sherley
```

Note: Ralph Shirley was a New Thought proponent of the time.

Chapter 1

Positive and Negative Thought

Your mind or spirit is continually giving out its force or thought, or receiving some quality of such force, as an electric battery may be sending out its energy and may be afterwards replenished. When you use your force in talking, or writing, or physical effort of any sort, you are positive. When not so using it, you are negative. When negative, or receptive, you are receiving force or element of some kind or quality, which may do you temporary harm or permanent good.

All evil of any kind is but temporary. Your spirit's course through all successive lives is toward the condition of ever-increasing and illimitable happiness.

There are poisonous atmospheres of thought as real as the poisonous fumes of arsenic or other metallic vapors. You may, if negative, in a single hour, by sitting in a room with persons whose minds are full of envy, jealousy, cynicism or despondency, absorb from them a literally poisonous element of thought, full of disease. It is as real as any noxious gas, vapor or miasma. It is infinitely more dangerous, so subtle is its working, for the full injury may not be realized till days afterwards, and is then attributed to some other cause.

It is of the greatest importance where you are, or by what element of thought, emanating from other minds, you are surrounded when in the negative or receiving state. You are then as a sponge, unconsciously absorbing element, which may do great temporary harm or great permanent good to both mind and body.

During several hours of effort of any kind, such as talking business, walking, writing, or superintending your household, or doing any kind of artistic work, you have been positive, or sending out force. You have then to an extent drained yourself of force. If now you go immediately to a store crowded with hurried customers, or to a sick person, or a hospital, or a turbulent meeting, or to a trying interview with some disagreeable individual full of peevishness and quarrelsomeness, you become negative to them. You are then the sponge, drinking in the injurious thought element of the crowded store, the sickly thought element from the sick-bed or hospital, the actual poisonous and subtle element from any person or persons, whose minds put out a quality of thought less healthy or cruder than your own.

If you go fatigued in mind or body among a crowd of wearied, feverish, excited people, your strength is not drawn from you by them, for you have little strength to give. But you absorb, and, for the time being, make their hurried, wearied thought a part of yourself. You have then cast on you a load of lead, figuratively speaking. As you absorb their quality of thought, you will in many things think as they do and see also as they do. You will become discouraged, though before you were hopeful. Your plans for business, which, when by yourself, seemed likely to succeed, will now seem impossible and visionary. You will fear where before you had courage. You will possibly become undecided, and in the recklessness of indecision buy what you do not really need, or do something, or say something, or take some hasty step in business which you would not have done had you been by yourself, thinking your own thoughts, and not the clouded thoughts of the crowd around you. You will possibly return home fagged out and sick in mind and body.

Through these causes, the person whom you may meet an hour hence, or the condition of mind in which you are on meeting that person, may cause success or failure in your most important undertakings. From such a person you may absorb a thought which may cause you to alter your plans, either for success or failure.

If you must mingle among crowds, or with minds whose thoughts are inferior to your own, do so only when you are strongest in mind and body, and leave as soon as you feel wearied. When strong, you are the positive magnet, driving off their injurious thought-element. When weak, you become the negative magnet, attracting their thought to you; and such thought is freighted with physical and mental disease. Positive men are drivers and pushers, and succeed best in the world. Yet it is not well to be always in the positive or force-sending state of mind; if you are, you will divert from you many valuable ideas. There must be a time for the mental reservoir of force or thought to fill up as well as give forth. The person who is always in the positive attitude of mind--he or she who will never hear new ideas without immediately fighting them--who never takes time to give quiet hearing to ideas which may seem wild and extravagant, who insists ever that what does not seem reasonable to him must necessarily be unreasonable for every one else, such a mind will certainly, by constantly maintaining this mental attitude, be drained of all force.

On the other hand, the persons who are always negative or always in the receiving state, those who "never know their own minds" for two hours at a time, who are swayed unconsciously by everyone with whom they talk, who allow themselves, when they go with a plan or a purpose, to be discouraged by a sneer, by a single word of opposition, are as the reservoir, ever filling up with mud and trash, which at last stops the pipe for distributing water; in other words, they have their force-sending capacity almost destroyed, and are unsuccessful in everything which they undertake.

As a rule, you must be positive when you have dealings with the world, for very much the same reason that the pugilist must be positive when he stands before his antagonist. You must be negative when you retire from the ring--from active participation in business. You will tire yourself out by constantly confronting opponents, even in thought, in any sort of contest.

Why did the Christ of Judea so often withdraw from the multitude? It was because, after exercising in some way his Immense power of concentrated thought, either by healing or talking, or by giving some proofs of his command over the physical elements, at which times he was positive and expended his force, he, feeling the negative state coming upon him, left the crowd, so that he should not absorb their lower thought. Had he done so, his force would have been dissipated by carrying such thought that is, by getting in sympathy with it, feeling it and thinking it, just as you may have done when a person, full of troubles, comes to you, and spends an hour telling those troubles to you, literally pouring into you his load of anxious thought. You sympathize, you are sorry, you desire strongly to help, and, when he leaves, your thought follows him. In such case, your own force is used up by the feeling of sympathy or sorrow, while it might otherwise have been applied to something far more beneficial and profitable in result both to yourself and him.

An orator would not spend an hour previous to his speech in public in carrying bushels of coal upstairs to relieve a tired laborer, for if he did, his strength, brilliancy, inspiration, the force required for his effort, would be mostly used up in the drudgery of carrying coal. The ideas which he puts forth may prove the direct or indirect means of relieving that laborer in some way, and even thousands of others.

You must be positive and restrain the outflow of your sympathetic force very often in the cases of private individuals in trouble, in order to have power to do all the more for them. In politics and professions, the men who live longest and who exercise most influence are those who are least accessible to the masses; for if they are constantly mingling with all manner of people, and so absorbing varied atmospheres, much of their power is wasted in carrying it. Look at the long list of prominent American politicians who have died in the prime of life, or but little past it, during the last few decades; Seward, Grant, Morton, M'Clellan, Logan, Wilson, Hendricks, Chase, Stanton. Not keeping themselves positive-- ignorant exposure to all manner of inferior thought atmospheres when negative-- has been a most important factor in these premature deaths.

Great financiers like Jay Gould avoid the crowd and hubbub of the Stock Exchange. They live relatively secluded lives, are not easy of access, and transact much business through agents. In so doing, they avoid hurried and confused thought atmospheres. They surround and keep themselves as in a fortress, in the clearer thought-element of the world of finance, and from it derive their keen sightedness on their plane of action. They realize the necessity of so doing without possibly being able to define the law. Many methods are quite unconsciously adopted by people which bring successful results in many fields of effort, and which are adopted through the unconscious action and teaching of the laws governing thought.

If you are now very much in the company of some person whose quality of thought is inferior to your own, you are certainly affected injuriously, through absorbing that person's thought since you cannot be positive all the time, to resist the entrance of his thought. When wearied, you are negative, or in a state for receiving his or her thought, and then it must act on you. As so it acts on you, unconsciously you may do many things, in conformity with his or her order of thought, which you would have done differently, and possibly better, had you not been exposed to it and absorbed it.

If so you absorb the element of fear or indecision from anyone, will you act in business with your own natural confidence, courage, energy and determination? It matters not what is the relation to you of those whose temporary or permanent association may thus do you harm, whether that of parent, brother, sister, wife or friend; if their mental growth is less than yours, and if therefore they cannot see as you see, you are very likely to be injured in mind, pocket and health through their constant association. For such reason, Paul the apostle advised people not to be "unequally yoked together in marriage." Why? Because he knew that of any two persons living constantly together, yet occupying different worlds of thought, one would surely be injured; and the one most injured is the highest, finest and broadest mind, which is loaded down, crippled and fettered by the grosser thought absorbed from the inferior.

If you are in active business sympathy or relation with any person who is nervous, excited, irritable, destitute of any capacity for repose, always worried about something, and on the rush from morning till night, though you are separated by hundreds of miles, you will, when in the receiving state, have that person's mind acting injuriously on yours, and you will have thereby sent to you much of his or her cruder thought-element, which, agitating and disturbing your mind, will, in time, work unpleasant results to the body.

Your only means of avoiding this is to cease such relation and common sympathy and effort with them as soon as possible,--to put them out of your mind,--to fix and interest yourself in some other diversion or occupation whenever your thought goes out to them. For every time that you so think, you send out your actual life and vitality in their direction, and thus doing you may transmit a current of life and force which will give them relative success in many undertakings, a success that you may lack, for you are transferring your capital stock of force, while you should use it for yourself. The cruder minds can only appropriate a part of this. The rest is wasted. They may be kept alive by it and prosper, and in return send you only element which brings on you disease, lack of energy and barrenness of idea.

Proper association is one of the greatest of agencies for realizing success, health and happiness. Association here means something far beyond the physical proximity of bodies. You are literally nearest the person or persons of whom you think most, though they are ten thousand miles distant.

If you have been long in association with a person, so absorbing thought-element inferior to your own, you cannot, if you sever the connection, immediately free yourself from the inferior thought-current flowing from him to you, though thousands of miles may intervene. Distance amounts to little in the unseen world of thought. If such a person is much in your thought, his mind still acts on yours, sending you grosser and injurious element. You must learn to forget him if you wish to escape injury. That must be a gradual process. In so forgetting you cut the invisible wires binding you together, through which there have been sent elements injurious to you.

Does this sound cold, cruel and hard? But where is the benefit of two persons being so tied together in thought or remembrance, if one or both are injured? If one is injured so also must be the other in time. But the superior mind receives more immediate injury, and many a person fails to attain the position where he or she should stand, through this cause.

Through this cause also there come disease, lack of vigor, corpulence and clumsiness. The cruder element so sent you by another, and absorbed by you, can materialize itself in physical substance, and make itself seen and felt on your body in the shape of unhealthy and excessive fat, swollen limbs, or any other outward sign of disease and decay. In such case, it is not really your own unwieldy or deformed body that you are carrying about. It is the inferior body of another person sent you in thought; as year after year this process goes on, the cumbrous frame which you so carry becomes at last too heavy for your spirit, and then it drops off. You are "dead," in the estimation of your acquaintances, but you are not really dead; you have simply tumbled down under a load which you could no longer bear.

Even a book in which you are greatly interested, which draws strongly on your sympathy, and has much to say on the mental or physical distress of the person so drawing on your sympathy, can, if you read it in the negative or receiving state, bring to you some form of the physical or mental ailments alluded to therein. Such a book is the representative of the mind of the individual whose history it contains, acting on yours, and bringing to you in thought-element all that person's morbid and unhealthy states of mind, which for a time settle on you and become a parasitical part of you. In this way great harm may be done to sensitive people through reading novels and even true stories full of physical or mental suffering.

If a character to which you are strongly attracted is described as being confined for years in a dungeon, suffering physical and mental pain from such confinement, and in the pages of that book if you follow such life and become absorbed in it, you do actually live therein. You will, if so reading such history day after day, and getting thoroughly absorbed or merged in it, find your vitality or your digestion affected in some way. The law operates, though you may never dream that the cold which you have taken more easily, through lack of vitality, the headache or weakness of digestion, is owing to a mental condition brought on you temporarily through living in the thought of that book while in the receiving state of mind. These are unhealthy books; and so are plays which work strongly on people's emotions in the dramatic representation of scenes of horror, distress and death. The health of thousands on thousands is injured through attracting and fastening on themselves, while in the negative or receiving condition, these unhealthy currents of thought and their consequent unhealthy mental states.

While eating, one should always be in the receptive condition, for then you are gathering material element to nourish the body; and if you eat in a calm, composed, cheerful frame of mind, you are receiving a similar character of thought. To eat and growl, to argue violently or intensely with others, to eat and still think business and plan business, is to be positive, when of all times you should then be negative. It is like working with your body while you eat. You send, while so arguing or grumbling, that force from you which is needed for digestion. It matters little whether you grumble or argue in speech or in thought.

There is also injurious result to you when any person at the table is for any reason--any offensive habit, any peculiarity of manner or mood-unpleasant to you, and you are thereby obliged to endure instead of enjoying his company, for all endurance means the putting out of positive thought-- in other words, working in mind to drive off the annoyance. Especially the dinner in the latter part of the day should be the day's climax of happiness--a union of minds in perfect accord with each other--the conversation light, bright, lively and humorous--the palates appreciative of artistic cookery, and the eye also regaled with the appointments of the table and the dining-room. In such a condition and in such receptive state you absorb a spiritual strength, coming from the thought of all about you as they will absorb yours. But if you eat in a social dungeon, in the barrack of a restaurant, where only material food is given, in an unhappy family, full of petty jealousies and complaining, in a boarding-house manger, you may exhaust yourself in resisting or enduring annoyances, thereby lessening the power of digestion and assimilation of your food; and you absorb also more or less of the discontent or moodiness of those about you, and so carry away a load worse than useless--a load which is the real cause of an imperfect digestion, of consequent physical weakness and mental unrest, or irritability.

When you are much alone, you attract and are surrounded by a quality and current of thought coming from minds similar to your own. It is for this reason, that in moments of solitude your thought may be more clear and agreeable than when in the company of others. You live then in another and finer world of ideas. You may deem these ideas but as "idle thoughts"; you may not dare to mention them before others; you may long for company, and may take such as you can get, or you may have it forced upon you. With it your ideal world is shattered, and seems possibly absolute nonsense. You enter into your neighbors' current of thought, their line of talk and motive. You chatter and run on as they do; you criticize, censure, judge and possibly abuse others not present; when you are again by yourself, you feel a sense of discontent with yourself, and a certain vague self-condemnation for what you have been saying. That is your higher mind, your real self, protesting against the injury done it by the lower mind--or not possibly so much your lower mind as the lower thought which you absorb while in that company, and which for a time becomes a parasitical part of you, as the ivy-vine may fasten itself to the oak, from the root to the topmost branch, drawing its nourishment in part from the oak, giving it poison in return, and at last so covering it up that the tree is concealed and is eventually killed thereby.

In a similar manner are refined minds often buried, concealed and prevented their true expression by the lower and parasitical thought, which, unconscious of the evil it can do them, they enter among, associate with and allow to fasten upon them. They are not themselves, and perhaps from their earliest physical life never have been themselves, so far as outward expression goes. They are as oaks buried and concealed by the poisonous ivy. But you may say: "I cannot live alone and without association." True. It is not desirable or profitable that you should. It is not good for man or woman to live alone. It is most desirable, profitable and necessary that you should be fed by the strong, healthy, vigorous, cheerful thought-element coming from minds whose aspiration, ideal and motives are like your own.

When you cut off association or the flow even of your thought from those who are injurious to you, you prevent not only the intrusion of their evil quality of thought but you open the door for the better. You will then by degrees attract, in physical form, those who can give you at once more entertainment and more help. Your highest thought is an unseen force or link, ever connecting you with higher minds akin to your own. These cannot act on you to any extent so long as you continue association or are linked in thought with the lower. Such link or association bars the door to the higher.

How much real comfort, strength, cheer or entertainment do you get from your daily associates? Are they live company? Who does the entertaining, you or they?, who must ever keep up the conversation when it flags? Are you never bored by their dullness, by all which you have heard over and over again, and if, when on hearing and rehearsing it you do not express discontent in your speech, do you not in your secret thought? How much of the association that you seek, or that seeks you, is really more endured than enjoyed, and is, in fact, only "taken up with "because of the lack of better.

You will never tire of your true and most profitable associates, who, having opened themselves to the higher, are ever drawing in new idea, and with this a new life, which they will give to you, as you give them in return. These are the "wells of water springing up unto everlasting life." These are the "savors of life unto life, and not of death unto death," as are minds to each other who, month after month and year after year, only think in a rut, talk in a rut and act in a rut. These are the dead who should be left to " bury their dead." True life is a state of continuous variety; it involves, through opening the mind in the right direction, and keeping it so open, an endless association with other and like minds, giving ever to each other, and receiving unfailing supply of strength, vigor and the elements of eternal youth.

The fountain of youth, and endless youth, is a spiritual reality, as are many other things which are deemed idle vagaries, and have been erroneously sought on the physical stratum of life. The fountain of endless youth, youth of body as well as mind, lies in the attainment of that mental attitude or condition which is instantly positive to all evil, cruder and lower thought, but negative or receptive to higher and constructive thought, full of courage, devoid of all fear, deeming nothing impossible, hating no individual, disliking only error, full of love for all. but expanding its sympathy wisely and carefully.

Chapter 2

Some Practical Mental Recipes

None of us can expect to believe and live up to new laws, principles, or methods of life all at once. Though convinced of their truth, there is an unyielding, stubborn part of us which is hostile to them. That part is our material mind or mind of the body.

There is a supreme power and ruling force which pervades and Rules the boundless universe. You are a part of this power. You as a part have the faculty of bringing to you by constant silent desire, prayer, or demand more and more of the qualities, belongings, and characteristics of this power.

Every thought of yours is a real thing--a force (say this over to yourself twice). Every thought of yours is literally building for you something for the future of good or ill.

What, then, Is your mind dwelling on now in any matter? The dark or the bright side? Is it toward others ugly or kind? This is precisely the same as asking, "What kind of life and results are you making for yourself in the future?"

If now you are obliged to live in a tenement house or sit at a very inferior table, or live among the coarse and vulgar, do not say to yourself that you must always so live. Live in mind or imagination in the better house. Sit in imagination at better served tables and among superior people. When you cultivate this state of mind your forces are carrying you to the better. Be rich in spirit, in mind, in imagination, and you will in time be rich in material things. It is the mood of mind you are most in, whether that be groveling or aspiring, that is actually making physical conditions of life in advance for you.

The same law applies to the building up of the body. In imagination live in a strong, agile body, though yours is now a weak one.

Do not put any limits to your future possibilities. Do not say: "I must stop here. I must always rank below this or that great man or woman. My body must weaken, decay, and perish, because in the past so many people's bodies have weakened and perished."

Do not say: "My powers and talents are only of the common order and those of an ordinary person. I shall live and die as millions have done before me."

When you think this, as many do unconsciously, you imprison yourself in an untruth. You bring then to yourself the evil and painful results of an untruth. You bar and fetter your aspiration to grow to powers and possibilities beyond the world's present knowledge. You cut from you the higher truth and possibility.

You have latent in you, some power, some capacity, some shade of talent different from that ever before possessed by any human being. No two minds are precisely alike, for the Infinite Force creates infinite variety in its every expression, whether such expression be a sunset or a mind.

Demand at times to be permanently freed from all fear. Every second of such thought does its little to free you forever from the slavery of fear. The Infinite Mind knows no fear, and it is your eternal heritage to grow nearer and nearer to the Infinite Mind.

 We absorb the thought of those with whom we are most in sympathy and association. We graft their mind on our own. If their mind is inferior to ours and not on the same plane of thought, we, in such absorption, take in and cultivate an inferior and injurious mental graft.

If you will keep company with people who are reckless and unaspiring, who have no aim or purpose in life, who have no faith in themselves or anything else, you place yourself in the thought current of failure. Your tendency then will be to failure. Because from such people, your closest associates, you will absorb their thought. If you absorb it, you will think it. You will get into the same mood of mind as theirs. If you think as they do, you will in many things find yourself acting as they do, no matter how great your mental gifts.
Your mind surely absorbs the kind of thought it is most with. If you are with the successful you absorb thought which brings success. The unsuccessful are ever sending from them thoughts of lack of order, lack of system, lack of method, or recklessness and discouraged thought. Your mind if much with theirs will

certainly absorb these thoughts exactly as sponge does water. It is better for your art or business that you have no intimate company at all than the company of reckless, careless, slipshod, and slovenly minds.

When in your mind you cut yourself off from the unlucky and thriftless, your body will not long remain so near theirs. You get then into another force or current. It will carry you into the lives of more successful people.

When you don't know what to do in any matter of business, in anything--wait. Do nothing about it. Dismiss it as much as you can from your mind. Your purpose will be as strong as ever. You are then receiving and accumulating force to put on that purpose. It comes from the Supreme Power. It will come in the shape of an idea, an inspiration, an event, an opportunity. You have not stopped while you so waited. You have all that time been carried to the idea, the inspiration, the event, the opportunity, and it also has been carried or attracted to you.

When in any undertaking we put our main dependence and trust in an individual or individuals and not in the Supreme Power, we are off the main track of the most perfect success.

The highest and real success means, in addition to wealth, increasing health, vigor, and a growth never ceasing into powers and possibilities not yet realized by the race.

As regards your business, don't talk to anybody, man or woman, regarding your plans or projects, or anything connected with them, unless you are perfectly sure they wish for your success. Don't talk to people who hear you out of politeness. Every word so spoken represents so much force taken out of your project. The number you can talk to with profit is very small. But the good wish of one real friend, if he give you a hearing but for ten minutes, is a literal, living, active force, added to your own, and from that time working in your behalf.

If your aim is for right and justice you will be led to those you can trust and talk to with safety. Your spiritual being or sense will tell you whom you can trust.

When you demand justice for yourself, you demand it for the whole race. If you allow yourself to be dominated, brow-beaten, or cheated by others without inward or outward protest, you are condoning deceit and trickery. You are in league with it.

Three persons engaged in any form of gossip, tattle, or scandal generate a force and send it from them of tattle, gossip, and scandal. The thought they send into the air returns to them and does them injury in mind and body. It is far more profitable to talk with others of things which go to work out good. Every sentence you speak is a spiritual force to you and others for good or ill.

Ten minutes spent in growling at your luck, or in growling at others because they have more luck than yourself, means ten minutes of your own force spent in making worse your own health and fortune. Every thought of envy or hatred sent another is a boomerang. It flies back to you and hurts you. The envy or dislike we may feel toward those who, as some express it, " put on airs," the ugly feeling we may have at seeing others riding in carriages and "rolling in wealth,' represents just so much thought (i.e. force) most extravagantly expended, for in its expenditure we get not only unhappiness but destroy future fortune and happiness.

If this has been your common habit or mood of mind, do not expect to get out of it at once. Once you are convinced of the harm done you by such mood, a new force has come to gradually remove the old mind and bring a new one. But all changes must be gradual.

Your own private room is your chief workshop for generating your spiritual force and building yourself up. If it is kept in disorder, if things are flung recklessly about, and you cannot lay your hands instantly upon them, it is an indication that your mind is in the same condition, and therefore your mind as it works on others, in carrying out your projects, will work with less effect and result by reason of its disordered and disorganized condition.

Ill-temper or despondency is a disease. The mind subject to it in any degree a sick mind. The sick mind makes the sick body. The great majority of the sick are not in bed.

When you are peevish, remember your mind is sick. Demand then a well mind.

When you say to yourself, "I am going to have a pleasant visit or a pleasant journey," you are literally sending elements and forces ahead of your body that will arrange things to make your visit or journey pleasant. When before the visit or the journey or the shopping trip you are in a bad humor, or fearful or

apprehensive of something unpleasant, you are sending unseen agencies ahead of you which will make some kind of unpleasantness.
Our thought, or in other words, our state of mind, is ever at work "fixing up "things good or bad for us in advance.

As you cultivate this state of mind more and more you will at last have no need of reminding yourself to get into such mood. Because the mood will have become a part of your everyday nature, and you cannot then get out of it, or prevent the pleasant experiences it will bring you.

Our real self is that which we cannot see, hear, or feel with the physical senses-- our mind. The body is an instrument it uses. We are then made up entirely of forces we call thoughts. When these thoughts are evil or immature they bring us pain and ill-fortune. We can always change them for better thoughts or forces. Earnest steady desire for a new mind (or self) will surely bring the new mind and more successful self. And this will ever be changing through such desire for the newer and ever more successful self.

All of us do really "pray without ceasing." We do not mean by prayer any set formality or form of words. A person who sets his or her mind on the dark side of life, who lives over and over the misfortunes and disappointments of the past, prays for similar misfortunes and disappointments in the future. If you will see nothing but ill luck in the future, you are praying for such ill luck and will surely get it.

You carry into company not only your body, but what is of far more importance, your thought or mood of mind, and this thought or mood, though you say little or nothing, will create with others an impression for or against you, and as it acts on other minds will bring you results favorable or unfavorable according to its character.

What you think is of far more importance than what you say or do. Because your thought never for a moment ceases its action on others or whatever it is placed upon. Whatever you do has been done because of a previous, long held mood or state of mind before such doing.

The thought or mood of mind most profitable in permanent results to you is the desire to do right. This is not sentiment, but science. Because the character of your thought brings to you events, persons, and opportunities with as much certainty as the state of the atmosphere brings rain or dry weather.

To do right is to bring to you the best and most lasting result for happiness. You must prove this for yourself.

Doing right is not, however, doing what others may say or think to be right. If you have no standard of right and wrong of your own, you are acting always on the standard held or made by others.

Your mind is always working and acting on other minds to your advantage or disadvantage whether your body is asleep or awake. Your real being in the form of a thought travels like electricity through space. So when you lay the body down to sleep, see that your mind is in the best mood to get during your physical unconsciousness the best things. For if you go to sleep angry or despondent your thought goes straight to the unprofitable domain of anger or despondency, and will bring to your physical life on awakening, first the element and afterwards that ill success which anger and despondency always attract.

Health is involved in the Biblical adage, " Let not the sun go down on your wrath." Every mood of mind you get into brings to you flesh, bone, and blood of a quality or character like itself. People who from year to year live in moods of gloom or discouragement are building elements of gloom and discouragement into their bodies, and the ill results cannot be quickly removed.

The habit of hurry wears out more bodies and kills more people than is realized. If you put on your shoes hurriedly while dressing in the morning you will be very apt to be in a hurry all day. Pray to get out of the current of hurried thought into that of repose. Hurried methods of doing business lose many thousands of dollars. Power to keep your body strong and vigorous--power to have influence with people worth holding--power to succeed in your undertakings comes of that reposeful frame of mind which while doing relatively little with the body, sees far ahead and clearly in mind.

So, when in the morning, be you man or woman, you look at what is to be done and begin to feel yourself overwhelmed and hurried by the household cares, the writing, the shopping, the people to be seen, the many things to be done, sit right down for thirty seconds and say, " I will not be mobbed and driven in mind by these duties. I will now proceed to do one thing--one thing alone, and let the rest take care of themselves until it is done." The chances are then that the one thing will be done well. If that is done well, so will all the rest. And the current of thought you bring to you in so cultivating this mood will bear you to far more profitable surroundings, scenes, events, and associations than will the semi-insane mood and current of hurry.

All of us believe in many untruths today. It is an unconscious belief. The error is not brought before our minds. Still we go on acting and living in accordance with our unconscious error, and the suffering we may experience comes from that wrong belief.
Demand, then, every day ability to see our wrong beliefs. We need not be discouraged if we see many more than we think we have at present. They cannot be seen and remedied all at once.

Don't take a "tired feeling" or one of languor in the day time for a symptom of sickness. It is only your mind asking for rest from some old rut of occupation.

If your stomach is disordered make your mind responsible for it. Say to yourself, "This disagreeable feeling comes of an error in thought." If you are weak or nervous, don't lay the fault on your body. Say again, "It is a state of my mind which causes this physical ailment, and I demand to get rid of such state and get a better one." If you think any medicine or medical advice will do you good, by all means take it, but mind and keep this thought behind it: " I am taking this medicine not to help my body but as an aid to my spirit,"

Your child is a mind which having lost the body it used in a past physical existence (and possibly of another race and country), has received a new one, as you did in your own infancy.

Tell your child never to think meanly of itself. For if it becomes habituated to such thought, others will feel it and think of the child first and of the grown-up person afterwards as of small value.

Nothing damages the individual more than self-deprecation, and many a child Is weighted down with the elements of failure before it goes into the world through years of scolding, snubbing, and telling it that it is a worthless being.

Tell your child in all its plans to see or think only success. To keep in the permanent mood of expecting success, brings causes, events, and opportunities, which bring success.

Let us also tell this to ourselves very often, for we are but children also, with physical bodies a few years older than the infants.

We have as yet but the vaguest idea of what life really means, and the possibilities it has in store for us. One attribute of the relatively perfected life to come to this race is the retention or preservation of a physical body so long as the mind or spirit desires it. It will be a body also free from pain and sickness, and one which can be made or unmade, put on or taken off, at will.

Say of anything that "it must be done" and you are putting out a mighty unseen power for doing. When your mind is in the mood of ever saying "must," whether you have in mind the particular thing you aim at or not, still that force is ever working on your purpose. But we need to be careful as to what that force of "must" is put on. "Must" without asking for wisdom as to where it shall be placed may bring you terrible results.

Always in your individual aims and purposes defer to the Higher Power and Infinite Wisdom. The thing you may most desire might prove a curse. Be always, then, in the mood of saying, "There is a Power which knows what will bring me the most permanent happiness better than I do. If my desire is not good let it not come, for in its place I shall have something better."

If you send your thought in sympathy to everyone who calls for it, you may have very little left to help yourself. It is necessary to have great care in the choice of those on whom we put our love and thought. One may help build us up; another tear us down. We need to ask for wisdom that we may know whom to receive in close association.

As you are a part of God or the Supreme Power, and a peculiar part, you can always estimate yourself as the very best of such peculiar part. No one else can approach or equal or excel you, as you represent and put out your own peculiar powers, gifts, or shades of mind and character. You will in time command the world of your own mind, and while others may compel your admiration, you will do yourself a great injury if you worship them or abase yourself or grovel before them even in mind.

Idolatry is the blind worship of anything or any body save the Infinite Force from which alone you draw life, power, and inspiration.

The thought of a woman coming to you, or a man, in sympathy or love, with ideas, aims, and aspirations equal to or above yours, may prove to you a source of strength of muscle, health of body, and clearness of mind. His or her thought so flowing to you is a real element. If a man or woman inferior to you mentally is your companion or much in your thought, your mind will be much less clear and your health will eventually suffer.

Be you man or woman, your life cannot be complete and you cannot build yourself rapidly into higher and higher powers until you meet and recognize spiritually your eternal complement or completement in the other sex. And from such complement there is no departure.

When we eat and drink let us remember that with every mouthful we place and build a thought into our selves in accordance with the mood we are in while eating. So be sure to be bright, hopeful, and buoyant while eating, and if you cannot command such mood of mind, pray for it. To ask night and morning of the Supreme Power for the highest wisdom (that is, the greatest good and happiness), and to demand this in that frame of mind which acknowledges the superiority of that Wisdom over your own, is certainly to put yourself in the current of the greatest and most enduring health and prosperity. Because another and better current of thought then begins to act on you and will gradually carry you out of errors and into the right. It will lead you by degrees into different surroundings, different ways of living, and will in time bring you the association you really need and what is best for you.

Chapter 3

Self Teaching; or,

The Art of Learning How to Learn

It is a commonly received opinion, that in youth it is easier to learn than in after years; that at "middle age," or after, the mind becomes, as it were, set in a rut or mould, which does not readily receive new impressions. This idea is expressed in the adage: "You can't teach old dog new tricks."

People have made this a truth by accepting it as a truth. It is not a truth. If your mind is allowed to grow and strengthen, it will learn more easily and quickly than during the infancy of the body. It will learn more and more quickly *how*, to learn any new thing. Learning *how* to learn, learning how to grasp at the principles underlying any art, is a study and a science by itself.

The child, in most cases, does not learn as quickly as many suppose. Think of the years often spent at school, from the age of six to sixteen or eighteen, and how little, relatively, is learned during that period. But this time of life is not regarded as of so much importance as that after eighteen or twenty. He or she would be deemed to have a dull intellect, who should require fourteen years to gain only so much as what a large proportion of children gain from the age of six to twenty.

It is possible for any man or woman whose mind has grown to that degree, that they can acknowledge that every possibility exists within themselves to learn any art, any profession, any business, and become skilled therein, and this even without teachers, and at the period termed "middle age," or after, providing,

First, That they are in living earnest to learn.

Second, That they fight obstinately against the idea of "can't," or that they are too old to learn.

Third, That in all effort to become proficient in their new calling, they cease such effort as soon as it becomes fatiguing or irksome, and that they make of such effort a recreation, and not a drudgery.

Fourth, That they allow no other person to argue, sneer, or ridicule them out of the truth that the human mind can accomplish anything it sets its forces persistently upon.

Fifth, That they keep their minds in the attitude of ever desiring, demanding, praying for whatever quality or trait of character or temperament they need to succeed in their effort; and that whenever the thought of such effort is in mind, it shall be accompanied with this unspoken thought: "I will do what I have set out to do."

There should be no "hard study" at any age. Real "study" is easy and pleasing mental effort; as when you watch the motion of an animal that awakens your curiosity, of a person that interests you. You are studying when you admire and examine the structure of a beautiful flower; you are studying the method and style of an actor or actress when they most hold and compel your attention and admiration. All admiration is in reality study. When you admire anything that is beautiful, your mind is concentrated upon it. You are quite unconsciously examining it. You remember, without effort, many of its features, or characteristics. That unforced examination and attention is study.

To "study hard " is to try to admire; to try to admire is to try to love; to try to love, or to be forced by others to try to love, generally ends in hating the thing or pursuit so forced upon you,--one reason why so often the schoolboy hates "to learn his lesson."

The experience of those who have gone before us in any art, trade, occupation, or profession, is unquestionably valuable, but valuable only as suggestion. There is a great deal laid down as rules and "canons of art" which shackle and repress originality. The idea is constantly, though indirectly, impressed on learners, that the utmost limit of perfection has been reached in some art by some " old master," and that it would be ridiculous to think of surpassing him.

Now, genius knows no "old master." It knows no set form of rules made for it by others. It makes its own rules as it goes along, as did Shakespeare, Byron, and

Scott in literature and the first Napoleon in war; and your mind may have in it the seed of some new idea, discovery, and invention, some new rendering of art in some form, which the world never saw before.

Any man or woman who loves to look at trees and flowers, lakes and rivulets, waves, waterfalls, and clouds, has within him or her the faculty for imitating them in the effects of light, shade, and color,--has, in brief, a taste for painting.

You say, "People to be artists, must have the art born within them." I say, "If they admire the art, they have within them the faculty for advance in that art."

You say, "But because I admire a rose, or a landscape, it is no sign I can ever paint either." I say, "Yes, you can, providing you really want to."

But how! Put your effort on it for an hour, half an-hour, fifteen minutes, a day. Begin. Begin anywhere. Anything in this world will do for a starting point. Begin, and try to imitate on paper a dead leaf, a live one, a stone, a rock, a log, a box, a brickbat. A brickbat lying in the mud has lying with it light, shade and color, and the laws governing them, as much as a cathedral, and is a better foundation than a cathedral to begin on. Begin with the stub of a pencil, on the back of an old envelope. Every minute of such work after beginning is so much practice gained. Every minute before such beginning, providing you intend to begin, and do not, is so much practice lost, as regards that particular art.

Mind, however, you make of such practice a recreation, just as boys do in ball throwing and catching, or as the billiard player does who takes up the cue for half-an-hour, matched only against himself, or as the horseman does who exercises the horse for practice before the race. When the work becomes irksome, when you get out of patience, because your brickbat won't come out on the paper like the original, drop it, wait for your patience-reservoir to fill up, and take for your next copy a log, a tree trunk, or anything else.

You say that you should go to a teacher of this or that art, so that you can become " properly grounded in its principles," and that, by such teacher's aid, you shall avoid blundering and stumbling along, making little or no progress.

Take up any trade, any handicraft, any art, all by yourself, and grope along in it by yourself for a few weeks, and at the end of that time you will have many well-defined and intelligent questions to ask about it, of someone more experienced in it than yourself,--the teacher. That is the time to go to the teacher. The teacher should come in when an interest in the art or study is awakened. To have him before is like answering questions before they are asked.

You cannot teach a dog to paint. The intelligence using the dog's organization has not grown to an appreciation of such imitation of natural objects. But you can teach him to draw a cart, to "point" to game in the cover, to swim out to the water-fowl you have shot, and bring it to you. Why? Because the dog has these instincts, or desires, born in him. The trainer, his teacher, brings them out. Some men and women have no more admiration for a beautiful landscape than the dog. Of course, neither can ever be taught to paint, because they have not the desire to paint, nor the admiration of the thing to be painted.
"Then, whatever a man or woman really desires to do, is to be taken as some proof that they can do it? " you ask. "Yes; that is the exact idea." *Desire to accomplish is a proof of ability to accomplish.* Of course, such ability may be weighted down and kept back by many causes, such as ill-health of body, ill-health of mind, unfavorable surroundings, and, perhaps, greatest of all, utter ignorance that such desire is a proof of the possession of power to accomplish the thing desired.

How did you learn to walk, and how did you learn to talk? Could anyone have taught you, if desire to walk and talk had not been born with you? Did you go to a walking teacher, or a talking teacher? Did you not learn both accomplishments after ten thousand failures? So far as you can remember, was it not rather an amusement than otherwise, to learn both, or at least, was there any idea of work associated with these early efforts?

You place a boy or girl by the water-side, and give them full liberty, and they will learn to swim as naturally as they learn to walk, because the desire to swim is in them. If, after learning, they see a better swimmer, they will naturally try to imitate him; and all this endeavor, from first to last, will be for them far more recreation than work. The better swimmer who comes along represents the teacher; and the boy and girl who can already swim fairly well, and are anxious to swim better, represent pupils who are in a condition to be taught.

Think for a moment, how much it was necessary to teach your body in training it to walk. First, to balance yourself upright on two feet without falling. Secondly, to balance yourself on one foot without falling. Thirdly, to move the body.

Fourthly, to give it the direction in which you wanted to go. And yet we call walking a "mechanical," and not a mental, effort.

If you are determined to paint, and love the creations of nature and art well enough to try and imitate them, you will be constantly studying effects in light and shade on rocks, stones, cliffs, towers, steeples. You will observe and study, and be rejoiced at the many changing aspects and colors of the sky, as you never were before. You will discover, as you continue to observe, that nature has a different shade of color for every day of the year, and almost every hour of the day. You will suddenly find in all this a new and permanent recreation, without money and without price. You will then find new interests and new sources of amusement in studying the works of painters and their methods, which will be revealed to you just so fast as your appreciation *grows* up to them.

The same principle will apply to any branch of mechanics or art,--to anything. Of course, it is best to pursue that for which you have the most inclination, that is, admiration. If you are in any occupation that does not suit you, and you want to engage in some art that does suit you, if you have fifteen minutes in the day to spare, begin on that art.

If it is painting, paint a brickbat in some idle moment as well as you can, and only as a means of amusement. If it is carving, you have always the means for practice, if you have a jack-knife and a bit of wood. If it be music, a banjo or guitar with but a single string will give you means for practice. For you must commence in the simplest way, even as you crept before you walked. There must be imperfect effort before there can be relatively perfect result.

Because, when you do so begin, you begin to practice with one instrument far more ingenious and complicated than any you can buy for use in your art; namely, your mind.
If we begin in this way, we begin something else; we begin drawing toward us ways, means, helps, and agencies unseen, but powerful, to help us. We are not to expect success in an hour, a day, a month, a year. But if we persist, a relative success is coming all the while. The effort of this month is better than that of last. There may come periods of weariness and discouragement; periods when, as we look back, we seem to have made no advance; periods, in fact, when we seem to have gone back, when we seem to be doing worse than at the start; periods when we lose all interest in the work. It makes us sick to look at it, even to think of

taking it up again; and a certain sense of guilt at our neglect intensifies the sickness.

That is a mistake. If, in our music, our painting, our profession, our business, be it what it may, we strive for some certain result, and fail, time after time, and week after week, to affect it, yet we are still advancing towards it.

We may not see such advance. That is because the advance is not in the direction we think it should be. There may be a screw loose in a part of our mental being that we have taken no note of, which keeps us back. That screw, in very many cases, lies in the state of mind in which we take up our work or pursuit.

We may be too anxious or impatient. We take up the pen, the brush, or the tool, in a hurried frame of mind. We want to do too many things at once. Or we endeavor to crowd the doing of several things in too short a limit of time. Or we are unable to dismiss all thought, save what bears on the effort now in hand.

All such moods are destructive to the best effort. They take much of our force from that effort. A common result is that we can do nothing to suit us. We throw down our work in disgust. We may not take it up again for weeks. We do take it up at last, perhaps, in a listless, indifferent frame of mind. We do not then set our hearts on doing anything perfect, or making it come up to our ideal in a moment, and that Is the very time when we produce some new effect; when we hit the idea we have aimed at; when we are surprised at the apparently accidental development of a new power within us.

There is a great mystery in this,--a mystery we may never solve,--the mystery that whatever purpose this power within us we call mind sets itself upon, fixes itself upon persistently, that purpose it is accomplishing, that purpose it is carrying out, that purpose it is ever drawing nearer to itself, not only when we work for it with the body and the intellect; we are also *growing ever towards it when it seems for the time forgotten*, or when we are asleep.

That persistent purpose, that strong desire, that never-ceasing longing, is a seed in the mind. It is rooted there. It is alive. It never stops growing. Why this is so, we may never know. Perhaps it is not desirable to know. It is enough to know that it is so. There is a wonderful law involved in it. This law, when known, followed out, and trusted, leads every individual to mighty and beautiful results.

This law, followed with our eyes open, leads to more and more happiness in life; but followed blindly, involuntarily with our eyes shut, leads to misery.

To succeed in any undertaking, any art, any trade, any profession, simply keep it ever persistently fixed in mind as an aim, and then study to treat all effort towards it as play, recreation. The moment it becomes "hard work," we are not advancing. I mean by "play," that both body and mind work easily and pleasantly. It matters not what a man or woman is doing, whether digging sand or scrubbing floors, when the mind is interested in that work and the muscles are full of strength, such work is play, and is more apt to be well done. When the muscles are exhausted of their power, and will alone drives the body forward, the occupation soon becomes work, drudgery, and is much the more apt to be ill done. I begin low down in illustration, as low as sand, mud, brickbats; but the principle is the same, be the worker a hod-carrier or a Michelangelo.

The science of learning to learn, then, involves largely that of making recreation of all effort. This is not as easy as it may seem. It involves a continual prayer for patience, patience, patience.

"Patience to play?" you ask. Yes. When we are amused by any effort of our own, be it effort of the eye, in seeing sights that please it, or effort of the ear, in hearing sounds that please it, or effort of muscle in exercising them, that is the very time when we are most attentive and most absorbed. The very time when we forget there is such a thing as patience, is the very time we most exercise patience.

That is the mood we need to cultivate. Because moods of mind determine the character and quality of effort. The painter writes out his mood in his picture; a mistake, a blur, a defect, a daub, may write out in that picture too much hurry to get ahead. He took up his brush, possibly, full of irritation, because his wife asked him for more money for household expenses; result, he puts a woman in that picture twelve feet high as proportioned to other objects, when she should have been but four. What put on that extra and needless eight feet? A mood born of household expenses. Or the scrubber wrote out her mood of mind on the floor. Where? In that neglected corner, where the last dust of summer lingers alone. Why? Because her mood of hurry to be through with her work is there written; or her mood of dishonesty, in doing as little as possible for the money to be received; or her mood of anxiety concerning the sick child, left at home in some squalid tenement; or the poor woman's mood born of physical weakness, in thus trying to do a man's work, with no nutritious food in her stomach, and no money to buy any till the work is done.

My very practical friend, you who despise all "art flummery," all and everything that is not "business," and smells of wood, or stone, or leather, or bank-bills, this cultivation of the mood is of vast importance to you, also; because, when you meet your brother Hard Cash, to have a wrangle over bargain and sale, the man who is in the coolest mood, the most collected mood, the mood most free of other thought, or care, the man who is in the least hurry, the man who throws overboard all anxiety as to results, the man who is not too eager, who can lie back in his chair and make a joke or laugh at you, when millions are trembling in the balance, who keeps all his reserve force till it is needed, that is the man who can play the best hand in your game, and make the best bargain. That is the man who gains his end by some knowledge of spiritual law; and spiritual law can be used for all purposes, and purposes relatively low as well as high; and in some things the wicked, so-called, of today, are better informed in certain phases of spiritual law than those who call themselves good.

How shall we get ourselves, then, into the most desirable mood for doing our best? By praying for it, asking for it, demanding it, in season and out of season. We can wish an earnest desire in a second, no matter where we are. That is a prayer. It is a thought that goes out, and does its work in bringing us another atom of the quality desired. That atom is never lost. It adds itself to and adds its strength to all the other atoms of the same quality so gained. So you call this simple? Is the method too easy? Remember, we are indeed fearfully and wonderfully made; and when Solomon wrote this he had an inkling of the existence of powers wrapped up in human bodies, that startled him, and would us, did we more fully realize them.

Possibly this question may be asked: "What is the use of cultivating, or encouraging others to cultivate any form of art, when for thousands the struggle is so hard today for bread?" Or, in other words, "What is the use of educating people to wants and desires they cannot satisfy?" Or, "What bearing and benefit has art cultivation in righting the 'great wrongs' of the hour?"

It is of the greatest possible benefit. Art, art appreciation, art cultivation, refines human nature. Refinement demands finer surroundings, finer food, finer houses, cleaner houses, cleaner clothes, cleaner skin. You can't make people clean, neat, tasteful, by telling them they "ought" to be so. They must have brought out of them some calling, some occupation, some work which will implant ever-increasing desire for more of the elegancies of life. Much of what is called the "oppression" of the strong over the weak, the rich over the poor, comes because so many of the poor do not aspire above a pig-pen under the window, a mud-puddle in the back-yard, and a front garden growing tomato cans, dead cats, and old hoop-skirts. Much of the money today given in charity to the poor, is really poured from one rich man's pocket into that of another, and relieves only a temporary distress.

You roll half a ton of coal this winter into the poor man's cellar. His family is warmed for the hour. The profits go into the safe of the coal corporation. Its heat warms human beings with little ambition above animals. You encourage that man's boy or girl to paint ever so roughly with the cheapest of watercolors, to mould forms in clay, to have any faculty awakened which shall show them what a beautiful world they really live in, and soon with this there may come a growing distaste for the mud-puddle in the back-yard, and the display of hoopskirts and tomato cans in the front. Show these children that they have within them more or less of this mighty and mysterious element--mind, and that through its exercise they can become almost anything to which they aspire, and that the more of the Infinite Spirit they call to themselves, the more will the have to strengthen, beautify, enrich, invigorate, and electrify their souls and bodies, and you have then started them on the road of doing for themselves, by the powers in themselves. They are then on a road leading away from both charitable soup-kitchens and gin-shops.

If they cultivate the love of grace and beauty in any direction, they cultivate also an ability for expressing such grace and beauty. If they follow the law of persistent demand for improvement in such grace or beauty, whether it be by the exercise of pen or tongue, of painting or sculpture, or self-command, or polish of manner, or the art of actor, elocutionist. musician, or worker on stone, worker in metal, cultivator of plant, tree, flower, they will at last do something a *little better* than anyone else can do, in their peculiar way, and through their self-taught, peculiar method; and when they can do this, the world will gladly come to them, and bring them its dollars and cents, for what they can please it with.

None of us know what is in us till we try to bring it out; A man, or woman, may go their whole life with some wonderful power, some remarkable talent which would benefit and please mankind, feeling it ever from time to time, struggling for expression in a desire to use it, in a longing to express it, yet having it ever forced back by that fatal thought, "I can't."

"It's no use." "It's ridiculous, the idea of my aspiring to such a thing." We are treasure boxes, holding wondrous powers. We brought these treasures with us into the world from an immeasurably far-off past--a past we may not compute--a past the spirit, born into being, the tiniest atom, the faintest movement, drawing to itself ever, age after age, through unconscious exercise of desire or demand, more and more of power, more and more of complex organization, more and more of variety of talent, more and more of the marvelous power coming through combination and re-combination of element, until at last the man is born, the woman is born, blind at first, blind as millions now are regarding the wealth within them; blind to faith and belief in themselves, until the veil is pulled from their eyes, and then they shall soon spring up into gods, destined to a career of eternal life, eternal growth, and eternal and illimitable happiness.

Chapter 4

Love Thyself

Christ's Precepts say: "Love thy neighbor as thyself." Some people incline to forget the two last words "as thyself," and infer that we should love others even better than ourselves. So far has this idea been carried that it has led in cases to entire sacrifice and neglect of self so that good may be done to others. There is a justifiable and righteous love for self. There can be no true spiritual growth without this higher love for self. Spiritual growth implies the cultivation and increase of every faculty and talent. It means the making of the symmetrically developed man and woman. Spiritual growth, fostered by unceasing demand of the Supreme Power, will bring power to keep the body in perfect health--so as to escape pain and disease--and will eventually carry man above the present limited conditions of mortality. The higher love of self benefits others as well as ourselves.

When we love a person, we send that person our quality of thought. If it is the aspiring order of thought, it is for that person a literal element and agency of life and health in proportion to his or her capacity for absorbing and assimilating it. If we think meanly of ourselves--if we are beggarly in spirit--and are content to live on the bounty of others, if we care little for our personal appearance --if we are willing to get money by questionable means--if we believe there is no Supreme and overruling Power, governing our lives by an exact law, but that everything is left to chance, and that life is only a scramble for existence, we send in thought such beliefs to that person, and if our love is accepted it is only a means to drag down instead of a power to elevate.

How can we send the highest love to another if we do not have it for ourselves? If we are careless and unappreciative of the body's great use to us--if we never give it a thought of admiration or gratitude for the many functions which it performs for us --if we regard it with the same indifference that we may have for the post to which we hitch a horse, we shall send that same quality of sentiment and thought to the person of whom we think most, and the tendency will be to generate a similar disregard for themselves. Either they will do this, or seeking light of the Infinite, they will find themselves obliged in self-protection to refuse the love which we send them, because of its coarser and grosser quality. This is sometimes the error of mothers, who say: " I don't care for myself so that my son or daughter's welfare is assured. I give and devote my whole life to them."

This means: "I am content to grow old and unattractive, I am content to slave and drudge so that my children may receive a good education and shine in society. I am an old and decaying weather-beaten hulk and can't hold together much longer; the best use which I can make of myself is to serve as a sort of foot-bridge for them in the shape of nurse, grandmother and overseer of the nursery and kitchen, while they are playing their parts in society." The daughter receives this thought with the mother's inferior, self-neglecting love. She absorbs and assimilates it. It becomes part of her being. She lives it, acts it out, and thirty years afterwards is saying and doing the same and laying herself upon the shelf with the rest of the cracked teapots for her own daughter's sake.

Ancestral traits of character, as bequeathed and transmitted from parent to child, are the thoughts of the parent absorbed by the child. When in thought, desire and aspiration we make the most of what the Infinite has given us (inclusive of these wonderful bodies), we shall have continual increase, and such increase will overflow of its own accord and benefit others. The highest love for self means justice to self. If we are unjust to ourselves, we shall be unavoidably unjust to those to whom we are of the greatest value. A general who should deprive himself of necessary food and give all his bread and meat to a hungry soldier, might in so doing weaken his body, and with his body weaken his mental faculties, lessen his capacity for command, thereby increasing the chances for the destruction of his entire army.

What is most necessary to know, and what the Infinite will show us if we demand, is the value which we are to others. In proportion to our power for increasing human happiness, and in proportion as we recognize that power, will the needful agencies come to us for making our material condition more comfortable. No man or woman can do their best work for themselves or others who lives in a hovel, dresses meanly and starves the spirit by depriving it of the gratification of its finer tastes. Such persons will always carry the atmosphere and influence of the hovel with them, and that is brutalizing and degrading. If the Infinite worked on such a basis, would the heavens show the splendor of the suns? Would the fields reflect that glory in the myriad hues of leaf and flower, in plumage of bird and hue of rainbow?

What in many cases prevents the exercise of this higher love and justice to self is the thought; "What will others say, and how will others judge me, if I give myself what I owe to myself?" That is, you must not ride in your carriage until every needy relative has a carriage also. The general must not nourish his body properly because the hungry soldier might say that he was rioting in excess. When we appeal to the Supreme and our life is governed by a principle, we are not actuated both fear of public opinion or love of others' approbation, and we may be sure that the Supreme will sustain us. If in any way we try to live to suit others, we shall never suit them; the more we try, the more unreasonable and exacting do they become. The government of your life is a matter which lies entirely between God and yourself; when your life Is swayed and influenced from any other source you are on the wrong path.

Very few people really love themselves. Very few really love their own bodies with the higher love. That higher love puts ever-increasing life in the body and ever-increasing capacity to enjoy life. Some place all their love on the apparel which they place on their bodies; some on the food they put in their bodies; some on the use or pleasure they can get from their bodies. That is not real love for self which gluts the body with food or keeps it continually under the influence of stimulants. It is not a real love for self which indulges to excess in any pleasure to be obtained from the body. The man who racks and strains his body and mind in the headlong pursuit of pleasures or business, loves that business or art unwisely. He has no regard for the instrument on which he is dependent for the materialization of his ideas. This is like the mechanic who should allow a costly tool, by which he is enabled to do rare and elaborate work, to rust or be otherwise injured through neglect. That is not the highest love for self which puts on its best and cleanest apparel when it goes out to visit or promenade and wears ragged or soiled clothes indoors. That is love of the opinion or approbation of others. Such a person only dresses physically. There is a spiritual dressing of the body when the mind in which apparel is put on is felt by others. Whoever has it in any degree will show it in a certain style of carrying his clothes which no tailor can give.

The miser does not love himself. He loves money better than self. To live with a half-starved body, to deny self of every luxury, to get along with the poorest and cheapest things, to deprive self of amusement and recreation in order to lay up money, is surely no love for the whole self. The miser's love is all in his money-bags, and his body soon shows how little love is put in it. Love Is an element as literal as air or water. It has many grades of quality with different people. Like gold, it may be mixed with grosser element. The highest and purest love comes to him or her who is most in communion and oneness with the Infinite Mind, is ever demanding of the Infinite Mind more and more of its wisdom. The regard and thought of such persons is of great value to anyone on whom it is directed. And such persons will, through that wisdom, be wisely economical of their sympathy for others and put a great deal of this higher love into themselves in order to make the most of themselves.

Some people infer from their religious teachings that the body and its functions are inherently vile and depraved; that they are a clog and an encumbrance to any higher and more divine life; that they are corruptible "food for worms," destined to return to dust and molder in the earth. It has been held that the body should be mortified, that the flesh should be crucified and starved and subjected to rigorous penance and pains for its evil tendencies. Even youth, with its freshness, beauty, vigor and vivacity, has been held as almost a sin, or as a condition especially prone to sin. When a person in any way mortifies and crucifies the body, either by starving it, dressing meanly, or living in bare and gloomy surroundings, he generates and literally puts in the body the thought of hatred for itself. Hatred of others or of self is a slow thought-poison. A hated body can never be symmetrical or healthy. The body is not to be refined and purged of the lower and animal tendencies being made responsible and continually blamed these sins--by being counted as a clod and an encumbrance, which it is fortunate at last to shake off.

Religion, so-called, has in the past made a scapegoat of the body, accused it of every sin, and, in so doing and thinking, has filled it with sin. As one result, the professors of such religion have suffered pain and sickness. Their bodies have decayed, and death has often been preceded by long and painful illness. "By their fruits ye shall know them." The fruits of such a faith and condition of mind prove error therein.

There is a mind of the body--a carnal or material mind--a mind belonging to the instrument used by the spirit. It is a mind or thought lower or crude than that of the spirit. But this mind of the body need not, as has been held, be ever at war with the higher mind of the spirit. It can, through demand of the Infinite, be made in time to act in perfect accord with the spirit. The Supreme Power can and will send us a supreme love for the body. That love we need to have. Not to love one's body is not to love one expression of the Infinite Mind.

We are not inferring that you "ought" to have more than reasonable love for your body, or that you "ought" in any respect to do or act differently from your deeds, acts and thoughts as they are at present. Regarding others, "ought" is a word and idea with which we have nothing to do. There is no reason in saying to a blind man: "You ought to see." There is no more reason in saying to anyone: "You ought not to have this or that defect of character." Whatever our mental condition may be at present, which we must act out. A man cannot, of his individual self, put an atom more of the element of love in himself than he now has. Only the Infinite Mind can do that. Whatever of in character and belief we have today, we shall act out today in thought or deed. But we need not always have that mind.

The Overruling Mind will, as we demand, give us new minds, new truths, new beliefs, and as these supplant and drive out old errors there will come corresponding changes for the better, in both mind and body. And these ever-improving changes have no end. There is to these changes but one gate, as there is but one road. That gate and road lie in an unceasing demand of the Infinite to perfect us in Its way.

"There is a natural body, and there is a spiritual body." In other words, we have a body of physical element which can be seen and felt, and we have another body which is intangible to our physical senses. When we are able to love, cherish and admire our physical body as one piece of God's handiwork, we are putting such higher love-element not only into that physical body but also into the spiritual body. We cannot of ourselves make this quality of love. It can come to us only through demand of the Infinite. It is not vanity or that lower pride which values more whatever effect its own grace and beauty may have on others than it values that grace and beauty. The higher love for the body will attend as carefully to its external adornment in the solitude of the forest as it would in the crowded city. It will no more debase itself by any vulgar act in privacy than it would before a multitude.

God gives one personal beauty and symmetry in physical proportions, should not he or she, thus favored with a gift from the Supreme, admire these endowments? Is it vanity to love and seek to improve and increase any talent which we may find in ourselves? If God made man and woman "in His own image," is it an image to be loved and admired, or regarded with hatred and distrust? Why, the religious belief of less than a hundred years ago actually courted ugliness, and inferred that it was more creditable than beauty. Had some of those solemn-faced professors been delegated to make an angel after their own ideal, they would have turned out a duplicate of themselves.

The Infinite, as we demand, will give us wisdom and light to know what we owe to ourselves. People have been over-ridden with the idea of their duties to parent, relative or friend. The road to heaven has been marked out as one full of sacrifice and self-denial for the sake of others, and of little good or pleasure for self. If Christ should be taken as an example in this respect, we find a very different course inferred. When charged with lack of attention to his mother, he asked; "Who is my mother?" When the young man pleads, as an excuse for not immediately following Christ, that filial duty demanded he should go and bury his father, the Messenger of a new and higher law said: "Let the dead bury their dead." In other words: If father or mother or sister or brother are steeped in a lifelong course of trespass and sin--if their lives have been one continual violation of spiritual law, bringing the inevitable penalty of disease and pain--if they are hardened and fossilized in their false beliefs, and regard your opinions as visionary and impractical you cannot, without injury, have fellowship with them. If you pretend for the sake of peace to agree with them, you are living a lie, and when you act or live a lie you materialize it and put it in your body, where it is a breeder of pain and unrest.

If others cannot see the law of life as clearly as you, and in their blindness go stumbling on and filling themselves with decay and disease, it is not in the line of the highest justice that you should be called on to nurse them every time that they are sick, to absorb their sick and unhealthy thought, to give them your life and vitality (for this you do when you think much of any one), and to be dragged down with them. You are not responsible for their blindness, nor can you open their eyes and make them see what is proven to you to be truth. Only the Infinite can do that. You do those who are in this lower and material current of thought no real good in ministering to them physically or spiritually. You may, having the stronger mind, bolster them up for a time, and, throwing your mind in theirs, you may give them your strength, but you cannot do this always, and when your influence is removed, as some time it must be, they will fall back to their old condition. What then have you accomplished You have taken so much force out of yourself that you owed to yourself; you have taught them to depend on you and not on what everyone must learn to depend on--the Supreme Power. Let the dead then, who are still above ground, bury their dead. Give them a thought and wish for their highest welfare whenever you do think of them, but leave them in God's care.

When you put the Higher Love into yourself --when you reserve your forces to raise yourself higher in the scale of being--when it is your aim and unceasing, silent prayer to be raised out of the current of the lower and material thought into that spiritual condition beyond the reach of physical disease--when you aspire to have every sense and faculty refined and strengthened beyond the present lot of mortals--when you begin to realize, through the proofs coming to you, that these are possibilities, then you are a real benefit to everyone. You are then proving a law. You are showing that there is a road out of the ills which afflict humanity, and when others, seeing these things evidenced in your own life, ask how you obtain them, you can reply: " I have grown, and am ever growing, into a higher and happier condition of mind and body, through knowledge of a law, and that law is as much for you to live by as for me." You may be able to say: " I believe in the existence of the Great Overruling Power which will show me ever the happier way of life as I demand wisdom of that Power. I had little faith in the existence of that Power at first, but I was prompted to pray or demand ability to see its reality. Now my faith in its reality is growing firmer."

To throw our whole being, care and thought into the welfare of others, no matter who they may be, without first asking of the Supreme if it be the wisest thing to do, is a sin, for it is an endeavor to use the forces given us by that Power as we think best. The result is damage to self and a great lessening of ability to do real good to others. Between the Supreme Mind and ourselves there should exist a love which is at once a love of ourselves and a love of that Mind. We must love what we draw from it, since what we draw and make part of self is drawn from God, and is a part of God. Every thought which we give to the Supreme Wisdom enriches us and directs us in the lasting path of happiness. Every thought which we give to others who are not actuated by the Higher Wisdom is unwisely bestowed. That Wisdom will direct our thought, love and sympathy to those on whom it can be bestowed without injury. To have our thoughts ever flowing spontaneously toward the Infinite Mind is to be one with God and a wise lover of self, as we feel ourselves more and more parts of God manifest in the flesh.

If we give sympathy and aid, material or moral, to others as they call for it, and without reservation or judgment, people will take all that we have to give and come open-mouthed for more. They will keep this up until we are exhausted. No outsider will put a limit to your giving. You must do that yourself. What is called "generous impulse" is sometimes another name for extravagance and injustice to somebody. Those who fling money to servitors and overpay largely for trifling services often owe that money to others, or they may owe it to themselves. In the really spiritual domain of being, we find this injustice perpetrated. on a still larger scale. Sympathetic natures sometimes give their whole lives to others. Giving thus their life and force to others becomes a fixed habit. They grow unable to restrain or control their sympathy. It overflows at everybody's call. They deprive themselves of things really needed and take up with the poorest in order to satisfy a mania for the squandering of time, force, effort and thought on others. A widely spread idea prevails that we can never give too much or do too much for others. It argues that salvation is more readily attained by such reckless expenditure of self than in any other way. No matter how barren it makes our lives--no matter of how much we deprive ourselves, it is to be made up to us tenfold in time.

We deem this a great mistake. We believe there is a Divine Economy which orders that when we give even our thought, we must give only as much as will really benefit others. Reckless prodigality throws dollars to children when cents would do them as much good. Reckless prodigality of sympathy (force) often gives ten times more to a person than that person can appropriate. What people cannot appropriate is lost for them, and when you have sent it once out you cannot recall it.

Undoubtedly to some, the idea of giving so much love to self will seem very cold, hard and unmerciful. Still this matter may be seen in a different light, when we find that "looking out for Number One," as directed by the Infinite, is really looking out for Number Two and is indeed the only way to permanently benefit Number Two. The gifts conferred by the Supreme Power are "perfect gifts," and a "perfect gift" once received by us goes out and benefits many others. So soon as one person on this planet receives the "perfect gift" of immortality in the flesh, involving perfect health and freedom from all pain and disease, that gift will be contagious, for health is catching as well as disease. The cornerstone of all symmetrical growth and constant increase of mental and physical power is the reservation and care of our thought-forces. This wisdom can only come as we demand it of the Supreme Power.

I am often asked: "How do you know what you assert?" Or: "Have you proved these assertions to yourself?" I know what I assert to be true, because I have seen its beneficial results as regards health and condition in life made evident. Other proofs are constantly coming. But what is clear to me is really no permanently convincing demonstration to any other person. That kind of proof you can only get from yourself and by the exercise and growth of your share of power given you by the Infinite. In the physical world we can safely accept the statement of a navigator who asserts his discovery of a new island. The island looks the same to every physical eye. But on the spiritual side of life spiritual things do not appear the same to all eyes. There are, so to speak, spiritual islands and spiritual realities which one person can see and another cannot see. You will see and get proof of these in proportion as you grow, and very possibly when you tell these things to others, they will call you a visionary, or will ascribe the material proof of such growth to some material cause. In the spiritual life every person is his or her own discoverer, and you need not be grieved if your discoveries are not believed in by others. It is not your business to argue and prove them to others. It is your business to push on, finding more and increase of your own individual happiness. Christ said to those of his time: "Though one rose from the dead you would not believe him." In this respect the world has not much changed since Christ used a material body on Earth.

Chapter 5

The Art of Forgetting

In the chemistry of the future, thought will be recognized as substance even as the acids, oxides and all other chemicals of today.

There is no chasm betwixt what we call the material and spiritual. Both are of substance or element. They blend imperceptibly into each other. In reality the material is only a visible form of the finer elements which we call spiritual.

Our unseen and unspoken thought is ever flowing from us, an element and force, real as the stream of water which we can see, or the current of electricity which we cannot see. It blends with the thought of others, and out of such combination new qualities of thought are formed, as in the mixture of chemicals there are formed new substances.

If you send from you in thought the elements of worry, fret, hatred or grief, you are putting in action forces that are injurious to your mind and body. The power to forget implies the power of driving the unpleasant and hurtful thought or element, and bringing in its place the profitable element, to build up instead of tearing us down.

The character of thought which we think or put out affects our business favorably or unfavorably, It influences others for or against us. It is an element felt pleasantly or unpleasantly by others, inspiring them with confidence or distrust.

The prevailing state of mind, or character of thought, shapes the body and features. It makes us ugly or pleasing, attractive or repulsive to others. Our thought shapes our gestures, our mannerism, and our walk. The least movement of muscle has a mood of mind, a thought, behind it. A mind always determined has always a determined walk. A mind always weak, shifting, vacillating and uncertain, makes a shuffling, shambling, uncertain gait. The spirit of determination braces every nerve and sinew; the thought-element of determination fills every muscle.

Look at the discontented, gloomy, melancholy and ill-tempered men or women, who manifest in their faces the operation of the silent force, which is their unpleasant thought, cutting, carving and shaping them to their present expression. Such people are never in good health, for that force acts on them as poison, and creates some form of disease. A persistent thought of determination on some purpose, especially if such purpose be of benefit to others as well as ourselves, will fill every nerve with strength. It is a wise selfishness that works to benefit others along with ourselves. In spirit, and in actual element, we are all united. We are forces which act and re-act on each other, for good or ill, through what ignorantly we call "empty space." There are unseen nerves extending from man to man, from being to being. Every form of life is in this sense connected together. We are all "members of one body." An evil thought or act is a pulsation of pain thrilling through myriads of organizations. The kindly thought and act have the same effect for pleasure. It is, then, a law of nature and of science that we cannot do a real good for another without doing one also to ourselves.

To grieve at any loss, be it of friend or property, weakens mind and body. It is no help to the friend grieved for. It is rather an injury; for our sad thought must reach its object, even if passed to another condition of existence, and is a source of pain to that person.

An hour of grumbling, fret, or fear, whether spoken or silent, uses up so much element or force in making us less endurable to others, and perhaps making for us enemies. Directly or indirectly, it injures our business. Sour looks and words drive away good customers. Grumbling or hating is a use of actual element to belabor our minds. The force which we may so expend could be put to our pleasure and profit; even as the force we might use with a club to beat our own body can be employed to give us comfort and recreation.

To be able, then, to throw off (or forget) a thought or force which is injuring us, is a most important means of gaining strength of body and clearness of mind. Strength of body and clearness of mind bring success in all undertakings.

They bring also strength of spirit; and the forces of our spirits act on others whose bodies are thousands of miles distant, for our advantage or disadvantage. The reason is that there is a force belonging to all of us, separate and apart from that of the body. It is ever in action, and ever acting on others. It must be in operation at each moment, whether the body be asleep or awake. Ignorantly, unconsciously and hence unwisely used, it plunges us into mires of misery and error. Intelligently and wisely used, it will bring us every conceivable good.

That force is our thought. Every thought of ours is of vital importance to health and true success. And so-called success, as the world terms it, is not real. A fortune gained at the cost of health is not a real success.
Every mind trains itself, generally unconsciously, to its peculiar character or quality of thought. Whatever that training is, it cannot be immediately changed. We may have trained our minds unconsciously to nourish evil or troubled thought. We may never have realized that brooding over disappointment, living in a grief, dreading a loss, fretting for fear this or that might not succeed as we wish, was building up a destructive force which has bled away our strength, created disease, unfitted us for business, and caused us loss of money and possibly loss of friends.

To learn to forget is as necessary and useful as to learn to remember. We think of many things every day which it would be more profitable not to think of at all. The ability to forget is the ability to drive away the unseen force (thought) which Is injuring us, and to change it for a force (or order of thought) which can benefit us.

Demand imperiously and persistently any quality of character in which you may be lacking, and you will attract increase of such quality. Demand more patience or decision, more judgment or courage, more hopefulness or exactness, and you will increase in such qualities. These qualities are real elements. They belong to the subtler, and as yet unrecognized, chemistry of Nature.

The discouraged, hopeless and whining man has unconsciously demanded discouragement and hopelessness. So he gets it. This is his unconscious mental training for evil. Mind is "magnetic," because it attracts to itself whatever thought it fixes itself upon, or that to which it opens itself. Give space to fear, and you will fear more and more. Cease to resist its tendency, make no effort to forget it, and you open the door and invite fear in; you then demand fear. Set your mind on the thought of courage, see yourself in mind or imagination as courageous, and you will become more stout of heart. You demand courage.

There is no limit in unseen nature to the supply of these spiritual qualities. In the words: "Ask and ye shall receive," the Christ implied that any mind could, through demanding, draw to itself all that it needed of any quality. Demand wisely, and we draw to us the best.

Every second of wise demand brings an increase of power. Such increase is never lost to us. This is an effort for lasting gain that we can use at any time. What all of us want is more power to work results, and build up our fortunes,--power to make things about us more comfortable, to ourselves and our friends. We cannot feed others if we have no energy to keep starvation from ourselves. The power to do this is a different thing from the power to hold in memory other people's opinions, or a collection of so-called facts gathered from books, which time often proves to be fictions. Every success in any grade of life has been accomplished through spiritual power, through unseen force flowing from one mind, working on other minds far and near, and as real as the force in your arm which lifts a stone.

A man may be illiterate, yet he may send from his mind a force affecting and influencing many others, far and near, in a way to benefit his fortunes, while the scholarly man drudges with his brain on a pittance. The illiterate man's is then a greater spiritual power. Intellect is not a bag to hold facts. Intellect is power to work results. Writing books is but a fragment of the work of intellect. The greatest philosophers have planned first, and acted afterwards, as did Columbus, Napoleon, Fulton, Morse, Edison and others, who have moved the world, besides telling the world how it should be moved.

Your plan, purpose or design, whether relating to a business or an invention, is a real construction of unseen thought-element. Such thought-structure is also a magnet. It commences to draw aiding forces to it so soon as made. Persist in holding to your plan or purpose and these forces come nearer and nearer; they become stronger and stronger, and will bring more and more favorable results.

Abandon your purpose, and you stop the further approach of these forces, destroying also so much of unseen attracting power as you have already built up. Success in any business depends on the application of this law. Persistent resolve on any purpose is a real attractive force or element, drawing constantly more and more aids for carrying out that resolve.

When your body is in the state called sleep, these forces (your thoughts) are still active. They are then working on other minds. If your last thought before sleep is that of worry, of anxiety, of hatred for anyone, it will work for you only ill results. If it is hopeful, cheerful, confident and at peace with all men, it is then the stronger force, and will work for you good results. If the sun goes down on your anger, that wrathful thought will act on others, while you sleep, and bring only injury in return.

Is it not a necessity, then, to cultivate the power of forgetting what we wish, so that the current which attracts the ill, while our body rests, shall be changed to the current which attracts the good alone? Today thousands on thousands never think of controlling the character of their thought. They allow their minds to drift. They never say of a thought that is troubling them: "I won't think of it." Unconsciously then they demand what works them ill, and their bodies are made sick by the kind of thought on which they allow their minds to fasten.

When you realize the injury done you through any kind of troubled thought, you will then commence to acquire the power of casting it aside. When in mind you commence to resist such injurious thought, you are constantly gaining more and more power for resistance. "Resist the devil," said the Christ, "and he will flee from you." There are no devils save the ill-used forces of the mind. But these are most powerful to afflict and torture us. An ugly or melancholy mood of mind is a devil. It can make us sick, lose us friends, and lose us money. Money means the enjoyment of necessities and comforts. Without these we cannot do or be our best. The sin involved in "love of money" is to love money better than the things needful which money can bring.

To bring to us the greatest success in any business, to make the greatest advance in any art, to further any cause, it is absolutely necessary that at certain daily intervals we should forget all about that business, art or cause. By so doing we rest our minds, and gather fresh force for renewed effort.

To be ever revolving the same plan, study or speculation, what we shall do or shall not do, is to waste such force on a brain-treadmill. We are in thought saying to ourselves the same thing over and over again. We are building of this actual, unseen element, of this thought, the same constructions over and over again. One is a useless duplicate of the other.

If we are always inclined to think or converse on one particular subject; if we will never forget it; if we will start it at all times and in all places; if we will not in thought and speech fall into the prevailing tone of the conversation about us; if we do not try to get up an interest in what is being talked of by others; if we determine only to converse on what interests us, or not converse at all, we are in danger of becoming "cranks" or monomaniacs.

The "crank" draws his reputation on himself. He is one who, having forced one idea, and one alone, on himself, has resolved, perhaps unconsciously, to foist that same idea on everybody else. He will not forget at periods his pet theory or purpose, and adapt himself to the height of others. For this reason he loses the power to forget, to throw from his mind the one absorbing thought. He drifts more and more into that one idea. He surrounds himself with its peculiar atmosphere, or element, and it becomes no less real than any other which we can see or handle.

Others near him feel the influence of this single idea, and feel it disagreeably, because the thought of one person is felt by others near him through a sense as yet unnamed. In the exercise of this sense lies the secret of your favorable or unfavorable "impressions" of people at first sight. You are in thought, as it flows from you always, sending into the air an element which affects others for or against you, according to its quality, and in proportion to the acuteness of their sense which feels thought. You are influenced by the thought of others in the same way, be they far or near. Hence we are talking to others when our tongues are still. We are making ourselves hated or loved while we sit alone in the privacy of our chambers.

A nonconformist often becomes a martyr, or thinks himself one. There is no absolute necessity for martyrdom in any cause, save the necessity of ignorance. There never was any absolute necessity, save for the same reason. Martyrdom always implies lack of judgment and tact in the presentation of any principle new to the world. Analyze martyrdom, and you will find in the martyr a determination to force on people some idea in an offensive and antagonistic form. People of great ability, through dwelling on one idea, have at last been captured by it. The antagonism which they drew from others they drew because they held it first in their own mind.

"I come not to bring peace," said the Christ, "but a sword." The time has now come in the world's history for the sword to be sheathed. Many good people unconsciously use swords in advising what they deem better things. There is the sword (in thought) of the scolding reformer, the sword of dislike for others because they won't heed what you say and the sword of prejudice because others won't adopt your peculiar habits. Every discordant thought against others is a sword, and calls out from others a sword in return. The thought which you thus put forth is the thought that you receive back, and it is therefore after the same kind.

The coming empire of peace is to be built up by reconciling differences, making friends of enemies, telling people of the good that is in them rather than the bad, discouraging gossip and evil-speaking by the introduction of subjects more pleasant and profitable, and proving through one's life that there are laws, not generally recognized, which will give health, happiness and fortune, without injustice or injury to others. Its advocate will meet the sick with the smile of true friendship, for the most diseased people are always the greatest sinners. The most repulsive man or woman, the creature full of deceit, treachery and venom, needs your pity and help of all the most, for that man or woman, through generating evil thought, is generating pain and disease for himself or for herself.

You are thinking of a person unpleasantly from whom you have received some slight or insult, an injury or injustice. Such thought remains with you hour after hour, perhaps day after day. You become at last tired of it, yet cannot throw it off. It annoys worries, frets, and sickens you. You cannot prevent yourself from going round on this same tiresome, troublesome track of thought. It wears out your spirit; and whatever wears the spirit, wears also the body.

This is because you have drawn on yourself the other person's opposing and hostile thought. He is thinking of you, as you are of him. He is sending you a wave of hostile thought. You are both giving and receiving the blows of unseen elements. You may keep up this silent war of unseen force for weeks and, if so, both are injured. This contest of opposing wills and forces is going on all about us. The air is full of it.

The struggle to forget enemies, or to throw out to them only friendly thought, is then as much an act of serf-protection as to put up your hands and ward off a physical blow. The persistent thought of friendliness turns aside thought of ill-will, and renders it harmless. The injunction of Christ to do good to your enemies is founded on a natural law. It is saying that the thought or element of good will carries the greater power, and will always turn aside and prevent injury coming from the thought of ill-will.

Demand forgetfulness when you can only think of a person or of anything with the pain that comes of grief, anger or any other cause. Demand is a state of mind which sets in motion forces to bring you the result needed. Demand is the scientific basis of prayer. Do not supplicate. Demand persistently your share of force out of the elements about you, by which you can rule your mind to any desired mood.

There are no limits to the strength which may be gained through the cultivation of our thought- power. It can keep from us all pain arising from grief, from loss of fortune, loss of friends, and disagreeable situations in life. Such power is the very element or attitude of mind most favorable to the gain of fortune and friends. The stronger mind throws off the burdensome, wearying, fretting thought, forgets it, and interests itself in something else. The weaker mind dwells in the fretting, worrying thought, and is enslaved thereby. When you fear a misfortune (which may never happen), your body becomes weak; your energy is paralyzed. But you can, through constantly demanding it, dig out of yourself a power which will throw off any fear or troublesome state of mind. Such power is the high road to success.

Demand it, and it will increase more and more, until at last you will know no fear. A fearless man or woman can accomplish wonders.

That no individual may have gained the full height of this power, is no proof that it cannot be really gained. Newer and more wonderful things are ever happening in the world. Some decades ago, and he who should assert that a human voice could be heard between New York and Philadelphia would have been called a lunatic. Now, the wonder of the telephone is an everyday affair. The powers, still unrecognized, of our thought will make the telephone of trivial importance. Men and women, through cultivation and use of this power, are to do wonders which fiction dares not or has not put before the world.

Chapter 6

The Law of Change

A condition of mind can be brought on you, resulting to you in good or ill, sickness or health, wealth or poverty, by the action, conscious or unconscious, of other minds about you, and also through the thought suggested to you by objects or scenes about you.

This is the secret of what in former times was called the "spell." Through the action of thought a state of mind can be brought on any person who may make them act conformably to such thought.

The "spell" is a matter of everyday occurrence in some form or other. To remain for an hour in sight of grand scenery casts on the mind a "spell" of pleasurable thought. To remain for an hour in a vault surrounded by coffins and skeletons would, through the associations connected with such objects, cast on you a "spell" of gloom. To live for days and weeks in a family, all of whose members hated you, or were prejudiced against you, would most likely cast on you a spell of depression and unpleasant sensation. To live in a family whose members were always sending you warm and friendly thought would produce a "spell" of pleasurable sensation.

If, when sick, you are obliged to remain for days and possibly weeks in the same room, your mind will become weary of seeing continually the same objects in it. Not only is the mind wearied at sight of these objects, but the sight of each one, from day to day, will suggest the same train of thoughts. This also soon becomes wearisome. Mind weariness, from this or any other cause, has a natural drift towards despondency. Matters present and future then assume their darkest aspect and the darkest side of every possibility comes uppermost. Despondent thought, as has been many times repeated, is force used to tear the body down instead of building it up.

This action and condition of thought is one form of the "spell." It is broken most speedily by a change to another place and another room.

For this reason "change of scene" is frequently recommended to the invalid. Change of scene and locality means not only a change of objects beheld by the eye but a change also in thought, as new ideas, and possibly a new condition of mind, come through seeing the new set of objects. The new condition of mind will "break the spell."

There is a much closer connection between things tangible and seen of the eye and things intangible than is generally imagined. In other words, there is a close connection between things material and thing spiritual.

The force or element which we call "thought" is all-pervading, and takes innumerable varieties of expression. A tree is an expression of thought as well as a man, and so are all that we call inanimate objects.

There is not a thoroughly dead or inanimate thing in the universe, but there are countless shades of life or animation. Many things seem dead to us, as a bone or a stone, but there is a life or force which has built that bone or stone into its present condition, and that same life or force, after that bone or stone has served a certain purpose, will take it to pieces again and build its elements into other forms. The unbuilding process we call decomposition. It matters not if the stone change or rid itself of but one atom in a thousand years. Time is nothing in the working of Nature's forces. Decomposition, then, is a proof of the existence of all-pervading and ever-working life or force. Otherwise, the stone or bone would remain without change through all Eternity. Incessant change is ever going on in the boundless universe; it is an inevitable accompaniment of all life; and the greater the life and force in you, the more rapid and varied will be the changes.

Everything, from a stone to a human being, sends out to you, as you look upon it, a certain amount of force, affecting you beneficially or injuriously according to the quantity of life or animation which it possesses.

Take any article of furniture, a chair or bedstead, for instance. It contains not only the thought of those who first planned and molded it in its construction, but it is also permeated with the thought and varying moods of all who have sat on it or slept in it. So also are the walls and every article of furniture in any room permeated with the thought of those who have dwelt in it, and if it has been long lived in by people whose lives were narrow, whose occupation varied little from year to year, whose moods were dismal and cheerless, the walls and furniture will be saturated with this gloomy and sickly order of thought.

If you are very sensitive, and stay in such a room but for a single day, you will feel in some way the depressing effect of such thought, unless you keep very positive to it, and to keep sufficiently positive for twenty-four hours at a time to resist it would be extremely difficult. If you are in any degree weak or ailing you are then most negative or open to the nearest thought-element about you, and will be affected by it, in addition to the wearying mental effect, first mentioned, of any object kept constantly before the eyes.

It is injurious, then, to be sick, or even wearied, in a room where other people have been sick, or where they have died, because in thought-element all the misery and depression, not only of the sick and dying but of such as gathered there and sympathized with the patient, will be still left in that room, and this is a powerful unseen agent for acting injuriously on the living.

Those "simple savages" who after a death burn not only the habitation but every article used by the deceased when alive, may know more of Nature's injurious and beneficial forces than we know. Living more natural lives, they unconsciously act according to the law, even as animals in their wild and natural state do, thereby escaping many of the pains and discomforts of the artificial life which we have made both for ourselves and the animals that we domesticate.

People who have some purpose in life, who travel a great deal, who are ever on the move and in contact with different persons and places, have, you will notice, more vitality, more energy, and physically preserve a certain freshness not evident with those who follow year after year an unvarying round of occupation, carrying them day after day to one certain locality, whether office or desk or workman's bench, just as a pendulum oscillates from side to side.

These last look older at forty than the active, changing person does at sixty, because their unvarying lives, the daily presence and sight of the same objects at their dwellings or places of business, contact with the same individual or individuals at meals and in leisure moments, and interchange of about the same thoughts year in and year out, weave about them an invisible web composed of strands or filaments of the same unvarying thought, and this web literally strengthens from year to year, exactly as strand after strand of wire laid together will form at last the massive bridge-supporting cable. But the unseen cable so made binds people more and more firmly to the same place, the same occupation, and the same unvarying set of habits. It makes them dislike more and more even the thought of any change. It is another form of the "spell" which they have woven for themselves. It is the sure result of always keeping your state of mind unchanged.

We do not live on bread or meat alone. We live also largely on ideas. The person ever planning and moving new enterprises, the person who throws his force into beneficial public movements and from either of these causes is led into a varied and ever-changing contact with individuals, receives and puts out a far greater variety of thought than the man who lives continually in a nutshell.

There is a time and use for retirement and solitude. There is a time and use for contact with the world. It is desirable to establish the golden mean between the two.

The person whose range of life and movement is narrow, who is doing nearly the same thing and seeing nearly the same things and people from year to year, has a tendency to feed mostly on the same old set of thoughts and ideas. Out of himself he generates the same order of old, stale notion and expression. Start him in a certain train of idea or association and he tells you time after time the same old story, forgetting how many times he has told it you before. He has about the same forms of expression for every occurrence and every hour of the day. He regards the world and things generally as about worn out. Lacking in life and variety of thought himself, he regards everything else as lacking in life and variety. For life is to us exactly as we see it through the spectacles which we so often unconsciously make to look at it. If our mental spectacles, through living unaware in violation of the Law, are blurred, cracked, discolored, and dim, the whole world will to us seem blurred, discolored, and dull in hue.

Such a person "ages," as we term it, very rapidly, because his physical body is as much an expression of his daily and prevailing order of thought as the apple is an expression or part of the apple tree. Feeding and living on the same set of ideas continually is analogous for feeding continually on a most limited variety of food. Both bring on disease. In some of the English prisons what are called "oatmeal sores" afflict the prisoners through being fed so much on that single article.

But the average mental condition shows itself on the body far more rapidly than any result from material diet. It is feeding on the same stale set of ideas, aided by living continually amid the same physical surroundings and with the same individuals, who are likewise subsisting mentally on the same stale mental diet, which whitens the hair, stoops the shoulders, wrinkles the face, and causes shrinkage of tissues and bodily inertia and weakness. Our land is full of people who at forty-five, through this cause, look older than others of sixty-five. It is full also of young men and women in a physical sense, who, through their poverty of idea and lack of real life, will be old, worn, and haggard within twenty years. They are in substance as much old fogies, "grannies," and "daddies" now as are those whom they ridicule as such. They are travelling in the same narrow rut of idea. Slang phrases and worn-out chaff, borrowed from others, constitute four-fifths of their talk and probably five-sixths of their thought.

To this class also belong many who are deemed of a high order intellectually, or of more "culture," whose thought after all is very largely a repetition of what they have heard or read, who look up to and idolize some human authority, living or dead, and have really very few ideas of their own, not possibly because new ideas occasionally do not suggest themselves to them, but they have not the courage to secretly entertain and familiarize themselves with such ideas. They smother them. They succeed at last in killing them and putting out the little light endeavoring to shine on them. When you destroy or so kill out of yourself the capacity for truthful idea to act upon you, you are killing also your body by degrees. You are cutting off the only source of new life for the body.

Of this order of minds the only claim to youth lies in that physical freshness belonging to the earlier growth and life of the body, which, owing to their mental condition, will fade in twenty years as surely as the absence of sunshine and water will soon wither the young and growing plant.

Such are now unconsciously weaving for themselves the web and "spell" of age and decay.

A constant renewal of physical life lies only in a never-ceasing change of mental conditions. New ideas beget newer and fresher views of life. There are millions on millions of truthful, new ideas ready to come to us, provided we keep the mind in the proper state to receive them. We have not to plod and "study hard" to receive them. There is no "hard study" in the kingdom of God or the kingdom of infinite good. If in the line of communication with that kingdom, we shall ever receive new thought, as the plant receives the sunshine and air, and like the plant just as much as suffices to give us life for the day and the hour. Every mind is now, or is to be at some period of its existence (not possibly in this present physical existence), a fountain for the reception of such new idea.

But new thought cannot come from books or from the ideas of others. These may for a time serve to start you on the road, or as temporary props or helps. But if you depend altogether on books or people for new thought, you are living on borrowed life. You, in so doing, keep your own mind closed to the inflowing of the element which its own individual needs call for, which is for it alone and for no other mind. You must draw your own sustenance from the infinite reservoir of truthful thought. Until you do so you are not a "well of water springing up into everlasting life," nor have you reached the initial point of that real and perfected existence which feels at home anywhere in the universe and can draw its self-sustaining life at any place in the universe.

No agency fetters more or does more harm to both mind and body than a very close and constant association with a mind or minds inferior to yours in tastes, in refinement, in breadth of views and quality of motive.

Such order of mind ever near you and with which you are much in sympathy, will infuse into yours more or less of its grosser desire or taste. It will blind you more or less to higher and healthier views and modes of life. You will, unconsciously to yourself, live and act out much of that mind's life. You will be peevish or cynical or mean in your dealings, when it is not the real you that is so thinking or acting, but the constant flow to you and reception by you of the grosser force or element of that mind, which you thus act out. You become, then, literally a part of the other and inferior mind. This will surely affect the body which in its material substance becomes a material expression of that lower mind grafted on yours. Unless you sunder this mental tie, the inferior graft may outgrow the original tree. You will become physically inert, lifeless, and be affected with some form of disease, because you are then giving that inferior graft your own thought or force. It can appropriate but a small part of that force, but from what it can, it draws its own stinted life. You are then giving of your gold and getting base metal in return. You are then giving of your life and getting a slow and living death in return. For the mind most clear and active in thought, considerate, wise and prudent, broadly but not recklessly benevolent in action, does give to others, and especially to those with whom it is in close sympathy, life and vigor, both of mind and body.

Talking openly has very little to do with the good or ill results coming of minds in close association and sympathy. It is not what people talk. It is what people *think* of each other that most affects them. A person always near you and ever thinking of you with dissatisfaction or peevishness, or putting out the thought of opposition to your aims and wishes, will eventually make you feel unpleasantly, be his or her words ever so fair. Such a person, under these circumstances, will at last injure you in mind and body. That person is throwing a "spell" on you.

On the contrary, the near presence of a person pleasantly disposed toward you, who wishes to bring you pleasure or benefit without "an axe to grind," will give you a feeling of rest and quiet, though such person may not say a word for hours. These different sensations are among the many proofs that thought is a literal element, in some way ever affecting us, and ever bringing results as it comes to us from others or is sent by us to others. In this last case the "spell" may be beneficial to you.

There is but one way of breaking the evil spell caused by continual association with the inferior mind or minds, which spell will surely prove fatal if continued in, and is indeed proving fatal to thousands at the present day. That method is an entire separation from such mind or minds. Such sundering of these injurious mental ties cannot, however, in every case be abrupt, or evils may result as great as those which it is sought to avoid. If a graft, however injurious, be roughly torn from the tree, the tree also is injured and perhaps destroyed. If your life has been one of long association with a lower mind, if both of you have, as previously stated, grown into a common life, and you are suddenly torn apart, the shock may prove to you injurious.

If one subsists for a long time on an injurious food, still a certain kind of life is derived from that food, and as the system has become accustomed to it, it cannot be immediately replaced by a healthier food. The system at first may not be able thoroughly to assimilate and digest such healthier food. There is a similar action and result as regards our mental diet.

Once be convinced of the evil resulting to you from any close, inferior association, and you will first assume in mind that such tie must be sundered. Assume this persistently; and half the work is done. That changed state of mind is the force then always working to free you, as your former state of mind, which endured, suffered, and submitted internally, was the force which bound you more and more firmly. The separation is now in your changed mental attitude simply a work of time. You have little to do, save to wait and take advantage of opportunities as they offer themselves. You have, in fact, committed yourself to another current of thought, and the forces coming of your changed mental condition and interior resolve are the spiritual correspondence of a great river to whose current you have committed yourself, and it is slowly bearing you away from your former enslaved condition. This is not a figurative illustration; change permanently a state of mind in which you have been for years; change unwilling submission into a hidden resolve no longer to submit; change endurance of near associations into a permanent and hidden resolve that you will separate from such associations; change that enforced content called "resignation to circumstances," as, for instance, resignation to the presence of inferior, squalid, and unpleasant material surroundings, into that positive internal mental attitude, which in plain language says--"I won't put up with this any longer; my body may be obliged to submit, endure, and suffer from these things temporarily, as it has done in the past, but in mind I will neither endure nor be resigned as I have been "--and you have placed yourself in the action of another power which will gradually bear you away from the old source of ill.

It is not so much what we *do* as what we *think* that brings results. By the force put out of what you permanently think are you carried, as on a current, to those results. You need do very little until you see that the time and opportunity has come for doing. It would be poor judgment for a man floating on a log down the Mississippi to keep on splashing the water and thereby using up his strength for the sake of "doing something." He had better remain quiet and take the chances of being picked up by a passing boat or steamer, or wait until he sees an opportunity of catching on to some near projecting headland. Then such strength as he may have been able to reserve will be used to some purpose. When you are in the right current of thought, you need in similar manner to reserve your strength until you meet the opportunity which that current will bring you, for as many injured through unwise and overmuch doing as by too little. If you don't know what to do, wait. When you wait till your hurry is over, you may see what really needs to be done.

Above all things, in any emergency or experience such as is suggested here, demand daily and hourly in silent thought the aid of a Higher Wisdom and Divine Power. There must come response to such demand. I do not assume to lay down a certain unbending rule to govern every individual life. Every individual life, when it places itself in the line of communication with its Higher Wisdom through a persistent mental attitude, asking silently for such wisdom, will make its own methods for riddance of the ills from which it desires to free itself, and such methods belong to it individually, nor can they safely be copied and used by anyone else. The Spirit of Infinite Good does not reveal itself alike to any two persons. The besetting error of our time is to copy or imitate other people's methods in everything, or to become blindly obedient to a book or the mind that wrote a book. Your mind, ever asking for Wisdom and Truth, is a power beyond any book and is now, or is to be, the reservoir into which ideas will flow which are different from those contained in any book. The power which generates and suggests new ideas is ever coming to the world. The book does not advance after it is written. But the mind which put ideas in that book may be ever going ahead and finding new meanings and broader interpretations for what it wrote years before.

If you wish to find out regarding the latest developments in chemistry or any material science, you do not have recourse to the books written a hundred years ago about such matters. You get the latest work on these subjects, and if possible you will go farther and get access to those now making such sciences their special studies, seeing that they may know something regarding them never yet written.

So even now in your own kingdom of mind there may be ideas and truths beyond any ever written, which you reject as "mere imaginings," or dare not assert either by word or act for fear of ridicule or opposition.

A book, like Paul, may plant new ideas in your mind; an individual like Apollo "may water" such ideas, but the awakened God in yourself can alone give the increase.

Complete isolation from their kind and loneliness is one terrible fear besetting some who live in associations which are really not congenial to them, but from which they dare not separate for fear of that loneliness. Try not to fear this. Permanent solitude is not in the order of Nature for anyone. Minds alike in thought were made to mingle and give each other pleasure. It is often the clinging to that order of association which, after all, only wearies you, and may oblige you often to play an enforced part to meet such association, that forms the barrier keeping you from your real companions. So long as (in mind) you accept the lower association, so long are you keeping the better away and sending it farther from you. So soon as you reject the lower (in mind), so soon do you set in motion the force to bring the better to you.

Chapter 7

Being Born Again

We do not yet know the full meaning or value of life.

The commonly held idea of existence runs thus: to be born, to grow from infancy to youth, from youth to maturity, from maturity to old age, from old age to death. During these stages, to gain possibly fame or fortune, but ever at the end to weaken, sicken, and die.

Man's real and ever-growing life is a condition so unlike this present existence, that there is scarcely a possibility of any realization thereof by comparison between the two. If you had never seen anything of a tree but its roots in the dark, damp ground, could anyone by means of words convey to you a realization of the beauty of its foliage and blossoms in the sunlight?

Our physical existence is the root from which in the future is to come an indescribable beauty and power.

Some speak lightly of their bodies, call them encumbrances, and entertain glowing anticipations, when rid of them, of a blissful life, entirely in the spiritual realm of existence.
This involves an error.

Because a certain physical life with ever-refining physical senses is in every stage of existence a necessity to the fullest completement of our lives.

The Christ of Judea spoke of the necessity of "Regeneration." "Ye must be born again," He says.

Reincarnated we all have been many times. Regeneration is a step beyond reincarnation.

Reincarnation means the total loss of one physical body and the getting of a new one through the aid of another organization. Regeneration means the perpetuation of an ever refining physical body without that total separation of spirit and body called death.

The cruder the spirit, the longer were the intervals of time between its getting for itself a new physical body through reincarnation.

As the spirit was quickened and gained power, these intervals became less in duration, numbering years in place of centuries. With still greater increase of power the spirit will seek the regenerative instead of the reincarnative process of perpetuating its life of the physical senses.

A spiritualizing and refining power has ever been and ever will be working on this planet. It has through innumerable ages changed all forms of being, whether mineral, animal, or vegetable, from coarse to finer types. It works with man as with all other organizations. It is ever changing him gradually from a material to a more spiritual being. It is carrying him through his many physical existences from one degree of perfection to another. It has in store for him new powers, new lives, and new methods of existence. That spiritual power has given him in the past new inventions. It illuminated his mind to see the uses of steam, electricity, and other material agencies. But far greater illumination is to come. A time is coming when he will not need iron, steam, and electricity to promote his convenience or enjoyment. New powers born out of his spiritual life will supersede the necessity of many of his present material aids.

There will come in the future a more perfected life, when, for the few at first and the many afterwards, there will be no physical death. In other words, every spirit will be able to use both its spiritual and physical senses, through the continual regeneration of its physical body.

Such making over and over again of the physical body will come of successive changes of mind. There will be continual separations from one old state of mind after another and entrances into new. We shall ever through regeneration be born into new individualities.

Regeneration may supersede reincarnation, because of our coming into a higher order of life, or receiving and being built of a higher order of thoughts. The spirit will then be ever changing its physical body for one still finer and more spiritualized. This is the process referred to by Christ as being "born again."

Life is an eternal series of regenerations. The whole aim and scope of all these writings is the endeavor to show what life really means; how the spiritual life rules the physical life; and how we are all growing from cruder to finer forms of life.

The spirit is regenerated when it shakes off the old physical body. It shakes off an old body because it is tired of carrying an instrument through which it cannot express itself. The old man or woman of decaying powers has as much mind or spirit as ever. But that mind cannot act on its body. It is cut off in a sense from that body. It is receding from that body and will finally quit it altogether. It recedes because, through ignorance, it has been drawing for years inferior thought and a monotonous round of thought to the body and endeavoring to make it over again with an old rotten material. It is like trying to repair a leaky roof with rotten shingles. This is the degenerative process of today and the cause of the decaying physical powers and death of the body.

But the more enlightened spirit will find out how to act on and replenish the body with newer and newer thought. This makes the body ever newer and newer and so keeps up the necessary connection between spirit and body.

We do not part with life in the loss of the physical body. But we do lose thereby one kind of life and a most important agency for the fullest enjoyment of life.

We lose in what is called death the use of that set of senses which we call the physical. We lose the power of living in a close connection with the world of physical things. It is most desirable to maintain a connection with the physical world, and the spirit on losing its body, contrary to general belief, laments the loss of such body and desires eagerly to have the possession and use of its former physical senses. Failing in this it uses, so far as it can. by a psychological law, the physical senses of those having bodies, which it can influence or control.

Every living man and woman has such influence brought to bear on him or her from the unseen side of life.

The "dead," as they are falsely called, resume imperfectly their lives on earth, through aid unconsciously given them by the living, or, more properly speaking, by those living with physical bodies.

If we do not wish to find out the new--if we instantly reject what some may call "new-fangled ideas"--if we want to go on in the old way of our fathers, then we invite the company and mind of spirits as ignorant as ourselves, who will only help on the decay of our bodies after getting from them all the use they can.

These are "unregenerated spirits." They have drawn to them little new thought since losing their bodies. They will by reason of the same ignorance through which they lost the last physical body, be drawn into another reincarnation, and perhaps another and another, until at last, gaining with each life more knowledge, they will know how to regenerate their bodies.

This regeneration will not come of any material medicines or methods. It will come of changing spiritual conditions. These spiritual conditions will cause the adoption of new habits and ways of life. But to adopt these habits before the spiritual condition prompts or demands them will do little good.

We have a life of the physical senses. We have another of the finer or spiritual senses. We live during the waking hours by the physical senses. We live another life during sleep by the spiritual senses. When these two lives are properly adjusted, they feed each other healthfully.

With such proper adjustment the physical senses receive a certain necessary supply of element from the spiritual while the body sleeps.

The spiritual being receives also from the material condition a certain vital supply. If your spirit loses its body these sources of mutual supply between body and spirit are for a time cut off.

The more perfected or regenerated life of the future means the consciousness of existence by both the physical and spiritual senses.

The life of the physical senses and that of the spiritual senses are necessary to each other. When they are joined together, and we become conscious of the use of both, life is relatively perfected and the spirit attains a degree of happiness not now to be imagined.

During all the centuries which have passed since Christ's time, can we point to any instance of this new birth or regeneration? If such regeneration is owing to a higher Faith and higher Law, can we say that any persons, no matter what may have been their reputation for piety or uprightness, whose bodies have finally sickened and decayed, have lived up to the highest Law?

"The wages of sin is death," says the Bible. We would prefer to say that the result of an unperfected life is the death of the physical body.
The body of every weak, shriveled, trembling old man or woman today is the result of sins committed in ignorance. Those sins lay in their thoughts. Out of such thought as it attracts the spirit builds first its spiritual body. The physical body is a material correspondence of the spiritual body. If the spirit believes in error it builds that error into the body. The result is decay.

For this result no blame can be imputed to those who suffer. They have lived up to all the light and knowledge they had. With more growth there will, in some condition of existence, come to them more knowledge. They will then see new methods of living and avoid the mistakes of the former less perfected life.

Charity comes of the knowledge that all people live up to the best light which they have. God alone can light up the darkened chambers of our and their minds. When we, leaving the faults of others alone, ask that our minds may be illuminated so as to see and avoid evil, which illumination alone will help all about us.

People weary of existence, because they think year after year the same set of thoughts and ideas over and over again. Eternal life and happiness come of a perpetual flow to us of new thought and idea. Thought is food for our spiritual beings. Our physical bodies are not nourished on one monotonous kind of food from year to year. Feed the spirit with the same thought (or try to) from year to year and it becomes sick. The sick spirit makes the sick body.

The Law of Eternal Life will not allow this repetition to go on. The Law says to us: "You were not made to run in ruts and grooves of fixed habit. You are not as John Smith or John Brown to be an eternal individuality without change, like a post rooted in the ground. You are to have a new mind for this period, and a superior mind with increased Powers of perception for the next period. You are ever, by drawing to you and adding to you new thought, to be as so many different individuals; as you live on, and this process of regeneration proceeds, you are born or changed into successive types of being, each one being finer than the last."

The regenerated life with a physical body means an ever-increasing life. It means a fresher capacity, with each day's waking, to sense that beauty in Nature which exists all around us. It means a new glory in each day's sunshine. It means a repose and restfulness whereby we can sit still and feel the spirit which animates the tree, the leaf, the ocean, the rivulet, the star, the flower, and every natural expression of the Infinite Mind. It means the daily flow to us of new thoughts which shall fill us with new life. It means that we shall rejoice in the realization and firmly grounded faith that we have in us the possibilities for development into numberless new lives. It means that power of so losing our material self in any effort which we may make that all sense of time shall vanish and ennui and mental weariness shall be destroyed. It means power to live without drudgery of mind and body, or that anxiety which is even worse than drudgery. It means at last the getting of enjoyment from all things. To get enjoyment from everything Is to get life from everything. To get life from everything is to get power from all things. To get power implies a control of all physical elements. This includes a power of ever holding an ever-refining physical body.

Ennui is sickness. When we don't know what to do with ourselves, when we try to kill time and everything seems "flat, stale and unprofitable, we have temporarily lost our hold of the Great Fountain of life, the Supreme Mind and Power. We are absorbing the wearied thoughts of thousands around us, who think the same thing from day to day and from year to year, whose minds in their play are treadmills, who are trying to get Life, exhilaration and variety entirely out of physical things.

The true and regenerative life cannot be obtained from material things. That is the reason why all that money can buy fails to satisfy. The monster of discontent and ennui rages as much in the palace as the hovel. Solomon was in the claws of this beast when he said: "Vanity of vanities, all is vanity." That exclamation is a libel on the Infinite Mind. It came from the Jewish king, because he was trying to get life and happiness out of wood and stone and metal, and flesh and blood and all things material. It cannot be done.

But when, through demand of the Supreme, you get new thoughts, the material thing of yesterday seems to you as a new thing of today. The very rock which you passed yesterday has a new idea associated with it today. It may not be an idea which you can put in words. It is something which you feel rather than think. Myriads of thoughts, coming at the physical sight of all material things about us, are so felt, but can neither be talked out nor written out.

The regeneration of the body comes in response to our increasing demand of the Supreme Power to be led in the path of the Highest Wisdom. It comes of a courage gained at last of persistent demand, whereby we shall *dare* to trust entirely to that power. This it is doubtful if any can do at present. We try to trust in God, but when the pinch comes and things look dark, we are tempted to adopt some of our worn-out material methods for averting the evil. But perfect trust in the Supreme Power can gradually come to us. When it does men will become more than mortal. Whoever attains to such perfect trust will be regenerated.

Demand then new thoughts, and an increasing nearness to the Supreme Mind, and in time you receive new life, and all things about you are, for you, imbued with new life or idea. You are then in the line of the regenerative process. Your spirit, as well as your body, is being born again and again. It is drawing to it ever new ideas, and becomes literally a new spirit, a new being. If the spirit is being thus renewed or regenerated, the body must be also.

As we become more spiritualized, as the material mind gives place more and more to the Spiritual Mind; in other words, as the regenerative process goes on, we shall, from time to time, find ourselves prompted to change many of our habits and modes of life. These changes will involve eating, sleeping, and association.

But we need not try to force these changes on ourselves. The regenerative process will involve the eating of less and less animal food, until we shall eat none whatever. But there would be nothing gained from ceasing to eat meat before the desire for It had gone.

 The regenerative process will impel us at times to seek solitude, because when alone with Nature the spirit absorbs and assimilates a finer quality of thought. But to enforce on ourselves the solitude of the hermitage or cloister when there is no real love for it does little good, as is proved by the fact that hermit and recluse have physically decayed and died like the rest.

This regeneration of the body will come to no one directly from any system of forms, habits, or observances. It will come because of a time ripe for it to come.

As this planet ripens spiritually all material things upon it partake of that ripening or development. The life of today, so different and superior to that of five hundred or a thousand years ago, is a part and a proof of that development. The earth ripened first from chaos to coarse development in the animal and vegetable kingdoms of ages ago, and then to its present relatively more refined condition. But this refining process is never to cease.

Perhaps you will say on reading this, "What has all this to do with me? What you say may be true. But it is all too far off, too indefinite. I want something to benefit me now."

This idea of the body's regeneration is for you a benefit now, if you can accept it. It cannot be displaced from your mind. It will first, as a tiny seed, stay there. It may for months or years show no sign of life and seem to be forgotten. But it will grow and have more and more of a place in your thought. It will gradually change the quality of your thoughts. It will gradually force out an old and false interpretation of life and bring in a new one. It will impel you to look ever forward to newer joys and make you cease groping among regrets and sad remembrances of your past, when you know that such thoughts bring decay and death to the body. We are built literally of our thoughts. When we realize that our regrets, our envying and jealousies, our borrowings of trouble, or our morbid contemplations of subjects ghastly and sickly, are literally things, and bad things, actually put in our bodies, as such thoughts, materializing themselves from invisible to visible element, turn into flesh and blood, and that as so built into ourselves they bring us pains, aches, weakness, sickness, wrinkles, bowed backs, weak knees and failing powers, we have a good and tangible reason for getting rid of them.

The body of a person given over to melancholy will be literally built of gloomy thoughts materialized into flesh and blood.

When a girl realizes more and more clearly that jealousy, peevishness, and pettish pouting moods will spoil her good looks and complexion, she will make efforts to rid herself of such thoughts. They will destroy her body. The Infinite Power for good wants all things and all people to be beautiful, healthful and symmetrical, and intends ever to increase this beauty, health, and symmetry. It works through a continual process of regeneration to keep them so. If it cannot affect such perpetual life and beauty with one physical organization, it mercifully lets it go to pieces and gives the spirit another.

When a man realizes that his angry mood, or his covetous mood, or his grumbling mood represents so much material put in his body, and that such element will give his body pain and make it sick, he has a good strong reason for having some care as to what his mind runs on, and for making the "inside of the platter clean."

Let us remember, so far as we can, that every unpleasant thought is a bad thing literally put in the body. Are some people unpleasant to us? Do their airs or affectations, or their stinginess or dishonesty, or their domineering manners, or their coarseness and vulgarity, offend us? Well, let us try and forget them. Why talk them over for an hour, holding the while all their disagreeable traits in our minds, and think of them, maybe, for hours afterwards, when we know that these unpleasant images which we carry in mind are *things* which are being literally put in our bodies to affect them injuriously and degenerate them? All such thoughts we must get rid of.

Such riddance is the commencement of getting a new body. It is in the way of a literal regeneration. If through long habit we find that we cannot by our own endeavor keep out of these injurious moods, if we find ourselves from time to time drawn into the current of tattle, or greed, or envy, we can cease all endeavor of our own and ask help of the Supreme Power to give us new and better thoughts. That Power, through our demand, will give us a new mind. The new mind will bring the new body.

About Prentice Mulford

New Thought Pioneer

Although Prentice Mulford was one of the earliest pioneers of the New Thought teaching, he is still comparatively little known or read, chiefly on account of the high price of the six volumes known as "The White Cross Library," in which form are published his essays in America.

Prentice Mulford was born in Sag Harbor, Long Island, USA in 1834. He was described as the strangest of men. He envisioned the airplane and radio and prophesized mental telepathy and practiced it. At 22 Prentice sailed to California. In Jamestown, California he was a gold miner, cook, school teacher, lecturer and observer of human nature, but made his fortune not from gold but by his interesting and imaginative articles and books. He was a fixture in San Francisco literary circles with the likes of Twain, Harte, and the Bohemian set in the 1860's. He wrote dozens of humorous short stories for the Overland Monthly, Golden Era, Californian, and other local journals. He referred to himself as "Dogberry".
In 1865 he became interested in mental and spiritual phenomena and lived in an old whaleboat cruising San Francisco Bay. After returning from a trip abroad, Prentice Mulford lived for the next 17 years as a hermit in the swamps of Passaic, New Jersey. It was there he wrote some of his finest works on mental/spiritual laws including his "The White Cross Library" dealing in the topic Thought Currents and How to Use Them.

His essays embody a particular philosophy, and represent a peculiar phase of insight into the mystery which surrounds man. The essays were the work, as the insight was the gift, of a man who owed nothing to books, perhaps not much to what is ordinarily meant by observation and everything or nearly everything to reflection nourished by contact with nature. To many his thoughts may seem but dreams; to others they are priceless truths.

That he was a wise teacher and no dogmatist is apparent from his own words "In the spiritual life every person is his or her own discoverer and you need not grieve if your discoveries are not believed in by others. It is your business to push on, find more and increase your own individual happiness."

To him, at any rate, is due the credit of having been a pioneer in the thought that is now influencing people throughout the world, and his influence is very apparent in the writings of all the teachers of the same school that have followed him.

At age 57, Mulford decided to return to Sag Harbor and write about Long Island after the Gold Rush but he passed away peacefully, without any apparent illness or pain, alone in his boat en route. After 30 years in an unmarked grave, Mulford's body was taken to Oakland Cemetery in Sag Harbor where a large stone was placed on his grave with these words, "Thoughts are Things".

About the Compiler and Editor

Richard Lanoue is an in-demand trainer, motivator and author. He takes pride in his ability to change peoples' lives through education, encouragement and empowerment. This work is the culmination of years of self-improvement and enlightenment. He lives in Texas with his best friend and wife, Stephanie, their Jack Russell Terrier, Annie and their Latino Cockatiel, Qi.

Richard owns his own business and is always looking for people to add to his list of success stories. Contact him right now to change your life forever.

He can be reached via email at scienceofliving@aol.com.